Hi. It's been a while. So much has happened this year, more than we can put to words, and it has all undoubtedly conditioned the way we produce and think NESS. Some references to this tremendous year will echo in the texts and dialogues that make this editorial constellation, as we all had to get used to thinking together while mediated by screens and different interfaces. We shared anxieties, worries, projections, desires and hopes, and in the meantime, like most of you, we reinvented how we work.

When NESS 2 Mad World Pictures was published in 2019, we were already in the process of editing NESS.docs 2, Landscape as Urbanism in the Americas, launched last March. Both publications were focused on the large scale, from the globe to the urban. It felt natural to think about objects when planning this issue. Intuitively we first imagined it implied a smaller scale conditioned by traditional categories such as closure and context, but readings, conversations, and the techno-bio-political shock of COVID-19 impacted our understanding.

That's why we decided to keep our playful theoretical spirit and reverse the rhetoric of the iconic quiz show *Jeopardy!*, by making the answer "What's an Object?" as the title of this issue's Dossier. By this we are also ambiguously proposing an enigma for our contributors and readers to respond to in different ways—sometimes even as buildings impersonated by our editorial team or other guests. Giving answers in the form of questions is a way of changing the perspective and opening up the conversation to new processes and reconfigurations.

Objects are linked to experiences that are not only about the haptic. Objects can transcend physical limits and measures. Objects can condition the way we inhabit, can give us shelter, inspire, be useful, be luxurious, be infinite, be intangible. An object, the phone with a camera was crucial to the Black Lives Matter movement. An object, a piece of paper with a vote has had the power to renew hope for democracy. Another complex object, a developing vaccine has dragged emotions and geopolitics for months. We could go on for hours enumerating how 2020 has made us re-signify other objects such as monuments, roofs, computers as means to access to education, streets, domestic spaces, etc.—and not take them for granted.

The dialogues and voices here represented intend to picture part of the questions we need to keep on discussing. I hope you join us in that spirit, and as always, we would love to hear your thoughts, we are just an email away: hello@nessmagazine.com

Pablo Gerson & Florencia Rodriguez

Credits

CHAIR & EDITORIAL DIRECTOR

Florencia Rodriguez
flor@nessmagazine.com

CHAIR & CHIEF EXECUTIVE OFFICER

Pablo Gerson
pablo@nessmagazine.com

CHAIR

Maximo Rohm
max@nessmagazine.com

EDITOR-IN-CHIEF

Isabella Moretti
imoretti@nessmagazine.com

EDITORS

Santiago Bogani
sbogani@nessmagazine.com

Renee Carmichael
rcarmichael@nessmagazine.com

Lisa Naudin
lnaudin@nessmagazine.com

Magdalena Tagliabue
mtagliabue@nessmagazine.com

ART DIRECTOR

Santiago Passero
spassero@nessmagazine.com

GRAPHIC DESIGNER

Ignacio Espert
iespert@nessmagazine.com

AUDIOVISUAL CREATOR

Natalia La Porta

PROOFREADER

Lisa Ubelaker Andrade

CONTRIBUTORS

Kebira Aglaou, Kumar Atre, Lily Baldwin, BCHO Architects, Carlos Bedoya, Stephen Burks, Luis Callejas, Ludovico Centis, Martin Cobas, Matevž Čelik Vidmar, Diego Arraigada Arquitectos, Penelope Dean, Olafur Eliasson, Sarah Entwistle, Ruth Estévez, Laura González Fierro, Bailey Hikawa, Matthias Hollwich, Wonne Ickx, Otto Ickx Estévez, Lina Ickx Estévez, Víctor Jaime, Carla Juaçaba, Jayne Kelley, Kéré Architecture, Manthey Kula, Malika Leiper, Gaspar Libedinsky, Megan Marin, Michael Meredith, Timothy Morton, Jeffrey S. Nesbit, Viveca Pattison Robichaud, Abel Perles, Hilary Sample, Agustin Schang, Saschka Unseld, SPBR Arquitetos, TAX / Alberto Kalach, Tolga Kemal Ünver, Rainer Weisbach

PHOTOGRAPHERS

Arturo Arrieta, Iwan Baan, Marlowe Broomberg, Matthieu Brouillard, Federico Cairoli, Luis Callejas, Martin Cobas, Ruth Estévez, Leonardo Finotti, Luis Gallardo, Pablo Gerson, Florian Holzherr, Wooseop Hwang, Onnis Luque, Erick Méndez, Isidoro Michan, Isabella Moretti, Jaime Navarro, Cristobal Palma, Fran Parente, Mariam Samur, Tommaso Sartori, Alberto Sinigaglia, Justin Skeens, Yvonne Tenschert, Colin Todd, Michael Vahrenwald

ACKNOWLEDGEMENTS

We want to especially thank the institutional support of the Future Architecture Platform, Martin Brück at the Bauhaus Dessau Foundation (SBD), the Museum of Architecture and Design in Ljubljana (MAO), and the Canadian Centre for Architecture (CCA).

To Felix and Bruno, our little partners.

Published in 2020 by
Lots of Architecture publishers

We care about cultural producers and the acknowledgement of the works and images here presented. We apologize for any errors or omissions.

4364 NW 113 CT
DORAL
FL 33178
USA
Tel: +1 (617) 674-2656

hello@lotsofarchitecture.com
ISSN: 2574-8351
LCCN: 2017203107
ISBN: 978-1-7320106-4-2

Printed in the USA

ONLINE

nessmagazine.com
instagram.com/ness_magazine
facebook.com/nessmagazine
twitter.com/NESS_magazine

COVER IMAGE

"Frame No. 42389," Software No. 12 DROOP by MOS (Michael Meredith, Hilary Sample, Zach Seibold, Mathew Staudt). Image courtesy MOS

–NESS®

NESS is a product of Lots of Architecture publishers: an editorial platform dedicated to Architecture, Life, and Urban Culture founded by Pablo Gerson and Florencia Rodriguez in 2017.

On Architecture, Life, and Urban Culture

$ 20 USD / € 18 / £ 16

FROM PHILOSOPHY TO SLANG, WORDS AND THE WAY WE USE THEM ARE BEING REINVENTED. THAT-NESS, COOLNESS, OR OTHERNESS ARE ALL SIGNIFIED TO INNOVATE CONTEMPORARY WAYS OF THINKING. NESS IS A SUFFIX THAT GIVES AN ADJECTIVE OR PRONOUN THE POSSIBILITY OF BECOMING A NOUN. NESS IS A MAGAZINE. IT INVOKES NEW IDEAS, SENSES, AND MEANINGS. IT IS PLAYFUL, SUGGESTIVE, AND EDGY. IN EACH ISSUE, WE INVITE DESIGNERS, THEORISTS, ARCHITECTS, AND CRITICS TO REIMAGINE THE WAY WE BUILD, SEE, AND TALK ABOUT THE WORLD. THINKING TOGETHER IS INVALUABLE.

Contributors

JAYNE KELLEY is an editor and writer based in Chicago. She is a Visiting Assistant Professor at the UIC School of Architecture, where she manages events and publications. From 2013 to 2017, she worked at the Canadian Centre for Architecture (CCA), most recently as managing editor in the publications division. She is a co-author of The *Western Town* (Hatje Cantz, 2013) and co-editor of *The Museum Is Not Enough* (Sternberg Press / CCA, 2019). Her writing has appeared in Clog, the Journal of Architectural Education, MAS Context, and Flat Out, where she is a member of the editorial board.

MARTIN COBAS is a PhD candidate in History and Theory of Architecture at Princeton University. His dissertation, "Liminal Creatures/Liminal Topographies: Rhetoric of Excess in the New World," explores the emergence of the creaturely and other enchantments of the modern in 20th century Brazil. He is a Professor of Architectural History and Design at the School of Architecture of the Universidad de la República, Montevideo, where he co-edits the journal Vitruvia. He has taught and published in Argentina, Brazil, Ecuador, the United States and the United Kingdom. He was co-founder of the office Fábrica de Paisaje. Cobas holds a master's degree in History and Theory of Architecture from the Harvard University Graduate School of Design.

LUDOVICO CENTIS is an architect and founder of the architecture and planning office The Empire. He is co-founder and editor of the architecture magazine San Rocco. Centis has a PhD in urbanism (Università IUAV di Venezia) and was partner at the architectural office Salottobuono from 2007 to 2012. Centis was the 2013-14 Peter Reyner Banham Fellow at SUNY-University at Buffalo and a participant of the CLUI Wendover Residence Program in 2015. He was awarded a 2018 Getty Library Research Grant in Los Angeles and is currently a Visiting School Head at the Architectural Association School of Architecture in London.

LAURA GONZÁLEZ FIERRO is an architect and curator based in New York. She was co-curator of "Walls of Air: The Brazilian Pavilion" at the 16th Venice Architecture Biennial, a research project that reflects on the borders of architecture in relation to other disciplines like geography, medicine, anthropology, social sciences, arts, law, and politics. She co-curates "In Situ: Conversations on Architecture and Beyond", a platform that explores contemporary architectural models and discourses from the Americas. She holds a master's degree from Columbia University GSAPP (2008) and founded FIERRO (2010), a human centric architecture and design studio with projects in the fields of architecture, design, and curatorial work.

PENELOPE DEAN is Associate Professor at the UIC School of Architecture. Her research focuses on contemporary architectural culture with an emphasis on the exchanges between architecture and the allied design fields from the late 1970s onwards. Dean's writings have appeared in Architectural Design, the Journal of Architectural Education, Harvard Design Magazine, Log, Hunch, Praxis, and Flat Out, and her work is supported by the Graham Foundation for Advanced Studies in the Fine Arts and a Visiting Scholars Residency at the Canadian Centre for Architecture in Montreal. She received a PhD from UCLA in Critical Studies of Architectural Culture and has served in various editorial capacities for Hunch, Content, KM3, and Crib Sheets. She is the founding editor of Flat Out.

Contents

TO BE KEPT IN THE LOOP
FOR FUTURE EVENTS
OR TO DISCUSS
COLLABORATIONS,
EMAIL US AT
HELLO@NESSMAGAZINE.COM

-NESS Talks

-NESS Talks is a series of online seminars exploring innovative topics through interactive dialogues with collaborators, thinkers, critics, and our readers. It aims to facilitate conversations that thrive on cultural agitation in an online, open, and accessible format that encourages a diversity of voices.

In July 2020, we inaugurated this series with the celebration and launch of the second issue of our monographic series "NESS.docs 2: Landscape as Urbanism in the Americas." It included panel discussions with the publication's editors Mercedes Peralta (Harvard Graduate School of Design), Florencia Rodriguez (NESS / Lots of Architecture -publishers), and Jeannette Sordi (Universidad Adolfo Ibáñez / New York Institute of Technology) and invited participants Luis Callejas (LCLA Office), Martin Cobas (Princeton University School of Architecture), Ana María Durán (Yale School of Architecture / University of California, Los Angeles / Pontificia Universidad Católica del Ecuador), Alfredo Ramírez (Architectural Association / Groundlab), and Elisa Silva (Enlace Arquitectura). Charles Waldheim (Director, Office for Urbanization, Harvard Graduate School of Design) gave a keynote address, and Marcela Ramos (David Rockefeller Center for Latin American Studies) introduced the Latin American context. Videos from Lucía Ardissone (Bulla), Diego Barajas (Husos), Alejandro Beals & Loreto Lyon (Beals Lyon Arquitectos), Bruno Emmer (RDR architectes), Guillermo Hevia García, Catalina Patiño (CAPA), Alfredo Ramírez, Camilo Restrepo (AGENdA agencia de arquitectura), Elisa Silva, and Nicolás Urzúa (Urzúa Soler Arquitectos) were also shown, making it a dynamic experience that opened up new narratives for thinking about landscape in Latin America.

NESS.docs 2 was produced with kind support from Harvard's David Rockefeller Center for Latin American Studies.

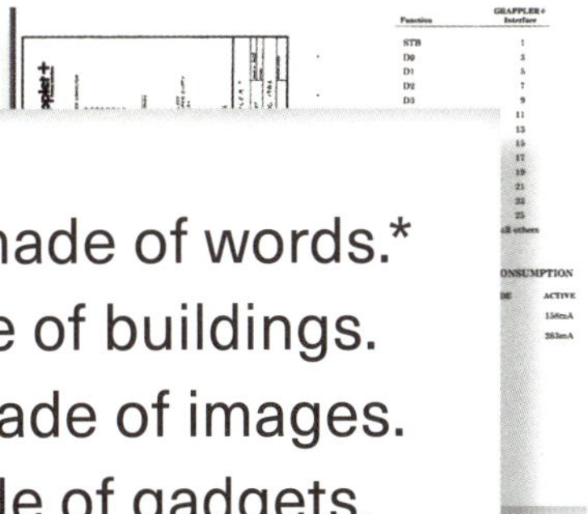

Machines made of words.*
Words made of buildings.
Buildings made of images.
Images made of gadgets.
Gadgets made of sounds.
Sounds made of drawings.
Drawings made of feelings.
Feelings made of videos.
Videos made of scrolls.
Scrolls made of voices.
Voices made of codes.
These are just a few
of our starting points.

*The American poet William Carlos Williams first called a poem a machine made out of words in the introduction to *The Wedge*, in Selected Essays of William Carlos Williams (NY: New Directions, 1969), p. 256.

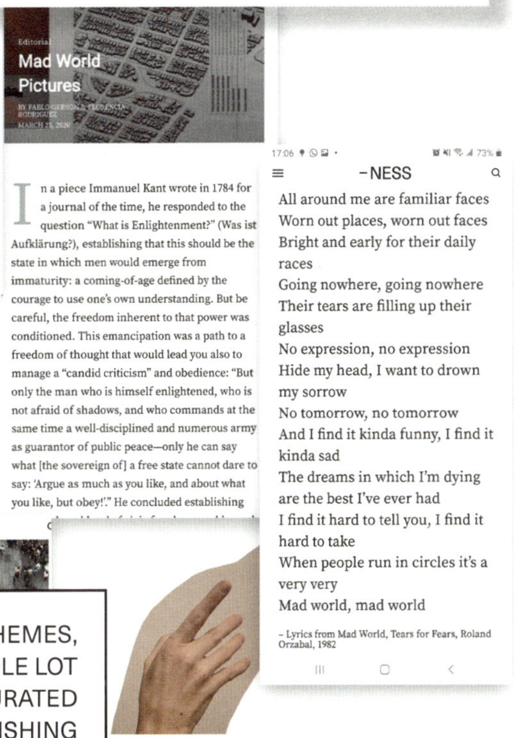

–NESS On Architecture, Life, and Urban Culture.
BROWSER PODCASTS REPORT–NESS STORE FOLLOW

Editorial 4—All is Full of Landscape

Is it really? In the 1990s, landscape was reiterated as a tool to open up new conversations, projects, and reflections that dialog between the natural and the artificial. This meant that it could determine cultural, social, ecological, and economic forms; and in the process, landscape either becomes an overarching concept or it gets itself caught up in the particularities of the different categories. As the term continues to be prominent in the wake of climate change and the constant desire for technological innovation, where can these traces be heard, felt, read, and seen? Coinciding with the late-March launch of NESS.docs 2 Landscape as Urbanism in the Americas, this editorial surveys and questions landscape in its different forms and scales—from books and films to exhibitions and real-world solutions. It does not try to redefine landscape or to provide an answer to its many iterations but instead encourages an exploration of how it manifests itself in and through a variety of experiences.

NESS #2 Mad World Pictures has landed!
Get your hands on a copy!

#NESSpicks

Beyond the Diary

Feels like Home: Chaptal Residence by Nathalie Eldan Architecture

Urban Reliefs: Pyramids Playground by AFA Group

In a piece Immanuel Kant wrote in 1784 for a journal of the time, he responded to the question "What is Enlightenment?" (Was ist Aufklärung?), establishing that this should be the state in which men would emerge from immaturity: a coming-of-age defined by the courage to use one's own understanding. But be careful, the freedom inherent to that power was conditioned. This emancipation was a path to a freedom of thought that would lead you also to manage a "candid criticism" and obedience: "But only the man who is himself enlightened, who is not afraid of shadows, and who commands at the same time a well-disciplined and numerous army as guarantor of public peace—only he can say what [the sovereign of] a free state cannot dare to say: 'Argue as much as you like, and about what you like, but obey!'." He concluded establishing

–NESS

All around me are familiar faces
Worn out places, worn out faces
Bright and early for their daily races
Going nowhere, going nowhere
Their tears are filling up their glasses
No expression, no expression
Hide my head, I want to drown my sorrow
No tomorrow, no tomorrow
And I find it kinda funny, I find it kinda sad
The dreams in which I'm dying are the best I've ever had
I find it hard to tell you, I find it hard to take
When people run in circles it's a very very
Mad world, mad world

– Lyrics from Mad World, Tears for Fears, Roland Orzabal, 1982

NESSMAGAZINE.COM INCLUDES REGULAR EDITORIAL THEMES, WEEKLY POSTS, PODCASTS, LECTURES, VIDEOS, AND A WHOLE LOT OF DYNAMIC-NESS TO EXPLORE. IT FUNCTIONS AS A CURATED AND ONLINE PLATFORM FOR ENTERTAINING AND PUBLISHING CRITICAL CONTENT ON ARCHITECTURE, DESIGN, AND URBAN CULTURE. IT EXPLORES, EDITS, AND DISSECTS IDEAS THROUGH A VARIETY OF VOICES AND FLARE. AS IT IS THE ULTIMATE INTERFACE FOR ENACTING OUR IDEA OF BRINGING PEOPLE TOGETHER AND CONNECTING DIFFERENT SECTORS—INDUSTRY, PRACTITIONERS, ACADEMIA, DECISION MAKERS, DESIGNERS, AND THE GENERAL PUBLIC—IT IS RICH IN EXPERIENCES THAT INSPIRE INTERACTION AND CONTRIBUTE TO THE EVOLUTION OF KNOWLEDGE.

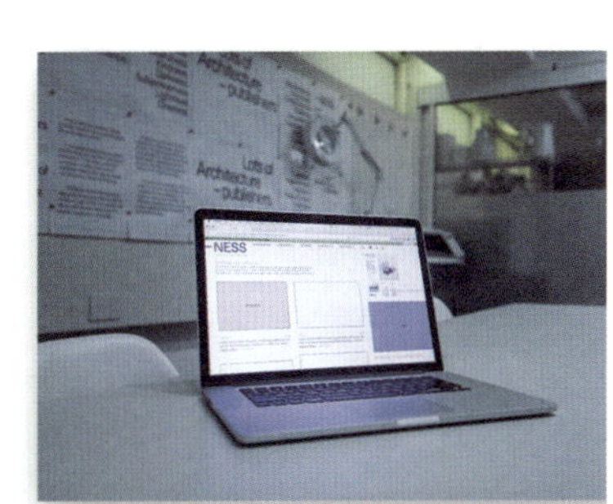

Terrain: A Docu-Dream

Terrain is a virtual reality film by Kumar Atre, designer and director of the New York-based office Rapt Studio, Lily Baldwin, a multi-faceted creative exploring dance and film in New York, Los Angeles, and Berlin, and Saschka Unseld, Emmy and Peabody Award winning German-born director and writer. It was presented in Venice VR Expanded, a satellite program of the 77th Venice International Film Festival, in September 2020. This is our experience moving through it.

WRITER AND DIRECTOR: Lily Baldwin & Saschka Unseld / CO-CREATORS: Lily Baldwin, Saschka Unseld, Kumar Atre / SPATIAL DESIGN: Kumar Atre with Rapt Studio / DIRECTOR OF PHOTOGRAPHY: Saschka Unseld / EDITOR: Lily Baldwin / ORIGINAL MUSIC & SOUND: Youguys Music / ADDITIONAL MUSIC: Sannety, Boris Rappo, Marasal Salmassi / FEATURING: Kumar Atre, Nanghiti Aviankoi, Lily Baldwin, Joy Falquet, Sasha Gravat Harsch, Madame Lisa Et Ses Filles, Lily Madera, Zeina Nassar, Charlotte Parfois, Clara Schramm, Daniil Simkin, Loula Weber / PRODUCERS: Jill Basmajian, Alethea C. Avramis, Marc Wientzek / CREATIVE PRODUCER: Marc Wientzek / BERLIN PRODUCERS: Yan Schoenefeld, Judith Lentze, Barbara Simon / GENEVA PRODUCER: Salar Shahna / CO-PRODUCER & CREATIVE CONSULTANT: Lou Savoir / CO-PRODUCER: Morgan Asdel / EXECUTIVE PRODUCER: Invr, Sönke Kirchhof / POST-PRODUCTION SUPERVISOR: Invr, Philipp Wenning / COLORIST: Jaime O'Bradovich / PRESENTED BY: Eams Productions, Happiness Machine, Dirty Bacon, Film Five, Talking Projects, Invr, Youguys Music, Company 3, Rapt Studio / FILMED IN: Geneva, Switzerland, and Berlin, Germany.

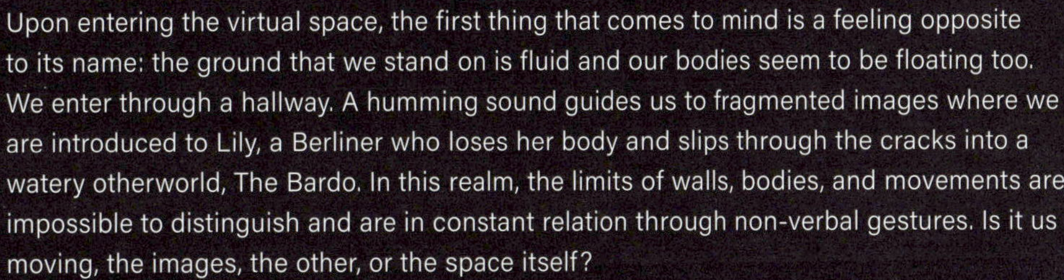

Upon entering the virtual space, the first thing that comes to mind is a feeling opposite to its name: the ground that we stand on is fluid and our bodies seem to be floating too. We enter through a hallway. A humming sound guides us to fragmented images where we are introduced to Lily, a Berliner who loses her body and slips through the cracks into a watery otherworld, The Bardo. In this realm, the limits of walls, bodies, and movements are impossible to distinguish and are in constant relation through non-verbal gestures. Is it us moving, the images, the other, or the space itself?

We join Lily in exploring bubble-like forms, made with 360-degree video, floating in a black expanse. In each, we find a person, dancing, whispering, or living. The filmmakers call these "Physical Interviews," or hyperreal encounters with people in their native environments. Editing becomes choreography: we can touch the intimacy of the other, not just watch them from scrolling distances.

A diverse community is formed that eventually helps Lily resurface on the streets of Berlin. We follow her. The space is again fragmented, but with the soundtrack of Lily laughing, we feel relief in its new normality. In the end, 'terrain' could be understood as the communities we form and not necessarily the ground we stand on.

Exiting the film to our habitual desktop view, we wonder if the tension between 'documentary' and 'dream' is an apt metaphor for today: is Terrain a micro experiment for the experiences of 2020? In any case, the digital gets under the skin, and we are active participants in a dance of being together, but different.

Sculpture for the Everyday

Artist Bailey Hikawa Designs Uncanny Phone Cases

#NESSpicks

Kame is a collection of sculptural and functional phone cases launched by artist and designer Bailey Hikawa in December 2018. Kame, meaning turtle in Japanese, is a metaphor for the shell of a brain. Each case is designed as a grip to hold the phone better and stand it up both vertically and horizontally, all while acting as a sculpture for the everyday. The concept for Kame comes out of the merging of Hikawa's art and design experience: a need to infuse the mundane with interactive and accessible sculpture. Kame may not fit in the pocket but it will hopefully inspire us to consider how we use our phones and the role we want our phones to play in our lives. Each case is fabricated in colored resin entirely by hand and finished in Hikawa's studio in Los Angeles, California.

Ph. Courtesy Bailey Hikawa

Gaspar Libedinsky

New Natures Through Material Exploration

"There is an intrinsic desire for inanimate objects that deserves to be investigated and re-signified," says Gaspar Libedinsky, architect, visual artist, and curator who lives and works in Buenos Aires.

Under the title "Kunstformen der Natur" (Arts Form in Nature), Gaspar Libedinsky presents this series of pictures. A progression of precise physical operations, such as compression, tension, and rotation transform each broom into a brushstroke. With a greater or lesser degree of control and accident, these pictorial compositions capture a universe that refers to the forms of nature that have yet to be discovered.

Libedinsky's work usually operates in the private and the public space mediating between the intimacy of the body and the urban scale.

Ph. Mariam Samur

Exploring the connection between space and literature, the exhibition displayed a series of objects that formed a collective landscape.

Ph. Luis Callejas

Norway Tells: LCLA office and Manthey Kula's Pavilion for the Frankfurt Book Fair

Ph. Luis Callejas

The competition asked participants to define a spatial concept and help determine how the different activities related to Norway's contribution would be developed; the designers thus focused on the notion of literature as space. Norway Tells—the name that the designers chose for the pavilion—is a collection of objects. Aluminum furniture and shapes create an interior landscape. The field of tables and their distinct forms do not evoke the Norwegian landscape directly, but make reference to the abstract geography contained in Norwegian literature—the imagined landscapes. Each of the tables is linked in shape and content to a Norwegian poem that contains indirect references to landscape.

There are two distinct spaces divided by a single wall. All activities that are attended by large groups happen behind the wall and facing the pavilion's large windows. Selected Norwegian artists and design objects are also presented in the interior scene. The proposal suggests that there is a strong connection between art, design, and literature in Norway.

After the book fair, the life of each character persists as some of the elements move to selected German libraries and bookstores. Each table was designed as a permanent object with precise craftsmanship with the intention to not only serve the temporary event, but to be able to stand outdoors or even become park furniture.

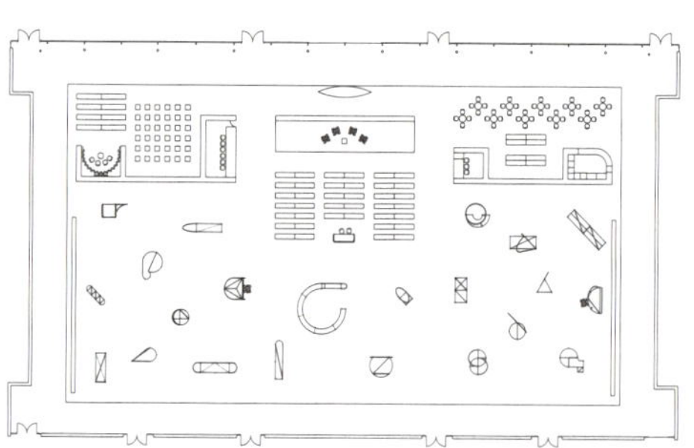

#NESSpicks_books

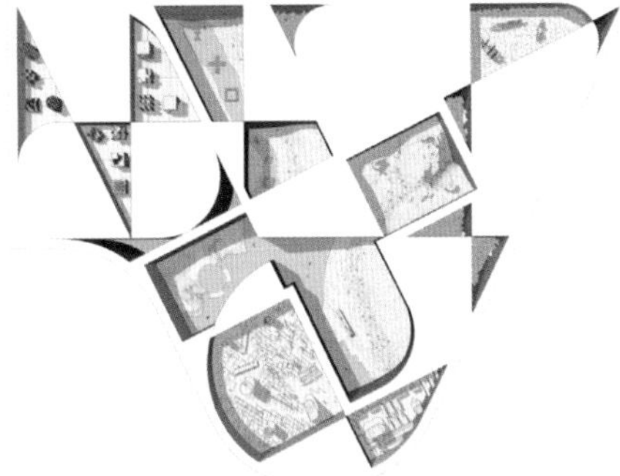

New Investigations in Collective Form

A Review of The Open Workshop's Latest Publication

JEFFREY S. NESBIT

Infrastructure and its associated technologies remain limited by their appearance of engineered rationality. And therefore, the potential utility and technological imaginary of infrastructural systems are confronted by its contingencies in culture, the environment, and politics. Perhaps the traditional discourse of 'infrastructural urbanization' understood infrastructure as existing in a space between skepticism and positivism.[1] With an oversaturation of digital software, the promise that infrastructure will become fully dematerialized is flawed. How do environmental and political challenges—and, more importantly—responses to those challenges, present themselves as a design formulation with infrastructure as its central figure? Cultural representation is the means for imagining alternative futures. In other words, the role of infrastructure and the material conditions from which infrastructures emerge are neither politically neutral nor culturally muted. Infrastructure is political. It becomes the social hegemony of power driven by consequential definitions of infrastructure and the agendas that it supports. While fifteen years ago landscape urbanist discourse engaged logistics, ecology, and impacts of decentralization, infrastructure now arises as a critical subject. Infrastructure becomes the operational method for producing political and cultural imaginations.

"New Investigations in Collective Form" (2019), authored and edited by Neeraj Bhatia, presents alternatives to the role of form as it intersects and constructs its politics of the commons. In 1964, while teaching in the early formation of the urban design program at Washington University in St. Louis, Fumihiko Maki wrote an essay entitled "Investigations in Collective Form." Maki illustrated the clear relationship "between the village and the houses... between village activities and individual family life." For Maki, this relationship between activity and object generated an architectural form through its collective memory, offering objects to be designed as a morphological sequence. Borrowing from Maki's title and theoretical relationality of collectivity and form, Bhatia expands this formula into contemporary questions of diversity and political indeterminacy to interrogate the role of design from within. Such questions of design and collectivity here is not the first time we have seen a return to Maki's "collective form:" Thom Mayne's book, "Combinatory Urbanism: The Complex Behavior of Collective Form" (2011) offers another example. However, I would argue for Bhatia the reference to Maki's project has little to do with morphological form itself, and that is precisely the point. Bhatia inherits the framework, flexibility, and temporal differentiation of a distributed collectivity and opens up the commons as political engagement—not a structure of space limited by its formal determinacy.

"New Investigations in Collective Form" begins with reflections from two key figures in the field—a foreword by Pier Vittorio Aureli and an introduction by Charles Waldheim. The

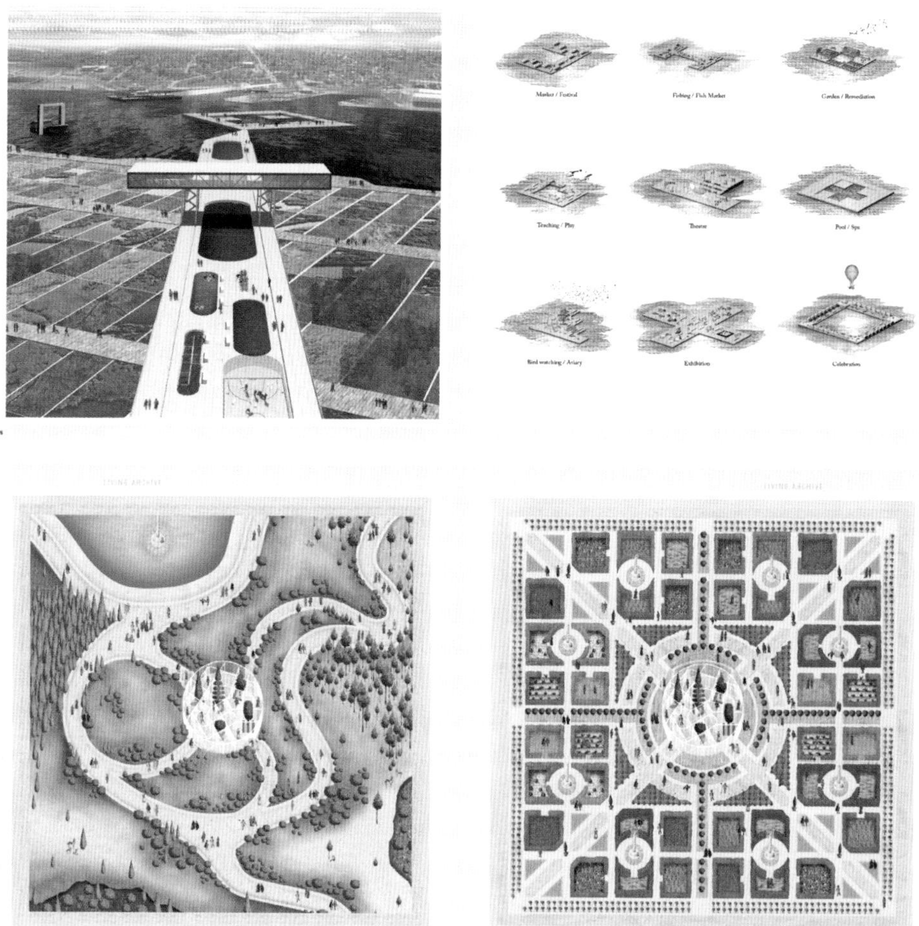

book provides five operative modes (living archives, rewiring states, commoning, articulated surfaces, and frameworks)—each complemented with an essay by notable design scholars in urbanism, ecology, and infrastructure. Contributors include Jenny Odell, Clare Lyster, Rafi Segal, Keith Krumwiede, Albert Pope. The volume concludes with an afterword by Peggy Deamer. In these various perspectives and discussions entangled in the 20th century discourse of the figure, field, and frame, it is not Maki who dominates the conversation. Instead, it is Hannah Arendt's "Human Condition" (1958) that continuously surfaces across the book. Arendt's reoccurring references in the text suggest form has agency in the shaping of collective actions. And perhaps more importantly, the "space of appearance" has been consistently suppressed by modes of power.[2] With this understanding, it becomes clear why the book structures a continuous framework for projects to interject design discourse surrounding the collective commons, while the essays tend to prompt new collective form as a driver for political and cultural representation. Although each of the contributions remains autonomous, they collectively encourage and elevate infrastructure's status as an instrumental role in politics 'and' design.

Along with essay contributions, *New Investigations in Collective Form* includes projects from The Open Workshop, a design research group based in Toronto, also led by Bhatia. These consistently well-articulated projects appear as a constellation of provocations for imagining future urbanisms. Intentionally breaching a range of scales and geographies, each project contributes to an overarching theme of culture, environment, and contemporary social politics. Many of the essays position the role of architecture as a central figure to curate and imagine collective society critically. Architecture thus resides in the space between—cleverly used as the backdrop to its functional form as the political subject. The so-called heterogeneous 'objects' are not formal gymnastics for the sake of form or lines to produce ever-expanded modes of connectivity. Instead, The Open Workshop's study in form intentionally blends architectural language through the infrastructural utility to critically reflect on the design discipline's status and cultivate new, productive ways to shape a better future and equitable society. Even the squared proportion of the book subtly points to the intellectual commitment of its contents. Platonically

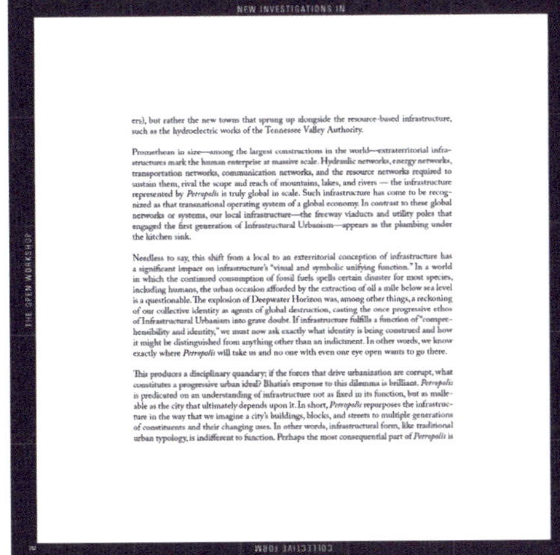

ers), but rather the new towns that sprung up alongside the resource-based infrastructure, such as the hydroelectric works of the Tennessee Valley Authority.

Promethean in size—among the largest constructions in the world—extraterritorial infrastructures mark the human enterprise at massive scale. Hydraulic networks, energy networks, transportation networks, communication networks, and the resource networks required to sustain them, rival the scope and reach of mountains, lakes, and rivers — the infrastructure represented by *Petropolis* is truly global in scale. Such infrastructure has come to be recognized as that transnational operating system of a global economy. In contrast to these global networks or systems, our local infrastructure—the freeway viaducts and utility poles that engaged the first generation of Infrastructural Urbanism—appears as the plumbing under the kitchen sink.

Needless to say, this shift from a local to an exterritorial conception of infrastructure has a significant impact on infrastructure's "visual and symbolic unifying function." In a world in which the continued consumption of fossil fuels spells certain disaster for most species, including humans, the urban occasion afforded by the extraction of oil a mile below sea level is a questionable. The explosion of Deepwater Horizon was, among other things, a reckoning of our collective identity as agents of global destruction, casting the once progressive ethos of Infrastructural Urbanism into grave doubt. If infrastructure fulfills a function of "comprehensibility and identity," we must now ask exactly what identity is being construed and how it might be distinguished from anything other than an indictment. In other words, we know exactly where *Petropolis* will take us and no one with even one eye open wants to go there.

This produces a disciplinary quandary; if the forces that drive urbanization are corrupt, what constitutes a progressive urban ideal? Bhatia's response to this dilemma is brilliant. *Petropolis* is predicated on an understanding of infrastructure not as fixed in its function, but as malleable as the city that ultimately depends upon it. In short, *Petropolis* repurposes the infrastructure in the way that we imagine a city's buildings, blocks, and streets to multiple generations of constituents and their changing uses. In other words, infrastructural form, like traditional urban typology, is indifferent to function. Perhaps the most consequential part of *Petropolis* is

COLLECTIVE FORM

differentiated forms found in the various projects—from Varna Library's "Reading Forest" to "A Room in the City"—deploy repeated geometry guided by muted, and often primitive types that do not enclose, but rather open up the 'hermetic objects' in the architectural subject. These are so ubiquitously repeated, almost as an infrastructural fiction, that the projects reach their highest agency and power. "New Investigations in Collective Form" enters into a broader discussion surrounding the appearance of politics. This body of design research offers critical questions for how the design fields will acknowledge and contribute to reimagining such "spaces of appearance." Bhatia has masterfully captured a much-needed resurgence on primitive form mechanics to cultivate new models for enabling collective space.

Jeffrey S. Nesbit is an architect, urbanist, and recently received his doctoral degree (DDes) from the Harvard University Graduate School of Design. He is the founding director of the experimental design group Haecceitas Studio and a post-doctoral research fellow in the Office for Urbanization, directed by Charles Waldheim and Mohsen Mostafavi. His research focuses on processes of urbanization, infrastructure, and the rise of "technical lands." Currently, Nesbit is studying the 20th century spaceport complex at the intersection of architecture, infrastructure, and aerospace history. He has written several journal articles and book chapters on infrastructure and urbanization. He is co-editor of "Chasing the City: Models for Extra-Urban Investigations" (Routledge, 2018), "Rio de Janeiro: Urban Expansion and Environment" (Routledge, 2019), and "New Geographies 11 Extraterrestrial" (Actar, 2019).

1 See Stan Allen, *Infrastructural Urbanism*, in *Points + Lines: Diagrams and Projects for the City* (Princeton: Princeton Architectural Press, 1999).

2 Hannah Arendt, *The Human Condition* (Chicago: University of Chicago, 1958), p. 204. Arendt points out that "power preserves the public realm and the space of appearance, and as such it is also the lifeblood of the human artifice, which, unless it is the scene of action and speech, of the web of human affairs and relationship and the stories engendered by them, lacks its ultimate raison d'être."

FUTURE ARCHITECTURE PLATFORM

Opening panel at Creative Exchange 2020.
Ph. Courtesy Future Architecture Platform

The Future Architecture Platform is a well-balanced ecosystem of European cultural players in architecture who perform specific roles within a complex architecture program. Founded by Matevž Čelik Vidmar, it connects multi-disciplinary emerging talents to high profile institutions like museums, galleries, publishing houses, biennials, and festivals. It provides talented conceptual thinkers and practitioners in architecture with opportunities to speak up, be seen, and be heard. This year, the platform organized Creative Exchange in which Agustin Schang participated along with nineteen other practices in a two-day marathon of talks, discussions, and amusement.

Ljubljana, 48 Hours at the Fužine Castle

Some Notes from February 2020

AGUSTIN SCHANG

Fužine Castle. Kaltenbrunn Ober-Krain, Joseph (Jožef) Wagner, around 1845, lithography, 49 x 63 cm. Courtesy Museum of Architecture and Design (MAO), Ljubljana.

I arrived in Ljubljana on a gorgeous sunny afternoon after a bumpy flight over the Alps. I had been selected to present a project at a two-day event called Creative Exchange 2020 at the Museum of Architecture and Design (MAO). I was lucky enough to have some time to do a little sightseeing before diving into a 48-hour non-stop conference about the future development of architecture. It was my first time in Slovenia, and spring was about to arrive: incredible sun, profuse green everywhere, plants about to bloom, and smiles all around. The conference started on Monday at 9 a.m. at the Fužine Castle. This renaissance construction, which houses the MAO museum, occupies a charming and quiet spot along the Ljubljanica River on the outskirts of the city. After arriving and having met some of the other guests during the bus ride, I was instructed to register to receive a badge with my name on it. That Wednesday, the event being held was described as the Matchmaking Conference: twenty-five fellows from Europe, the United States, and Australia were there to present their ideas and thoughts about the future of architecture. The conference operates as a connecting platform; each fellow has ten minutes to seductively present their projects to a room full of yet-unknown cultural agents and players. These operators represented twenty-six European architectural institutions, all of them members of the Future Architecture platform. They had designed, in pre-COVID times, an extensive 2020 program full of exhibitions, conferences, lecture series, and workshops. If you made a good match there, you had a probable chance of materializing your ideas in collaboration with strong European architectural institutions.

The presenters were distributed in five thematic groups: Research, Storytelling, Architecture as Cultural Production, Strategies, and Practice. The research team pitched future ideas about how tourism could reinforce local communities: women's cooperatives in Greece could expand through sharing models; flower farmers in Kenya could adapt corporate greenhouse models into larger sustainable cooperative based practices. Then came forecasting projects about strolling the globe online: one was about linking architecture and sites through the 45º North parallel, and the other looked to found a new institute to conduct linear research through multiple geographical coordinates. Tales of inhabitation and existence, depicting future visions and disruptions, were grouped under the Storytelling category. Drawings between the real and the imaginary were followed up by a series of London-based stories about possible worlds through the lens of climate and political disputes. We were transported to the Neretva river in Bosnia in search for hybrid spaces; to Pristina to reveal how the diaspora can transform fragments of the city; and to ex Yugoslavian cities to raise the question: can someone be called an 'architect' after renovating their own apartment. When architecture was called in to prove its capacity to expand cultural value, I shared my ideas about how one could treat buildings in order to see them. Based on a site-specific project, I argued that through different archives, modes of care, and affective readings, a dormant building in downtown Manhattan had been reactivated by its own community. I came all the way to this event in the hopes that there was someone out there in the audience that would be interested in hearing more about these architectural tools for the appreciation of everyday buildings. The stress and nerves of going on a blind date started dissipating after I discovered Future Architecture had created the perfect setup to find your best professional significant other.

During one of the coffee breaks, I ran into a very small exhibition about the building and its history. The national museum has operated in the Fužine Castle since 1992 and one of its primary programs is offering new experiences in the castle through different formats like that show. This Renaissance fort fashioned in an Italian style was constructed between 1528 and 1557. It was first owned by the Khisl family and after the expulsion of the Protestants, by Baron Wizenstein and the Jesuits of Trieste. There was a text on the wall that described this place as one of richest aristocratic residences in the area and also related some of the events that took place within those walls: "stories about entertainment practices of Ljubljana's high society in which young ladies were the most desirable brides." Some other sources mentioned there was a spa below the castle, on the banks of the river, next to a fish pond, and a row of trees accommodating a group of silkworms weaving wedding veils.

As I sat back on my chair in a semi-dark conference room, I started feeling a little anxious again as I realized that 24 hours had already passed, and I only had one more day to form an opinion. All the candidates, including myself, had been seen and heard, and it was time to listen to the platform members' plans in hope to be chosen. While this was happening, I could not stop thinking about the stories of brides, grooms, and single people walking around the palace, taking baths and massages at the spa, anxiously preparing for their dates and weddings. To find the perfect match is an art. Matchmaking is an art. In ancient times, astrologers were guided by the stars to sanctify matches approved by families; the old and wise men and women became essential advisors in helping to find 'the right one'. In some places in North America, marriage-age children were put to dance in line or in a square shape, while matchmakers camouflaged themselves in the ball ensemble advising families of any prospective romance before it went too far. Now that technology has overpassed its function as a tool and become an extension of our bodies, online dating enables fast connections under profile-based mechanisms. Age, gender, sexual orientation, location, appearance, and photos are required for an algorithm to decide whether or not you want to initiate contact. Everybody can customize their digital self, boost their work and career profiles, and then rely on a computational process for the perfect combination to happen. The acceptance of dating systems, however, has created something of a resurgence in the role of the traditional and professional matchmakers offering 'a chance to connect' and 'a chance to authenticate' prospect partners in ways websites cannot. As everybody was 'going online', Future Architecture decided to mediate between real people, boosting architects' social capacity, intelligence, and personal touch to make connections that would enlighten their future in the field. I wonder what is going to happen to all of that now, where will the brides, the grooms, the architects and the weaving silkworms go? Looking back at those days, today, isolated at home like the rest of the world, I realize that being at the Matchmaking Conference was probably being in the future already, very disruptive and very real, having all of us close to each other waiting nervously for the perfect match.

Full disclosure: I am still single.

Matchmaking for Cultural Players

Agustin Schang Interviews Matevž Čelik Vidmar, Founder of Future Architecture Platform

Agustin Schang:

How did the Future Architecture project start? I am interested in its development in regards to the European understanding of access, participation, and enjoyment of culture, and the availability of public resources for promoting these types of initiatives.

Matevž Čelik Vidmar:

I could say that the Future Architecture project was born out of a financial crisis that we were still experiencing in Slovenia in 2014. That year we organized the BIO 50, the design biennial, which was celebrating its fifty-year anniversary. Curator Jan Boelen conducted an edition of the biennial that abandoned the traditional design exhibition. BIO 50 has created new opportunities for young unemployed creators. They were able to participate in international teams and, under the mentorship of renowned designers, undertake new projects that addressed pressing issues related to the city, ecology, mobility, science, food production, etc. The design biennial had a major mobilizing moment for young professionals, and I wanted to launch a project that would similarly address young people working in the field of architecture. The Creative Europe Program's call for European Platforms, which provides financial support to cultural operators showcasing and promoting emerging creators and artists and stimulates a genuine and truly Europe-wide programming, came at the right time. I contacted friends across the continent, presented them with an idea for the platform, and together we submitted an application that was successful. At the time, European cultural platforms were a new type of culture project aimed at connecting emerging artists with cultural players. At the same time, the platforms are intended to act as aggregators for different fields of culture and to help guide EU policies. There are thirteen such cultural platforms in Europe today and ours brings together a variety of players in the field of architecture.

AS

Why did you decide to call the project Future Architecture? And besides the specific name, what are your insights on the idea of futurology, forecasting, the technology of the future in the architectural discipline?

MČV

As I thought about what should be the focus of a platform aimed at the emerging generation of professionals, I read "Future Practice" by Rory Hyde. This was a time when the discourse on architecture seemed extremely unproductive to me. It was dominated by anger over 'starchitects' who were criticized as responsible for the global crisis and the polarization between proponents and critics of individual notorious projects. It seemed extremely important for me to try to make this discussion more productive, to think about how our practice is developing, and how should we respond to the climate crisis or to increasing inequalities in the world. I wanted to turn the discussion on architecture that dealt with the past and the projects already completed, towards the future. I wanted to give young professionals in architecture a voice to describe how they see their profession and what projects they consider relevant to the future. I wished that, through the platform, architecture would become more futurological than it was at that time. But at the same time, I hoped that it would not be too speculative but grounded in an understanding of the past and present context.

AS

The Creative Exchange conference takes place every February in Ljubljana, Slovenia, at the MAO, where you are also the director. Could you expand on the relationship between that specific location in Eastern Europe, with its cultural and architectural history and tradition, and the impact this project has for the museum, its architectural audience, and the city?

MČV

Ljubljana is an ideal place for a sober and down-to-earth debate about the future of architecture. If we talk about Ljubljana as a specific location in architectural terms, then we are talking about Central Europe, the space that is culturally developing between the Adriatic Sea and Vienna, where the first Slovene architects studied, including Jože Plečnik, who is the most prominent personality of the local school, which is just celebrating its 100-year anniversary. Slovenia is a place that is paradoxically interspersed with cultures and at the same time very introverted. Our architectural culture is, on the one hand, strongly characterized by crossbreeding of various influences and, on the other, by pragmatism resulting from modest resources. The two together have, in many cases, led to interesting moments and innovations in architecture. When I took over the museum ten years ago, for me, one of the most important things was to relate history to what is happening today. I am convinced that temporality should not be a criterion for the mission of an architectural museum. The internationally acclaimed BIO and Future Architecture helped us redefine MAO's mission and convince the government to revise the museum's founding act. It is also important that with the creation of the platform, we have become one of the important centers of debate on architecture, which is undoubtedly good for the development of education and practices at the local level.

AS

The Future Architecture Creative Exchange conference is based on a very specific matchmaking format in which fellows are connected with institutions to develop future collaborations. The format seems borrowed from the entrepreneurial tech-startup world where developers and idea-promoters are linked with buyers, clients, and investors. How did you end up with this format? Are you thinking of trying new configurations?

MČV

When designing the platform, I didn't think as much about the matchmaking format at the conference as I did about the process of operating within the platform's annual cycle. I was thinking of designing an open system within which emerging talents and top institutions could come up with ideas and projects. The question was how to, within this cycle, give players enough time to introduce themselves to each other and how to provide enough time to produce interesting and relevant events and exhibitions. At the moment, we are not thinking about new configurations but optimizing existing ones. At the same time, we are talking about an overall yearly theme that could help the platform send out a clearer message about what it stands for and what it does. Each spring, we prepare a new European Architecture Program, featuring exhibitions, conferences, series lectures, workshops, and other events that will be offered to emerging talents. This program is part of an open call we launch every year in early November. Emerging talents must apply to them with a stand-alone idea, project, or work that, in their opinion, offers the answer or part of the answer to the question of what architecture will be like in the future. With their ideas, architects, researchers, curators, and others apply to participate in the European Architecture Program. From each application, each member institution can select the participants it deems best to contribute to its exhibition, conference or other event. The Board of Directors selects 25 applicants who are invited to attend the annual Creative Exchange Conference at MAO in Ljubljana. At the conference, they can meet with the artistic directors, curators, and producers of the participating institutions and discuss joint projects. Creative Exchange has become a central event, attended by more and more institutions beyond the platform, as well as many other young professionals working in the field of architecture. This is an event where you can meet the most interesting young people, who with their ideas are just entering the world of architecture, as well as a range of cultural players and promoters with interesting programs in the field of architecture.

AS

What are the themes that you and the members think could become relevant for future editions?

Matevž Čelik Vidmar welcoming participants of the Creative Exchange 2020. Ph. Courtesy Future Architecture Platform

MČV

Recently, we have talked a lot about two topics. The first one is about the 'mass' that defined architecture in the 20th century, in terms of housing, migration to cities. Today we are looking at mass-less architecture, which is less defined by physicality and more by the intangible. Another topic that is very much at the forefront is 'care,' a topic that talks about the dynamics of solidarity, collective self-organization and trust networks.

AS

How do you measure the success of

the project? I imagine this is very different for each of the member institutions: they all work around the idea of promoting architecture practices and ideas, but their scales, locations, mission statements, formats of operating are very different...

MČV

The success of a project is measured in different ways. The response to the platform as a whole is more important to us than the responses to individual projects within the platform. We want to know the reach and impact of the platform, not only in numbers, but also in real external effects. For example, we would like to understand to what degree the topics that young professionals bring up in the platform are relevant in daily practice. Very important information from the point of view of the Creative Europe program, for example, is whether the platform has helped the participants in their careers or what have the institutions learned from the platform and how have they changed their *modus operandi*. For example: dpr-barcelona has developed an interesting model of digital-analogue publishing with the help of the platform, which allows users to compose their own publications, share them, and print them on demand. The Young Architects program in MAXXI in Rome, originally intended for young Italian architects, today invites young architects from all over Europe to compete for the best proposal for the Summer Pavilion in front of the museum. Above all, institutions are beginning to understand that, whether small or large, whether private or public, wealthy or underfunded, they have great power when they are facilitating emerging talents with advanced ideas; together, they can actually create change in the architecture world.

> I wished that architecture would become more futurological through the platform than it was at that time. But at the same time I hoped that it would not be too speculative but grounded with an understanding of the past and present context.
> — MČV

AS

The ideas from the open call are very much connected with projects and emerging practitioners situated all around the world. What are your thoughts on the expanding global response the project is receiving every year? Has the platform followed up with the impact Future Architecture had on each fellow after their participation?

MČV

The European Union is funding projects to build stronger cooperation within Europe and to raise awareness of the benefits of joint projects across national borders. But the platform is not limited to Europe. We could implement almost one third of the project in so-called 'third countries.' These are countries that are not members of the EU and do not have any treaties signed with it. The project is therefore open and from the very beginning we have been working with Switzerland, which is technically a third country, just like the United States. Also part of the platform are organizations from Georgia, Ukraine, and Kosovo, which have only recently signed agreements with the EU. The global response suggests that there is a need for such a platform among young professionals. A space is needed where you can present ideas to relevant interlocutors, who are either your peers or someone who can help you take the step towards their implementation by giving you the space and time to present yourself. At the end of each year, Future Architecture fellows write their assessment of collaboration within the platform. We monitor the careers of Future Architecture alumni and plan their meeting at the end of the current cycle, in 2021.

AS

Archifutures is the digital/analog publishing platform FA is promoting as a repository of ideas and content. How do you decide on the content and ideas to be promoted? What does the platform think the future of the state of architectural publishing should be in terms of formats and languages?

MČV

Archifutures is a standalone project within the platform. The editorial team of andbeyond.xyz and the publishing team of dpr-barcelona decide independently on the content. It seemed to me that among the various platform companies we needed to have an innovative publisher, and I think we were able to find the perfect combination: dpr-barcelona interested in new publishing models and andbeyond.xyz as an exceptional and dedicated editorial team. My primary purpose was to provide Future Architecture a publication that would explain complex projects in an understandable way to a wider audience. At the same time, I wanted fellows to have the opportunity to present their work in a top-notch publication.

AS

How do you envision the future of this platform in terms of sharing and cooperating with the upcoming UK withdrawal from the EU, the potential regularity of borders shutdowns because of new pandemic outbreaks, etc.? Do you have any thoughts on how this could affect the project and discipline?

MČV

The platform itself will not be affected by the UK's departure from the EU. We have excellent cooperation with UK institutions, and we have every leverage to continue this cooperation without any disruption. The pandemic situation we are currently experiencing, however, is a great test for Europe. According to Slavoj Žižek, the fight against coronavirus can only be won if it is part of the overall ecological struggle. This is a big crisis and Europe should respond more closely to crisis situations in general. Collaborations in Europe, such as Future Architecture, are a more beautiful and simpler part of a European project. But they certainly need to be considered in this context. We may have to ask ourselves how to collaborate in the future. How many trips are urgently needed for us to work together? We may do more from home in the future. As far as architecture is concerned, I hope that before any new construction we will ask ourselves more thoroughly whether it is really needed and what the consequences for the environment are.

AS

Have you ever considered expanding the platform beyond Europe? The open call is global, but participating institutions are still all European. What would be necessary for the FA amplification to reach other regions and continents? What are the challenges and opportunities of going global?

MČV

I am constantly thinking about expanding the platform across Europe. In this case, the platform would simply need a larger team and you would have to start working out where to get the extra funding to maintain the larger platform. There are two ways to do this: with strong partners who are willing to invest in the platform, or by requesting to pay a call for ideas application fee. I think for now, the platform would lose more than it would gain by either of these two measures. The platform already is open globally, but I don't think it is necessary for it to continue to grow. Turning it into a big machine would make it lose a lot of the quality of exchange, which is now taking place at a very human, personal level.

Agustin Schang is an Argentine architect, curator, and cultural producer based in New York. He studied architecture at the Universidad de Buenos Aires and graduated in 2015 with a master's degree in Critical, Curatorial and Conceptual Practices in Architecture from Columbia University GSAPP with a thesis on archives, communities, and architecture. From 2013 to 2018, he was curator in residence at the Emily Harvey Foundation, the home of landmark performances by significant Fluxus and conceptual artists. He has collaborated on multiple cultural projects with institutions including the Columbia University GSAPP; New Museum's Ideas City; Friends of the High Line; Emily Harvey Foundation; The Leslie-Lohman Museum; The Shed; Istanbul Design Biennial; CCCB Barcelona; Fundación Proa; and Ministerio de Cultura de la Ciudad de Buenos Aires. Currently, he is curating the Architecture Program at AmericasSociety / Council of the Americas NY, a new initiative developed in alliance with Americas Society Visual Art's curatorial team.

Matevž Čelik Vidmar is an architect, writer, editor, researcher, and cultural producer. Between 2010 and 2020, he was the director of the Museum of Architecture and Design (MAO). Under his direction, the MAO has launched new programs and grew into a flagship national institution with international reach. He considers the understanding of new hybrid roles of public cultural institutions to be of key importance in our times and in the future. He has been a contributor to Oris magazine in Zagreb and, in 2007, he published "New Architecture in Slovenia" (Springer Wien New York, 2007). He stands behind the repositioning of BIO, the oldest design biennial in the world, which has been transformed from a design exhibition into a live experiment to explore the potentials of design to instigate social and economic change. Since 2015 he has been leader of the platform he created, Future Architecture Platform.

PERSONAL

London-born artist and architect Sarah Entwistle is based in Berlin. Her artworks are poetic forms that play with the domestic and the quotidian within a visual and formal language that explores spolia, the architectural practice of appropriating materials into new forms. It is hard not to notice that both art and architectural thinking are at play in her practice, and the way that these two worlds have merged together is a peculiar story. It was only through a chance discovery during her training as an architect at The Bartlett School of Architecture in London that she learned about her grandfather Clive Entwistle. A friend of Le Corbusier and a figure in the mid-century modernist movement in New York whose projects were mainly never built, he was an eccentric man whose cardinal points were "Architecture, Spiritually, Intellect, and Sex." Their relationship became a central theme in her practice, like a haunting of a person that she has never met. She accessed his archive and began manipulating, erasing, and reinterpreting his motifs into tapestries, ceramics, metal cut-offs, and a book "Please Send This Book to My Mother."[1] The artworks show forces in tension, a slow unravelling, in which Sarah's search for an identity—as an architect, artist, and woman—is woven throughout.

Sarah Entwistle photographed in her Berlin studio by her son, Marlowe Broomberg (2020).

Renee Carmichael: Let's start from the beginning because you have quite a diverse background. You began with anthropology, then you eventually became an architect. How did you arrive at your grandfather's archive?

Sarah Entwistle: Architecture was not on my horizon at all. I actually wanted to be an artist, sculptor, but I was skeptical of the path of art school. I felt uncomfortable with it and I didn't have a clear drive to be in that environment. Anthropology felt closer to my interests in human interactions with objects and how objects and people build relationships. After a year of studying Social Anthropology, I enrolled in The Slade, University College London (UCL) summer foundation course and had my mind blown in the library of The Bartlett School of Architecture, UCL. I had never even thought about the wider spectrum of what architecture can be, the metaphysics of it and the scale and scope of what it can hold, and so it was a really powerful moment. I decided to transfer into the architecture department, still with no knowledge of my grandfather's work. My father obviously at that point said, "this is wonderful and also confronting

MUSINGS

Sarah Entwistle Talks with Renee Carmichael

"An architect and his wife arriving in his own rather large airplane" (2020), handwoven tapestry, Sarah Entwistle with Kebira Aglaou.

for me because of your grandfather's story." It really came out of nowhere, this new passion in my life, and I dove deep into it. I graduated from my BSc at the Bartlett and then completed my diploma at the AA. Periodically in this time I had professors come to me, Peter Cook from Archigram, different people would say to me "oh, are you related to Clive Entwistle?" And so I thought he obviously has some kind of presence in the canon, but where is he? He's nowhere. I had a few conversations with my dad and began to fill in the story of Clive. I became more aware that he had an influence, a presence in the narrative of post-war European architecture. I would often have internal dialogues. Calling forth his presence for support, St. Clive!

> One aspect of my love for architecture is in the material processes, not just in the assembling and fabrication but also in the life span of a building, it's material degradation and decay.
> — SE

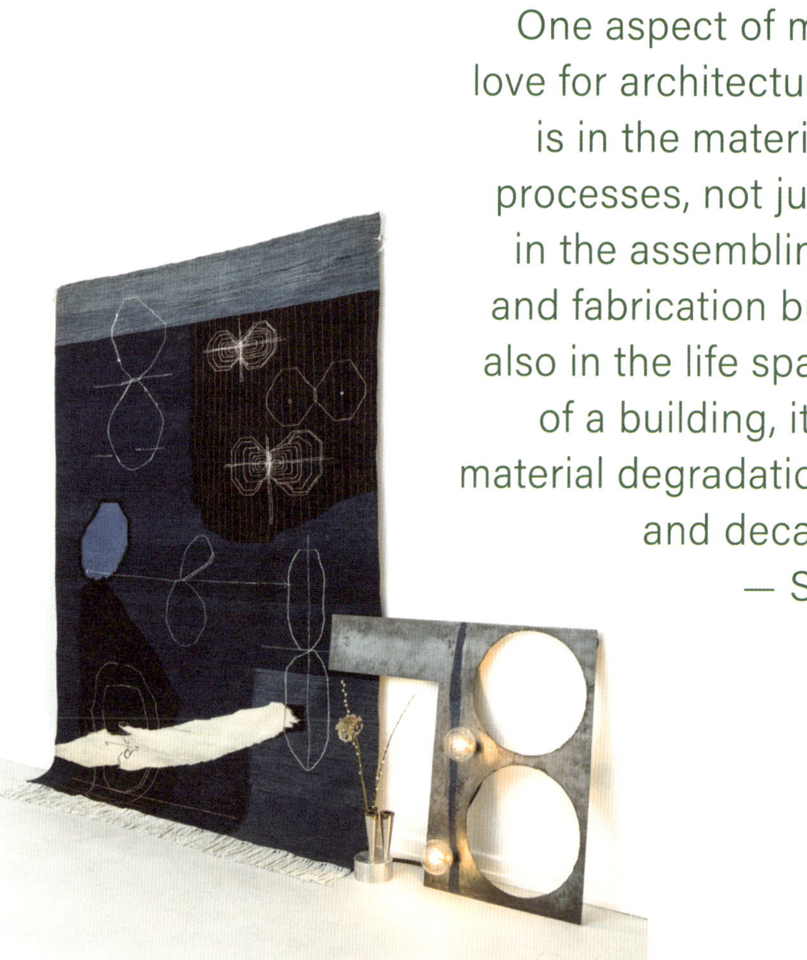

Exhibition installation for "All that I have acquired in life is yours for the taking and in fact you must take it" (2018), Etage projects, Copenhagen. Featured work The Almonds Pele, Honey, Oignons, Potatoes, Milk, Eggs, Triple Soda (2017), handwoven tapestry and steel lighting element.

After my first child was born, it was a pivotal moment because I simultaneously completed my architectural training (after a good decade of study and practice). Becoming a parent gave me immense courage, and I reconnected to my foundational desire to be an artist. I had the incredible opportunity to study at the Bartlett and AA, and flourished, but at the end I was conflicted about the practice of architecture; it was always the conceptual process that drove me, and I questioned myself throughout this time. I have to say it felt that, at some point, there was a force pushing me in that direction, it wasn't coming from my own personal desire to build and be a consummated architect. At this point I was teaching at the AA and my daughter was one year old and my father told me about the archive, which was in New York in a storeroom and was being moved to London. It's not really an archive, archive makes it sound too consolidated. It was everything Clive owned when he died, put into boxes, put into storage. That was in 1976. I was born in 1979. When I finally accessed the material, I felt this great sense of relief and the thought was there, "oh this is the person that wanted me to become an architect," this was the agen-

Selected pages from "Please Send This Book to My Mother." Sarah Entwistle, Sternberg Press (2015).

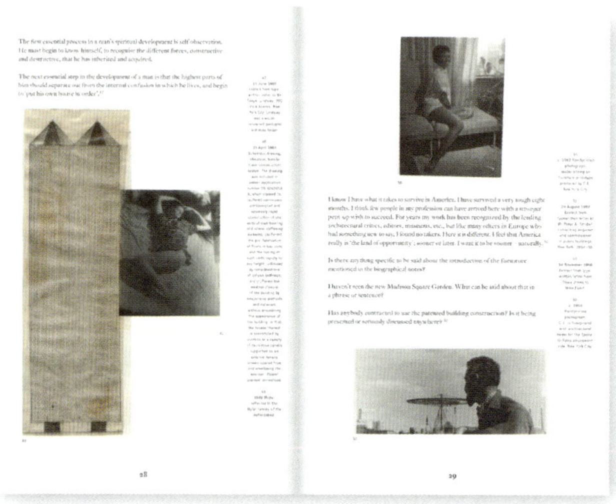

da because—essentially, he was from the time of epic gestures in architecture. He was the idealist and I had somehow channeled all of that energy but it didn't feel authentic to me and then I understood why.

Using his material became my means to stop being an architect. [laughs] I feel at different episodes I was Clive's channel and then he became mine. And there really is still this struggle within our dynamic.

RC: You can see a lot of these tensions that start to appear in your book "Please Send This Book to My Mother." Could you elaborate on how they might materialize in your carpets or your works? There is also an idea of control. He talks a lot about forces, about luck, about these forces that he can't control and it seems like your work also enters into that.

SE: Definitely, questions of control, force, forces, luck, are all themes that Clive was exploring and are drawn out in the book. Clive had a broad library of books, heavily annotated and marked up. These notations have become refrains that I have in mind and sometimes include graphically in the work. Carl Jung's book about synchronicity is part of his library, and I think there are many moments of synchronicity in my life that resonate with Clive's narrative. But our shared visual language has become the repeated motifs that cycle through the archive and then subsequently re-appear in real time in found materials or compositionally in my ceramics and tapestries. This Morse code reverberates between the raw material of the archive and my works. There is certainly a lot of tension for me around his relationship to women because that's a really central part of the archive and clearly relevant to our dynamic. There are many elements that are potent there, he was exploring BDSM (Bondage, Discipline, Dominance, and Submission / Sadomasochism), often as the dominant, and he at one point declares his cardinal points as architecture, intellect, sex, and spiritualism. And he really did live by those four drives. There's always been a tension for me between being seduced by him and then being him, embodying him. [laughs] There's a masochism and an egotism and other confronting forces, often judged as pathologies, that I'm aware of in me and compelled to explore through my work. The tapestry series I'm currently working on both highlight his most compelling architectural proposals and graphically degrade them. These are mostly towers, easily conflated with his phallicentric perspective, and then I use different gestures or markings from the archive that for me have feminist symbology to obscure and intercept the towers. These motifs are often developed from secondary gestures in the archive, smudges, doodles, or arbitrary line making; I amplify those. I use them to erase the structural imagery, the dominant architectural imagery of the archive. Dismantling his presence with these expressive gestures that are both his and mine. I feel with each work I'm unravelling him and abstracting the archive. The book was so immediately centered on him. It was the first project and it was intended to re-present him. To satisfy his restless need.

RC: You have a mythological family story that you are working with, but at the same time you have material elements. How did you start working with these materials?

SE: One aspect of my love for architecture is the material processes, not just in the assembling and fabrication but also the life span of a building, its material degradation and decay. Also the process of construction, much of what I use in the studio are found off cuts from building sites and fabrication yards, the leftovers and remnants of a process. The first installation I developed was for Le Corbusier's apartment in Paris, the exhibition was titled "He was my father, and I was an atom of him destined to grow into him." The apartment was unrestored at the time and largely untouched since Le Corbusier had lived there, emptied of furniture and belongings. The installation was a skewed re-furnishing of the apartment. The objects, both formally and materially, were drawing from the space and the archive, materializing an aspect of the mythology Clive perpetuated around his kinship with Le Corbusier. I centered myself as a mediator. The domestic context felt very apt and continues to resonate with my work and the play between the soft and hard furnishings of a space and the total architecture spatial language that the Bauhaus and modernism aspired for, this totalizing spatial experience. Through this project, I identified materials and techniques that I've returned to: hand built ceramics, sheet metal, and hand weaving. At the end of his life Clive was living in Morocco so I thought to build a bridge with that period of time. I met a weaver in Morocco, Kebira Aglaou,[2] and we have worked together since then. I give her complex compositions, with multiple layers and gradations in color and tone, and she is continually challenging the technology and techniques to translate and interpret the imagery, textures, and hatchings. That is something that resonated for me with the processes of translation in architecture from drawing to construction, the interpretive element and also the slippage between image and materiality, the physicality, the process which demands such labor and gesture. Kebira said to me when we met and discussed the background of the project, "your grandfather, he couldn't really get the job done, we are getting the job done with the weavings, we are finishing his project." [laughs]

RC: I took a lot of notes on your work and one of the words that stuck out was 'erasure.' You are doing that but at the

Selected pages from "Please Send This Book to My Mother." Sarah Entwistle, Sternberg Press (2015).

But our shared visual language has become the repeated motifs that cycle through the archive and then subsequently re-appear in real time in found materials, or compositionally in my ceramics and tapestries. This Morse code reverberates between the raw material of the archive and my works.

— SE

same time you are exploring a way that you can appear in these works.

SE: It's tricky because some people have issues with the fact that he is so present in the work and say that I should let him go. But I don't feel as dominated by him or his work as I once did, and I also don't feel like fully erasing him. One could say he was a sexist, masochist, narcissist... all these things, but he also had a lot of potency, curiosity, courage. Occasionally, lines he wrote come to mind that help me, like mantras. They often become titles for works. There's one that I was thinking about recently and he says "do not forget to do the things you do today again." I take from this that when one has a spiritual practice or a good habit you want to develop you have to remember to do it again and again; It's helpful, I can use that, that's a valuable thing so I don't want to erase that. Albeit he was writing it in the context of a really punitive letter to one of his lovers. [laughs] I produced a series works of marbling ink over archival drawings. The marbling grafts into the fibers of the drawings, literally erasing his work while at the same time invigorating the reproductions into new works. Erasure is certainly a central theme and an active process but it's not total, it's more a smudging out, a palimpsest, I guess this is true of all practices. Perhaps at some point Clive's presence will fade away.

RC: It's a kind of tension between erasure and, what you said, translation...

SE: Someone that would have known him wouldn't even recognize him in the book because it's fully interpreted in terms of how the material is put together. It's very much my agenda as well. I didn't show my father the book when I was working on it and he only saw it after it was produced. He was very supportive but it was emotionally confronting for him, he expressed concern that readers would find the figure of Clive derisible. I understand that there's a tragic aspect, he could be seen as a parody of a mid-century architect. I arranged the material intuitively, I didn't have a consolidated perception of who he was or how I wanted him to be received by a reader. A thread that I imposed for myself as I went along was that it was a love story, at different levels. His love story with his narrative, with this myth, but also with his lovers, his wife, and then also with the ideologies that he was looking at. This impacted the format of the book, which is soft cover and novel-sized. I didn't want it to be a historical biography because I'm not a historian and I also wasn't interested in a systematic processing of the material or narration of his story. I made a portrait of him, but I'm not his biographer. I did not make a reflective third person narration, it's more immediate as all the material visual and textual is from the archive. I think it can be quite disorientating. I often have the conversation where people say "there's a lot going on there." [laughs] And I want to keep all of these elements going but at the same time I hope to convey the forces at work and perhaps don't need the narration for people to access it to experience something from it.

RC: There is something in the way of reading, in the way of processing it, it really relates to the tapestries. It's interesting how you take this experience that you are trying to unweave and at the same time you are then weaving it as something else.

SE: Maybe it's quite helpful just to go back to the materials. Architectural methodologies often come into play. There is a practice that is definitely rooted in my architectural training. I think it is really critical for me that I couldn't have come to this practice as a fine artist. I remain an architect in this process. [laughs]

1 Entwistle, Sarah. *Please Send This Book to My Mother* (Berlin: Sternberg Press, 2015).

2 Kebira Aglaou was born in 1975 and lives in Morocco. She is an accomplished weaver who incorporates traditional and experimental techniques. Kebira helped start the female carpet cooperative *Nkob de Siroua*. She continues to develop her own compositions and collaborative pieces and has exhibited works in both regional and international fairs.

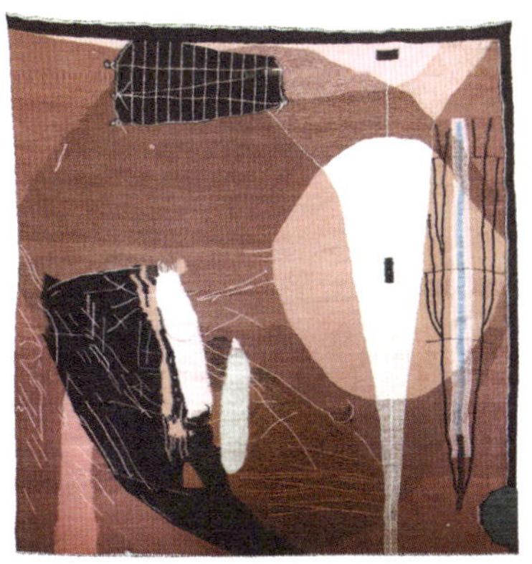

"Many small carrots and frail sticks" (2019), handwoven tapestry, Sarah Entwistle with Kebira Aglaou.

"Here behind my eyes I am no longer afraid" (2019), handwoven tapestry, Sarah Entwistle with Kebira Aglaou.

"You shout first, and I will shout after" (2019), handwoven tapestry, Sarah Entwistle with Kebira Aglaou.

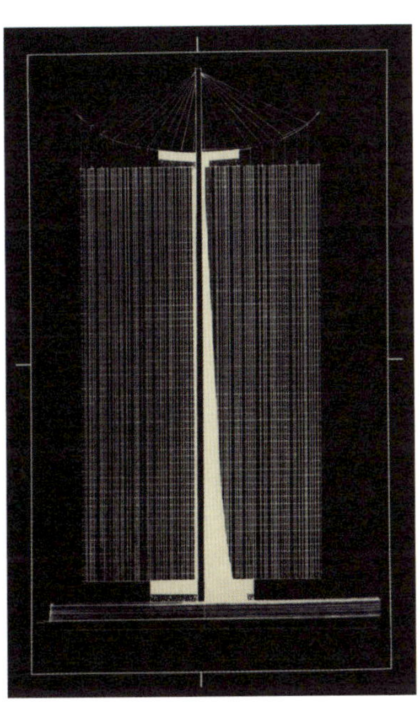

Elevation drawing for a proposed cable-suspended tower by Clive Entwistle (c.1964) for a Montreal location. Client: City Investing Company, New York. Unrealized.

Erasure is certainly a central theme and an active process but it isn't total, it's more a smudging out, a palimpsest, I guess this is true of all practices. Perhaps at some point Clive's presence will fade away.

— SE

Exhibition installation for "All that I have acquiered in life is yours for the taking and in fact you must take it" (2018) Etage project, Copenhagen. Featured work "Do not attempt to break the seal" (2018), handwoven tapestry, ceramic objects.

In a pleasant Zoom conversation, Brazilian architect Carla Juaçaba covered topics as diverse as working with raw materials and the need to make use of references that go beyond the traditional architectural imaginary. The dialogue, like her projects, suggests the construction of stimulating narratives in which readers—or users—become crucial participants.

Ph. Courtesy Carla Juaçaba

CARLA JUAÇABA

On the Open, the Theatrical, and the Fragile

MAGDALENA TAGLIABUE

Although Carla Juaçaba moved to London in early 2020, she emphasizes that no matter where she finds herself in the world, her work remains the same. She is originally from Rio de Janeiro, Brazil, and it was there that she established her independent practice in 2000. After completing the Humanidade Pavilion in 2012, she began to be recognized as a reference in the contemporary young Latin American architecture scene. Now, a few years later, her international commissions are increasing, as are the invitations she receives to lecture and teach at universities such as Harvard, Columbia, and Mendrisio.

After commenting informally on her recent move and the current state of affairs in Brazil, we turned to the Vatican Pavilion project in Venice, as it seems to synthesize many of her recent explorations. I was intrigued by its spatial vagueness and how its openness does not relegate programmatic concerns.

Is this a sculpture? Is this an installation? I like to say that this is architecture because there is a program, not because there is a roof or there are walls. You sit on a bench and look at the cross... It is the synthesis of a program that existed for ages... Even though you could maybe see it as sculpture, once you sit on it, it becomes architecture.

When reviewing Juaçaba's work, the idea of something else completing what has been designed seems to be a canon. This may be a consequence of her influence and collaboration with theater directors. For example, in the Venice pavilion she was inspired by the work of the fa-

mous contemporary London director Peter Brook, and in the well-known Humanidade Pavilion, the general concept and direction was co-authored with Bia Lessa, a Brazilian filmmaker, theater director, and curator. In her work, users and contingencies such as the weather—intangible and unpredictable—have the capability to impact the way the future unfolds. As it is seen in the slow, silent videos in which the tree's leaves, the greenness, and the reflection of the Venetian water is reflected in the mirrored stands of the Vatican pavilion.[1]

Peter Brook is a reference for me. It was very relevant to me to be in contact with him. Eighteen years ago, when I was very young, I participated in a workshop with his scenographer in Rio: Jean Guy-Lecat. From that moment on, it was very important to begin to see my profession through the lens of another discipline.

The intention to pose neutral, ethereal, and diluted scenes in some of her projects is intrinsic to their ephemeral condition. For both the Vatican pavilion and the Humanidade Pavilion, when the idea of becoming permanent was raised, a contradiction was embodied. In fact, this is what was fulfilled with the Vatican project.

This pavilion seems to dissipate, and the Vatican doesn't seem to appreciate things that are 'disperse.' Everything is so permanent for the Vatican. Of course, I was very happy for it to be made permanent, but before we knew it was going to stay there, we had all these questions: where are they going to move this chapel after? There were a few invitations to move it to different places, so I

Ph. Leonardo Finotti

HUMANIDADE PAVILION - Rio de Janeiro, Brazil, 2012

The scaffold structure is composed of five elements with walls 170 meters wide, 20 meters high and 5.4 meters apart. The structure creates a suspended walkway over Rio de Janeiro's landscape and becomes a temporary exhibition center. Auditorium, exhibition, and meeting rooms are separated from each other. Circulation on ramps in between the spaces generates the experience itself.

called Francesco dal Co, the curator, and we both thought it had to remain there because of its direct relation to the site.

While in line with theories based on tectonics and the proportions with which Brazilian architecture is traditionally defined, Carla Juaçaba's architecture also incorporates a freshness of experimental work through her relation to natural contexts. The Humanidade Pavilion acted like a scenography for the Rio de Janeiro coast. Built as scaffolding that could extend indefinitely, its origin is nothing more than the continuation of its pre-existing bases.

Impermanence is also part of the Humanidade Pavilion project. Very few materials were used, it is not a traditional construction. It is defined by the continuity of the elements that were already there. There were existing structural bases and the project was a continuity out of those bases. Both this project and The Vatican Chapel are definitely site-specific objects.

How can architects speak from other points of view that do not exclusively refer to the discipline? Carla Juaçaba reverses the question going through other references that influenced her poetic quality:

There is one carioca artist that I really like, Lygia Pape. She was very important at the school where I studied, the Universidade Santa Úrsula. Everything was very experimental and chaotic but, at the same time, everyone seemed to follow what she designed as a course or exercises and the way of doing them. You could describe her work as a variety. She never used the same material

Ph. Federico Cairoli

VATICAN CHAPEL - Venice, Italy, 2018

The Vatican Chapel was part of the 16th International Architecture Exhibition at the Venice Biennial. Ten different architects were invited to build ten chapels on San Giorgio Maggiore island in Venice, which had never been open to the public before. Four 12 by 12 centimeter and 8 meter-wide, polished steel beams make up the ensemble. One pair of beams creates a bench, the other pair a cross; both are traditional elements of the Catholic Church. The bases are built with concrete and hidden underground.

twice. It seems that in her work there is always something new. She uses gold lines [2] and everything looks very fresh. This diversity is something that I am very interested in.

When talking about Juaçaba's inspirations, Lina Bo Bardi was a clear starting point. The work of the Italian-Brazilian Bo Bardi synthesizes the idea of an essential balance between the contemporary and the ancestral anthropological syntaxis. Carla Juaçaba adds to this the performative aspect of the event. In Cadeira de Beira de Estrada (1967), the same element (a cane) repeated three times, needs a body to activate the counterweight so that the tripod is supported and functions as a chair. It is a joint between the stable and the malleable. The relationship between the object and its configuration, where the manipulation of the material is valued as much as the materials themselves, is typical of povera-art.

Both povera-art and povera-architecture communicate with a few elements. There is of course a relation between low-budget projects and this povera-art. When I went to Lina's house, for example, I was fascinated by it, but also by the wall that delimits the terrain. This perimeter wall is made in a really sloppy way with concrete blocks and with dirty joints between the concrete blocks. This 'not done well' appearance was the author's intention, of course, and I thought it was beautiful, the most fascinating part of the house.

Also, Peter Brook uses bamboo elements[3] in the theater; he changes a scene by playing with a few vertical elements. He proposes different

symbolisms by moving the bamboo poles. From a cross to a forest, it is a cross; it is a forest; it becomes many things with just one element.

Juaçaba's projects for exhibitions generally appear not as curatorial actions but as an opportunity to create different sets.[4] "Ministry for All" at the Storefront for Art and Architecture in New York was the result of her collaboration with the artist Marcelo Cidade. The structural logic of the seemingly hidden architectural elements was revealed through the unfolding of the façade of the iconic Storefront building. Like an unveiled veil, the skin that acts as an edge against the sidewalk became more and more permeable until it almost dematerialized. These layers, like hanging dry skins, travelled inside. The physical presence of the structure remains constant, so what happens inside is in perpetual flux, molding and influencing the social order.

In "Ministry for All," the curator was José Esparza Chong Cuy; he gave us a subject. The intention of this work was a little bit untraditional. I started working with moving out of its façade. Then, he invited Marcelo Cidade to project something on the inside with the façade material. Storefront is an over-consecrated place in New York and José's intention was to bring back the action of architecture and art. The name of the gallery is "art and architecture," and so he wanted to return to this point where the artist does not necessarily have a better position than the architect.

So, in a way, we were destroying the museum's consecrated image by reconstructing it with its own elements.

Ph. Federico Cairoli

CASA SANTA TERESA - Rio de Janeiro, Brazil, 2008

Invisible from the street, the house is like a pavilion that parallels the curves of a plot. It is located on a high level in a green and hilly area. No trees were removed. One level contains public areas and the other contains private rooms. Both areas are connected by a glass gallery adjacent to the street. On the opposite side, both sectors have panoramic views. Four different slopes make up a veneer roof structure covered with wood on the inside.

Ph. Federico Cairoli

BALLAST - Venice, Italy, 2008

Titled Freespace, the 16th International Architecture Exhibition at the Venice Biennial invited architects to reflect on the generosity of spirit and a sense of humanity. A set of concrete blocks act as sculptures scarcely placed in a park as a response to this type of democratic space. Without connections between the parts, the simple weight of the components balances with the arrangement of the different concrete blocks.

In the end it was incredible because all this nice and perfectly well-done image was destroyed by revealing what was inside the façade. And it seemed to be something really improvised. It was chaotic but amazing to see.

When I finished the Humanidade Pavilion project in Rio, I was invited to Brasilia to do something as a continuation of it. They wanted to copy and paste the Humanidade Pavilion there. For me, this was not a possibility as the pavilion was very site-specific and Brasilia's scale does not allow anything to fit inside. It was then when the idea of a 'ministry for all' came out. As Brasilia has this pristine image, I proposed a building which would have the same measurement, height, and distance between all of the ministry's buildings. It would be a public institution but made of scaffolds. Because we are living in this critical moment in Brazil, José wanted to take up this idea. It was very symbolic to make this reference.

These questions about context, which act as a general theme in her practice, guided our conversation inadvertently and somehow very naturally returned us to the starting point.

London is just a base point. I moved here because there was an invitation to teach in Switzerland, and at the same time, there are a few works in Europe that I am starting to develop. Certainly, this has been an opportunity to see my country from the outside.

Juaçaba is working in an installation for the Bienal da Pedra in the city of Alpendorada, Portugal. The determining factor of the invitation was the

Ph. Fran Parente

CASA VARANDA - Rio de Janeiro, Brazil, 2008

Along a continuous border between nature and the city, the house divides the field into two lengths. A cut in the roof becomes a 24 meter by 6 meter skylight that accentuates the division. The visuals go beyond the structure. Private rooms are at the extremes of the house, while the living room is in the center, acting as an open terrace. The steel structure was built in fifteen days. The roof is made of zinc aluminum tiles and was added in one day.

material: stone. In addition to this, she has recently completed a house where the main operation consisted in the realization of a façade made entirely of brick-type blocks. These blocks were nearly sixty centimeters long and are no longer produced.

Artists linked to povera-art, defended a dismantling of the hierarchy of materials, rejected consumerism, and were interested in conjunction of the force of nature and industrial modernity. The spirit of that era is present in the work of Carla Juaçaba, but her work also stakes a claim for an aesthetic poetic language that is often missing in contemporary architecture.

1 Vatican Chapel, Carla Juaçaba (video by Gabriel Kogan). https://www.youtube.com/watch?v=fY-mhUFsIDQ
2 Lygia Pape, "Ttéia 1," 2000.
3 Peter Brook, "A Magic Flute," 2011.
4 Juaçaba curated "Isostasy," LIGA, Mexico City, 2011, and "Viajem das Carrancas," Moreira Salles Institute, Rio de Janeiro, 2015.

Stephen Burks Man Made

Weaving process of the armchair Ahnda for Dedon, 2014

Stephen Burks Man Made is a New York-based design studio. All its stories begin with the hand: the hand that weaves, the hand that shakes, the hand that makes, the hand that protests, the hand that communicates. The studio's workshop-based practice engages craftspeople throughout the globe, bringing us closer to an immediacy of making that is deeply meaningful, expressive, and innovative. Building bridges between artisanal production and world distribution through contemporary design has been its mission for the last fifteen years, which is shown in an impressive portfolio including collaborations with brands such as Dedon, Missoni, Roche Bobois, and Living Divani. We talked to Stephen Burks, industrial designer and educator, and his partner Malika Leiper, cook, storyteller, and urban strategist.

Ph. Justin Skeens

NESS: Stephen, how did it all begin? What was your path to design?

STEPHEN BURKS: As a child growing up in Chicago, confronted with the architectural force of the city's modernism, my entry into the world of design came through buildings. The first time I set eyes upon Mies van der Rohe's, Crown Hall, I knew I wanted to study at the Illinois Institute of Technology. Studying there was a very spiritual experience. Those classical proportions, the way the light travels through the building, and the possibilities of its open plan really led me to want to study architecture and design. It was there in the basement of Crown Hall, at the Institute of Design originally known as the New Bauhaus, taking classes in visual training, color theory, graphic design, and architectural photography that my understanding of what it means to be a designer took shape. Years later, at Columbia University's Graduate School of Architecture Planning, & Preservation, I realized I was more inspired by how we engage with the things inside the building rather than the buildings themselves.

NESS: The Stephen Burks Man Made studio tagline is 'we bring the hand to industry,' tell us a little bit about what that means and how you arrived at this way of working?

SB: At around the turn of the millennium, after a successful exhibition with a French gallery, I began designing furniture with the small factories of the Italian companies B&B Italia, Boffi, Cappellini, Missoni, Moroso, and others. These early years were educational at an intimate scale for both hand and industrial production, working in harmony for the global success of brands barely half-a-century old. It wasn't until 2005, after my first trips to Africa as a product development consultant with Aid to Artisans, that I began to ask myself: if the economic transformation of postwar Italy was possible through investment in craft-based family businesses, why couldn't the same be done in other parts of the world?

The realization of what was possible by using craft in combination with industry through collaborations with artisans around the world led me to a fundamental belief in the creative and transformative power of communities of hands or "hand factories," as we call them. It was obvious that these hands have power and after working in

Armchair Ahnda for Dedon, 2015

Colombia, Ghana, Haiti, Kenya, India, Indonesia, the Philippines, Rwanda, Senegal, and South Africa, as well as all over Europe and the United States, our studio's practice is deeply rooted in the conviction that through our hands, we are all capable of design.

NESS: What about you, Malika? What was your journey as an urban strategist like and how did you and Stephen join forces?

MALIKA LEIPER: I spent my childhood in the rapidly urbanizing context of Phnom Penh, Cambodia. Growing up in a place like this, I developed an underlying awareness of the uneven processes shaping urban spatial production and the limits of modernist ideals. As I witnessed the primacy of speculative real estate and the changing East-Asian face of development transform my hometown, I questioned the role of the 20th century architect or designer as *auteur*. Instead, I began searching for the possibilities of design as a community development project engaged in a process of exchange rather than transaction. My graduate school thesis, for example, involved partnering with a non-profit in Lowell, Massachusetts, to design and build a bicycle parking facility for their community center. Through several workshops that led to a community-informed design, I sought to demonstrate how culturally sensitive infrastructural interventions could create a more inclusive and sustainable public realm. Ever since Stephen and I met at the Harvard Graduate School of Design, where he became the first industrial designer to join the Loeb Fellowship and I was completing a Master's in Urban Planning, we've been digging deeper into what it means to be citizens of the world contributing to a broader view of the built environment.

Variations.
Exhibition desisgn for Calligaris, Milan Furniture Fair, 2013

NESS: Stephen, you have often said that design is a Western concept. Can you please elaborate on that and how it applies to the studio's practice?

SB: The idea of Design with a capital D was in fact invented at the Bauhaus in Europe in the early 20th century. There it is a profession that you are educated in that teaches you to be in service of industry; to give form to and solve problems of industrial production. It is a very Western concept. While in the rest of the world people have been manipulating material, making the things they need in service of their communities for centuries, but even today we struggle to consider it to be design. The idea that one culture has the right to consider itself more 'advanced' than another or dictate taste or style and consider itself superior is wrong. Rather, the realization of dreams in physical form for the expression of culture exists within different time frames across the globe and everyone has the right to progress at their own pace regardless of the tools of design they choose to use.

When we look outside of our comfortable surroundings, we're often reluctantly forced to consider the other. Whether it be our next-door neighbor or an artisan on the other side of the world. Instead of seeing them as an obstacle to avoid or overcome, our practice is engaged in actively embracing the differences which encountering the other offers us in an open attempt to collaborate with or learn from cultures other than our own.

ML: Our home studio is a great physical manifestation of what Stephen is talking about. For us, there is no distinction between art, design, fashion, urbanism, or photography. We are more interested in how things are related rather than how they exist apart. The blackboard wall, for example, is replete with material samples, postcards, concepts, and hand sketches that blend together to create a cacophony of visual references. Our bookshelves are full of titles on art, design, architecture, urban history, and critical theory, to name a few. And all around our home, collectible design objects are intermingled with inspirational souvenirs from our international travels. Instead of trying to compartmentalize, categorize, and decontextualize, we prefer to explore the unknown in order to find possibilities that may not be so black and white.

All images courtesy Stephen Burks Man Made

SB: It's all in how you see it. Like the term "majority world" in opposition to phrases like "global south" or "the developing world," which are inherently value-driven, the majority world is a simple reference to the fact that the greater share of the world's population is living outside of a Western context. At the end of the day, we cannot achieve sustainability unless we embrace the ways other people are thinking, living, and making.

NESS: What projects are you working on at the moment?

SB: We recently began an ongoing relationship with the historic institution, Berea College Student Craft. As the first fully-integrated school in the American South, Berea College offers tuition-free education to its 1,600 students. In 2018, the studio was commissioned to develop a new collection of products within the four student craft departments—Broomcraft, Ceramics, Weaving, and Woodcraft. Entitled "Crafting Diversity," the project ties each physical object to the college's longstanding 'great commitments', which include the kinship and equality of all people, supportive and sustainable living, and the dignity of labor.

ML: It was crucial for us that the collaboration not only result in radically contemporary products but also in a new relationship to craft that speaks directly to the student's potential in the world today. The decision was made early on to pursue a participatory workshop-based model, which brought students into direct dialogue with the design process for the first time. The textile collection woven in cotton and sustainable bamboo thread was given the name Pixel in acknowledgment of the students' relationship to the digital world. For the placemat, which is woven on a handloom, students have the opportunity to choose their own color and position of stripes in the warp. In this way, the students are literally placing their hand into the objects they make—a testament to the value of the creativity of the students.

SB: By pursuing the possibilities of student-designed products, "Crafting Diversity" embodies our overarching commitment to extending craft traditions into the future.

NESS: How have you been coping since the global pandemic turned the world upside down and what are some projects you have on the horizon?

ML: Our time spent sheltering-in-place has opened up a window for a new way of working together. In addition to aiding in the launch of several new collections for BD Barcelona, Dedon, Living Divani, and Luceplan, we've reinvented our home as a laboratory to explore new ideas shaping domesticity, namely, how do we want to live in the future.

SB: This time spent working from home has forced many of us to consider—some of us for the first time—how we live, what we live with, and why. From this conceptual starting point, we are in the process of responding to requests for radically reimagining not just our own home as fertile ground for new ways of inhabiting our domestic environments, but also the ways in which new building developments inhabit neighborhoods and communities. It goes without saying that craft will be at the center of all of these explorations.

ML: These home experiments have already attracted the attention of galleries and museums, and we are in early-stage conversations about realizing them on a larger scale. A woven television kit assembled at home, a hooded screen intended to create privacy for Zoom calls in an open space, and even a lamp that responds to your position in the room are a few ways that we are exploring a new frontier where craft and technology intersect.

SB: The closer the hand gets to the act of making, the more potential there is for innovation, especially if, ultimately, the product or interior is made by its owners. For us, the future of craft lies in everyone's imagination and maybe, if we can help it, their participation.

CRAFTING DIVERSITY
Berea College Student Craft, 2018 - ongoing

In the spring of 2018, Stephen Burks began an ongoing collaboration with Berea College to develop a new collection of products for their Student Craft Department. Entitled "Crafting Diversity," the project ties each physical object to the college's longstanding 'great commitments,' which include the kinship and equality of all people, supportive and sustainable living, and the dignity of labor.[1] It was crucial that the collaboration not only resulted in a new collection, but also in a new relationship to craft that spoke directly to the students' position in the world today. Burks's decision to pursue a participatory workshop-based model was the starting point for a way of working, which brought students into direct dialogue with the design process for the first time. By pursuing a relational collaboration with design—as opposed to transactional—"Crafting Diversity" embodies the studio's overarching commitment to extending craft traditions into the future.

1 Margot Guralnick, "Crafts and Kinship: Broom Making, Weaving, and More at Berea College in Kentucky," 2020. Available online at: remodelista.com

BABEL - Parachilna, 2016

Babel is a lighting collection in anodized aluminum that refers to the ancient mythical tower of Babylon. Light and shadow are cast in equal measure from the recessed windows of its faceted architectural form.

TRYPTA - Luceplan, 2019

Trypta is an acoustic lighting solution that utilizes a custom designed 3D-knitted textile over three acoustic panels suspended from an aluminum extrusion that delivers both ceiling and surface illumination.

GRASSO - BD Barcelona, 2018

Grasso is a seating collection inspired by the imperfection of human skin. This different vision of beauty allowed Stephen Burks Man Made to imagine furniture of extreme visual comfort but also imperfect, fat, and overflowing. Grasso Ceramics were inspired by their upholstered counter-part's overstuffed voluminous forms with a nod to the coil basket weaving traditions of Senegal using hand painted metallic glazes.

ISLANDS
Living Divani, 2019

Islands is a collection of free-standing furniture that uses an extruded aluminum louver to create open or closed storage. Low cabinets, side tables, and shelving are currently in development.

Ph. Tommaso Sartori

DALA - Dedon, 2012

Dala means to take or to make in Tagalog, the language of the Philippines. The notion of an improvised casual seating was expressed through circular forms and artisan controlled weaving patterns that resulted in the first outdoor furniture ever made with recycled extruded polyethylene woven through expanded aluminum.

THE OTHERS - Dedon, 2017

The Others is a family of solar powered portable lanterns disguised as colorful companions for spending time indoors and out; they seek to remind us that we were all new in the neighborhood once.

ANWAR - Parachilna, 2015

Anwar means luminous in Arabic and is the first collection designed for the Spanish lighting brand. Electroplated in brass, copper, and graphite, its bold forms are illuminated in coiled tension and can be combined like powerful totems.

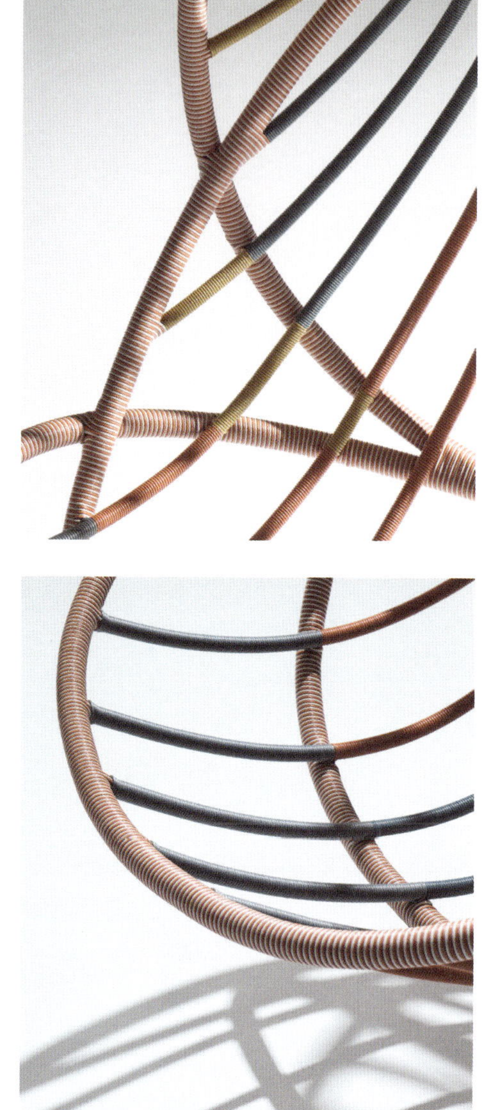

KIDA - Dedon, 2020

Drawing inspiration from his close collaboration with master weavers in the Philippines, Burks sought to reinvent the hanging chair. He developed a design that looks and feels less enclosed. This is the first collection to be wrapped rather than woven in Dedon Fiber.

Weaving in the Work of Stephen Burks Man Made

ISABELLA MORETTI

A quick glance at Stephen Burks Man Made's website reveals a close relationship with the bauhaus imaginary. The colorful layout of the website's backgrounds echo Josef Alber's Homage to the Square iterations. The aesthetic speaks to his first steps in design as a student taking courses in what once were the classrooms of the New Bauhaus in Chicago. "All of our contemporary life revolves around design," Stephen Burks says—a statement also reminiscent of his modern predecessors. Nevertheless, he detaches himself from the figure of the Designer of the 20th century and chooses a model more closely related to the first Weimarer phase of the renowned school, where craft was considered equally relevant to industrial production. Burks aims for a balance in what he lovingly calls "the artisan community hand factory," a hybrid model that sees the potential of both and places the hand where it is most useful.

Anni Albers reminds us of weaving's long tradition; a tradition that has been left essentially unchanged; its principle still relevant in times of mechanic production. In a 1963 lecture, she said: "With our fingers we can make infinite variables, with machinery only limited variance." [1] For several years now, Stephen Burks Man Made has been collaborating with the outdoor furniture business DEDON in four collections: The Others, Dala, Ahnda, and Kida. Founded in the 90s, DEDON combines modern industrial technology with craftmanship. They specialize in a waterproof synthetic fiber—now expanded into a comprehensive catalog of materials—that is woven by more than twelve hundred artisans in the Philippines. In his last trip to the factory, Burks was able to engage closely with the weavers to perform technical and material tests and innovate through an iterative process. Back in 2011, Burks presented an exhibition inspired by the traditions of Senegales basket weavers of the village of Thies in his first solo show at the Studio Museum in Harlem. Four years later, he traveled once again to do a self-initiated workshop; the resulting baskets were the first the community made with the guide of a drawing. The Thies community also influenced the Grasso Ceramics collection. With this in mind, Burks taught the workshop "What's in a Basket?" as a 2019 Loeb Fellow at the Harvard Graduate School of Design. Students brought random baskets to the classroom, and after carefully understanding their materiality through touch and drawing, they designed their own original baskets, constructed them by hand, and then translated the experience to the digital realm.

Coil baskets have a revealing potential. The anthropologist Tim Ingold was able to elaborate a theory on how to bypass the nature-culture division by encountering the waste-paper basket in his study and understanding its handmade construction as analogous to the growth of the gastropod shell.[2] Both idea and action are inherent to artisanal making; crafted objects carry within them stories that often speak to the personal, intimate, and make one wonder about the situations, places, and hands that made them. Donna Haraway explains in a film as she dearly holds a basket "...this beautiful Navajo Basket, which of course I have no right to own. One of the reasons I hold it up here is because it's also embarrassing. How is it that a daughter of conquest owns this object? [...] There is no way that we can touch without inheriting the whole thing. It's not that I feel guilty of holding this basket but the basket is also this eruption of a whole story of dispossession and dependence sovereignty of native American people [...] the basket remind[s] me of the details, the intimacy of inheritance."[3]

1 Anni Albers, "Untitled Lecture," New Haven, 1963. In: *On Weaving*, (New Jersey: Princeton University Press, 2017).
2 Tim Ingold, "On Weaving a Basket" in *The Perception of the Environment*, (London and New York: Routledge, 2000).
3 *Donna Haraway: Story Telling for Earthly Survival*, film directed by Fabrizio Terranova, 2016.
4 See the full article "Puff Dada" published by Pilar Villadas in September 2005 at nytimes.com.
5 Aid for Artisans creates economic opportunities for artisan communities where crafts and traditions are at risk. Their work facilitates product development, business training, and market access. More information at creativelearning.org
6 "Designer of the Day Stephen Burks" by Ryan Waddoups in *Surface Magazine*. Available online.
7 Arturo Escobar, *Autonomía y diseño: la realización de lo comunal*, (Buenos Aires: Tinta Limón, 2017).

As the first American to work in the international (mostly European) contemporary design scene,[4] Burks anchored his work in collaboration with artisans. The year 2005 marked a turning point: through the Aid to Artisans initiative,[5] he acted as a Product Development Consultant and traveled to Cape Town. For the first time, he was closely working with people who had forged a relationship with a particular material and technique for generations. Burks found his identity suddenly aligned with his work. Over the following five years, he became a nomad circling the world and meeting different communities. His conception of design changed with every trip; each artisan community influenced his radically aware practice.

Reviewing the global economy of artisanal craft is necessary in order to engage with the transformative potential of its practice. Building bridges between artisanal production and world distribution is also relevant 'designerly' knowledge that, when done with responsibility, can have real economic impact for communities. It is an opportunity for mapping design processes holistically and sincerely. Designers like Stephen Burks have turned to this challenge by partnering with new actors, beyond academia, such as Not for Profit Organizations and eco-conscious brands in a workshop-based practice. After two years' experience working with Aid to Artisans, Burks inaugurated an economic model called The Development Triangle. The artisan is positioned in the lower left corner of the triangle, the designer in the lower right, the company providing distribution on top, and the nonprofit organization in the center. According to Burks "The designer and the artisan have a collaborative relationship, an almost symbiotic relationship. I'm learning from them about making by hand and I'm teaching them about the relationship to industry and what contemporary design can contribute." Both designer and artisan build a business relationship for the company in terms of license and in terms of production respectively.

Basket weaving workshop Senegal, 2015

Nonprofit organizations are a key actor holding the triangle together through the management and oversight of each project. Aside from Aid to Artisans, Burks has worked with Artesanías de Colombia, Design Network Africa, and Ten Thousand Villages. As organizations with different business models (from nonprofit to public-private partnerships) they share the mission to empower makers (mostly women) and battle poverty in so-called 'developing' countries. In order to provide fair wages, preserve ancestral legacies, and foster consumer ethics, they facilitate access to markets—through fairs or commercial outputs such as online shops—marketing campaigns, design workshops, and business training. However, this approach is not infallible. In some cases, organizations abandon their initial goals or impose a model that becomes inviable after they withdraw, generating unforeseen damage to artisan communities or running the risk of becoming too paternalistic in their methods.

As design has become a category deeply embedded in the complexity (and collapsing) of our world, questions posed by Burks are vital: "Who gets to participate in contemporary design and why? How can we engage the other ninety percent of the population or the majority world in communicating by design?"[6] Following Arturo Escobar, design is an invitation to become "aware and effective weavers of the warp of life."[7] Thus weaving as a conceptual, artisanal approach highlights the process, the livelihoods touched, "the intimacy of inheritance," and has the potential to change our relationship to others and objects.

Like in the iconic US quiz show *Jeopardy!*, giving answers in the form of questions is a way of going beyond common sense, cheating facts or serious categories. It changes perspective and opens the game: Timothy Morton talks about the present with Florencia Rodriguez 68, Martin Cobas rifles through Lina Bo Bardi's cabinets 82, Isabella Moretti details the debates triggered by two models 92, Penelope Dean brings tables to the foreground 98, Ludovico Centis collects relics from his travels 104, curators from the Canadian Centre for Architecture reframe two archival objects 108. Finally, we ask Jayne Kelley, Laura González Fierro, and the Estévez Ickx family to embody one building; the NESS editorial team redraws single projects 112.

WHAT'S AN OBJECT?

(answer)

If the way we relate to objects is used to make up the contemporary self, how can we engage in a new conversation? With our usual playfulness for theorizing design, we gathered tales of entanglements, reenactments, and recollections.

Objects are like people. They're living, breathing things that have knowledge inside them about how to do things and have memory inside them so they can remember things. And rather than interacting with them at a very low level, you interact with them at a very high level of abstraction, like we're doing right here. [1]

If you were coming to **Earth from Mars** *it would be easy to observe that one species is entirely dominating the planet. But where would you meet this* **species***? What would be the first* **encounter** *be? Coming across a piece of space junk on the way in? Would you say, "Well, that's just a* **designed object** *and let me wait till I find out who made that." Or would your first thought be "Okay,* **contact with another** *creature?"* [2]

The shape is the object: at any rate, what secures the wholeness of the object is the singleness of the shape. [3]

Queer furnishing is not, therefore, such a surprising formulation: the word 'furnish' is related to the word 'perform' and thus relates to the very question of ***HOW THINGS APPEAR****. Queer becomes a matter of how things appear, how they gather, how they perform, to create the edges of spaces and worlds. / The objects with which we furnish 'rooms' or interior spaces are called furniture.* [4]

When humanists accuse people of ***"TREATING HUMANS LIKE AN OBJECT,"*** they are thoroughly unaware that they are treating objects unfairly. [5]

Embodiment is significant prosthesis; objectivity cannot be about fixed vision when what counts as an object is precisely what WORLD HISTORY *turns out to be about.* [7]

The souvenir is not simply an object appearing out of context, an object from the past incongruously surviving in the present; rather, its function is to envelop the present within the past. **Souvenirs are magical objects because of this transformation.** [6]

The object must either be 'expanded' to a full-fledged subject—a spirit; an animal in its human, reflexive form—or else understood as related to a subject. 8

The construction of meaning was displaced from the object itself to the spatial field between the viewer and the object: a fluid zone of perceptual interference, populated by moving bodies. 9

"The Tower acquires a new power: an object when we look at it, it becomes a lookout in its turn when we visit it, and now constitutes as an object, simultaneously extended and collected beneath it, that Paris which just now was looking at it." 10

Rather than viewing objects as too shallow to be the truth, we can treat them as too falsely deep to be the truth. 12

The most significant event of our times **is the rise in importance of the object.** 11

If object labeling is indeed ***THE REIGNING MEME FORMAT OF NOW,*** what does that say about now? 13

As if space itself is invisible, all theory for the production of space is based on an obsessive preoccupation with its opposite: substance and objects, i. e., architecture. 14

Up to now it has been assumed that all our cognition must conform to the objects; but all attempts to find something about them a priori through concepts that would extend our cognition have, on this presupposition, come to nothing. Hence let us once try whether we do not get farther with the problems of metaphysics by assuming that **the objects must conform to our cognition**, which would agree better with the requested possibility of an a priori cognition of them, which is to establish something about objects before they are given to us. 16

Objectivism constitutes the social world as a spectacle offered to an observer who takes up a 'point of view' on the action and who, putting into the object the principles of his relation to the object, proceeds as if it were intended solely for knowledge and as if all the interactions within it were purely symbolic exchanges. 15

New media live and die by the update: ***the end of the update, the end of the object.*** 17

For that we have to follow the things themselves, for their meanings are inscribed in their forms, their uses, their trajectories. 18

Could we classify the luxuriant growth of objects as we do a flora or fauna, complete with tropical and glacial species, sudden mutations, and varieties threatened by extinction? 19

THIS IS –NESS 3

(clue)

1 Steve Jobs in conversation with Jeff Goodell, "Looking for the NeXT Revolution: Steve Jobs," in *The Rolling Stone*, (June 16, 1994).
2 Beatriz Colomina, Mark Wigley, *Are we Human? Notes on an Archeology of Design*. (Zürich: Lars Müller Publishers, 2016), p. 18.
3 Michael Fried, "Art and Objecthood," 1967.
4 Sara Ahmed, *Queer Phenomenology: Orientations, Objects, Others* (Durham and London: Duke University Press, 2006), p. 167.
5 Bruno Latour in Beatriz Colomina, Mark Wigley, *Are we Human? Notes on an Archeology of Design*. (Zürich: Lars Müller Publishers, 2016), p. 165
6 Susan Stewart, *On Longing: Narratives of the Miniature, the Gigantic, the Souvenir, the Collection* (Durham and London: Duke University Press, 2007 [1993]), p. 151.
7 Donna Haraway, "Situated Knowledges: The Science Question in Feminism and the Privilege of Partial Perspective," in *Feminist Studies* (Vol. 14, No 3, 1998), pp. 575-599.
8 Eduardo Viveiros de Castro, "Exchanging Perspectives: The Transformation of Objects into Subjects in Amerindian Ontologies," in *Common Knowledge* (vol. 10, no. 3, 2004), pp. 463–484.
9 Stan Allen, "From Object to Field" In: *AD Architectural Design*, (67 n. 5-6, May June, 1997), p. 24.
10 Roland Barthes, *The Eiffel Tower and Other Mythologies* (Berkley: University of California Press, 1979), p. 4.
11 Fernand Léger, "Actualités," in *Variétés* (February 15, 1929), p. 522.
12 Graham Harman, *The Road to Objects*, *Continent*. 1.3 (2011), pp. 171-179.
13 Schwedel, Heather. "The Distracted Boyfriend Was Onto Something. We are Now Living in the Golden Age of 'Object Labeling' Memes." In: *Slate*, (March 22, 2018).
14 Rem Koolhaas, "Junkspace," in: *October*, (Vol. 100, Spring, 2002, The MIT Press), p. 176.
15 Pierre Bourdieu, *The Logic of Practice* (Stanford University Press, 1990), p. 53.
16 Immanuel Kant, *Critique of Pure Reason* (Cambridge University Press, 1998), p. 110.
17 Wendy Hui Kyong Chun, *Updating to Remain the Same. Habitual New Media* (Cambridge: The MIT Press, 2016), p. 14.
18 Appadurai, Arjun, *The Social Life of Things* (Cambridge: Cambridge University Press, 1986), p. 5.
19 Jean Baudrillard, *The System of Object* (London: Verso, 1996), p. 3.

View of "Din blinde passager," *Olafur Eliasson: In Real Life*, 2019. Ph. Pablo Gerson

THIS IS NOT NOW

Timothy Morton in Conversation with Florencia Rodriguez

Timothy Morton is a "white boy currently living in Houston, Texas," or so he says in conversation. However, that is not what he is known for exactly: as a member of the Object Orientated Ontology movement. He coined the term 'hyperobject' within ecological thinking, taking inspiration from Björk's 1996 single "Hyperballad." He is also the Rita Shea Guffey Chair in English at Rice University and author of several recent books including *Being Ecological* (2018), *Humankind: Solidarity with Non-Human People* (2017), and *Dark Ecology: For a Logic of Future Coexistence* (2016). NESS founder Florencia Rodriguez talked with Morton virtually, in what could be described as a dance of vibrating presents. Together, they feel to think through a future that is not yet frozen in forms, words, or stones. It is a journey from bits—eyebrow encrustations, viruses, spiders, and weirdly gross lifeforms—to liquidness—shimmering bodily fluids, the rhythms of the Smiths alongside scientific uniforms, alien architectures, and thump-ness. The dialogue is an experience of attuning between the everything and the nothing in possible dimensions: feel the flow and fade in between.

FLORENCIA RODRIGUEZ

As you know our publication is called NESS. The idea of naming it after a suffix was to point out that our normal vocabulary is becoming insufficient and we need to invent new words.

TIMOTHY MORTON

Oh, that's great. That's literally where I am at. I think feelings are from the future and ideas are from the past. Like when you go to therapy: you go to therapy because you are having feelings and you don't know what they mean yet, right? So, there is this 'not yet' quality about the feeling, and the word or the idea are just like the receipts that come out of the cash register of the process. You can think of it in terms of something I've been pondering in the last few weeks actually, which is this very interesting concept of the Marxist thinker, Raymond Williams, who died in the late 1980s, "Structure of feeling." You could certainly say that in a way, ideology—whatever that might be—is like a receipt-idea version of something that actually starts off as a kind of feeling, and the feeling is more important. For me, the hyperobject feeling is more important than the word hyperobject, and now we all have this feeling. We all have coronavirus in the air, we know that emotionally there is this thing that is terrifying on the scale of an individual and on this other scale is waking everybody up to panic, and it's doing all these other things in between.

And the same with Black Lives Matter. We now have this feeling of what global collective human action feels like, right? It's not yet an idea, it hasn't crystalized, it's much more sort of intangible, and it could fail. The strength, in a way, of the 'ness' of the structure of feeling is that it's flimsy. It's not yet, it hasn't become a statue. It hasn't become something that people can tear down, and in a funny way this is also talking about architecture. Because in a way, when people say, you know, "writing about music is like dancing about architecture," that's what you always do. It's just that sometimes you do it in this mechanical, repeated way, you just always go to the same subway station, or whatever. Schelling says architecture is frozen music, but it's more like frozen dancing. And a street protest like Occupy or Black Lives Matter is a way of making architecture that is not made of stone yet, so it's undermining some of the stone things which are like old frozen ways of dancing that we don't want to do any more.

FR

Exactly, it's like making space in a very direct way. I'm very interested in the idea of feelings being from the future. I was listening yesterday online to a public conversation you had with Olafur Eliasson, in which you were talking about something quite similar, about the intuition that takes place in art and the idea that art is also from the future. I think some of these notions are in a way very related to psychoanalysis. Or I might be reading it that way because I grew in this kind of 'Lacanian' cloud.

TM

I've been in psychoanalysis for 23 years and, if you're going to talk about it—and as I understand Argentina, where you are from, is a place where there is a lot of analysis—there's that difference between free association, which is more of an energy thing, and some kind of idea that you have that kind of pops out of that process.

I think very important to this idea of 'ness', is that the thing that seems like the accidental quality is the thing. Like the '-ality' or the '-icity' part of a word. Like Heidegger is arguing that time is temporality, that you cannot have different measurements without having a feel, kind of a time-feel. You cannot have different types of sex without sexuality, you cannot have different types of technology without technicity. These are pointing towards the thing that seems like the accident, like the tail of the dog is the thing that wags the dog.

How you live is not just building things out from the past, it is not just kind of building things out from pre-packaged fabricated things. In some ways the problem we have right now with fascism around the world, is that it's looking for the meaning in the fragments. "There must be something more real underneath what appears to us, all around us. There must be something underneath that is the real thing, that is the substance, there must be some meaning in this ancient Hindu symbol of the Swastika." Whereas in fact I think what 'ness' is saying is that the meaning is from the future. Or the meaning is the future, not just the future that you can predict which is just the past that you built out a little more, but the future in terms of the possibility that things could be different. That kind of future.

FR

And do you think that the future and those ideas are in a way capable of being understood?

TM

Absolutely. And I feel on the other hand that people like me often feel like we get paid to look clever by convincing everyone how paralyzed we are, and I don't understand how theory class turned into people like me performing intelligence by saying you wouldn't believe how screwed up everything is. "Your version of screwed up is so much less screwed up than it really is and I'm here to tell you how impossible things are." I think that, in a way, you could call it ideology or you could call it the past, or you could call it appearance, or you could call it memes, little viral bits of stuff, that's what viruses are, little parts, little bits of some single-cell organisms, DNA that popped out of the cell layer. The past is everywhere but that doesn't mean that the future isn't real. Ideology is everywhere but it doesn't mean that it is everything.

And in a way, it is much easier to think this way because it joins together these two theories in Marxism, these two ideas about alienation. First, the traditional, 'vanilla idea,' which is that we are alienated from some essence, that we have a basic humanity and that we have been alienated from it. The trouble is if you look for this essence in the past you are going down a path that ends with fascism, it ends with extreme forms of religion, like "once upon a time we were perfect and then all of sudden this bad thing happens and if we could only get rid of the bad thing then we would all be perfect." It's a recipe for disaster. We could make ourselves great again by this process... So, this idea is wrong, but it's sort of right for the wrong reasons. We are not alienated from the past—we are alienated from the future. Realizing how we are and being able to be nice to each and other life forms is something that we haven't done yet completely. It is very simple; it sounds crazy and sci-fi but it's really very simple. We are alienated from the future and the automated world we live in makes this future difficult if we keep just the systems going.

And second there is this other ideology theory, the cool-kid-theory-class-one, the Althusser theory, which is this idea that ideology is everywhere. The idea that you are somehow free of it and then you get imprisoned by it, is the basic form of it. And so, the alienation theory is right for the wrong reasons but the Althusser theory is wrong for the right reason, which is namely that it isn't true that we are completely imprisoned, it isn't.

Things could be different, but the way you can tell actually is that it doesn't look like that. The past is everywhere: look at my face, it's just a map of everything that I did to my face. This [pointing out his shirt] is a thing I bought several years ago, it is made in a factory. It's the past, how my hair didn't work today, it's the past. But that doesn't mean the future isn't real. The fact that it is everywhere doesn't mean that is everything. And the future is, in this sense, the unspeakable, ungraspable. It is the way in which my idea about this doesn't get rid of this. My appropriation of this thing doesn't get rid of how this is also a habitat for some little tiny encrustations that live in my eyebrow and little tiny bacteria living on my skin. This is the thing that is not exhausted by the way it gets appropriated or exploited. Which doesn't mean that it goes on forever, or that it's underneath the appearance, it just means that it has a kind of, what in Japanese it's called *yugen*: it's this mysterious depth quality.

And that's the future actually, especially with the way I talk, you don't know when the end of the sentence will be and the meaning is the future, it's haunting the present. It's not that everything is nonsense. If everything was nonsense, one thing would have to be not nonsense, a.k.a. this phrase "everything is nonsense." Like "everything is ideology:" this sentence has to not be for that to be true, this is a self-defeating concept, everything is a lie except for this sentence. The fact that everything looks a little fake and a lie is how things could actually be true. Take the example of fake news. Fake news wants you think that true and false are very different, fake news wants you to go this is the truth! News-news in a way is more ambiguous. News-news is like maybe this is a lie, actually maybe lie and true are overlapping. They are not exactly the same but they aren't completely different, but to get into the feeling of that properly you have to be in a non-patriarchal logic space. You have to accept that you can say some things that are a little bit true, or this much true, or this much false. You can say things that are paradoxical, you can say things that are true and lie at the same time.

So, I think that the safe position is that anything can be weaponized, anything can become ideology, anything can become a weapon, but that doesn't mean that everything is evil and that we live in this world and we can't get out. Funnily enough, it is like this 'ness' concept, it's like, in a funny way, truth is based on the feeling of true, a.k.a. truthiness is how things can be true, which doesn't mean that everything is a lie, it means that when you are a scientifically orientated person, the world feels uncertain and weird and insecure and shifty, and the feeling of being a scientist, minus all the money and the degrees and the technical apparatus and stuff, is more like the feeling of animism, like the spider who was nice to you yesterday, maybe today could be your worst enemy. You don't know yet, maybe they will be nice to you, you don't know that.

FR

I'm responding while thinking so many things at once. They pop into my head while listening to you. As I understand it, there is something about the truth that is more about a feeling than something objective, provable. And I want to try and make an effort to translate some of this to architecture and the space in which we live. Have you discovered something about this in the experience of sheltering-in-place?

TM

Sure, yes, I have. Well said. Here's the thing about the coronavirus situation. The official position is that the sheltering-in-place and the social distancing is called lockdown and then we should open it up again. I think it's the other way around. I think that the social distancing lockdown is opening up to the possibility of things being different. I think it's like looking out of your window and seeing another verse of Imagine with John Lennon. Like "Imagine there's no carbon... Imagine all the lifeforms walking down the street without being killed... Imagine there's no churning... Imagine there's no furnace that you're throwing yourself into, the fiery furnace of the COVID or the global warming or the Capitalism furnaces... Imagine they weren't there." Just imagine. And then of course, in a way it's very violent, it's about opening ourselves to being killed literally, it's about sending ourselves to our death, by going back into the churning machinery.

For me, what's happening is something that is very key to thinking about architecture, which is that it is not about measurable objects, it's about relationships between people. And by people we could also mean dolphins, and algae, and hedgehogs. Actually social distance, which is tape measure distance, is not social distance, that's intimacy. I'm not going to hurt you, I'm going to stand far away from you because I don't want to be hurt: that's a form of intimacy and it's a special new form of intimacy with beings that I don't even know if they are real. I may not even go to the supermarket, I may not even go into the future to see my future self, or my neighbor, dying of COVID in the future. I can't see them, but I care about them all of a sudden in a science way, and this thing here that I'm wearing, this is not a statement about my ego, this is me saying, "I have mercy on you, I don't want you to die." I don't want to die. Which is why white men, where I live, which is Houston, Texas, they think it's a gag, because that's how they treat everything else,

THIS
NOT

IS
HERE

Homage to Yoko Ono's retrospective art exhibition held in 1971 at the Everson Museum of Art in Syracuse, New York.

they think the world is a manipulable object, and that this means being humiliated, this is what they don't want really. It's not that they don't want freedom, freedom is maybe the 50-dpi jpg but the 3000-dpi jpg of what they want is not to look humiliated. In other words, closer to the Earth. And so somehow, we are doing architecture by dancing, by refusing to interact so close. It's a form of dancing, very slow motion, and it's like liquid architecture.

And also, it's showing how, what is called landscape architecture, which is supposedly the poor relation, the thing you think of after you do the building, is actually everything. The environment is everything and the building is always the crystal that appears in the liquid solution, like the copper sulfate crystal appearing in there, and that actually architecture-architecture or things made of stone are just like art that people are forced to appreciate whether they like it or not. And so, somehow this moment is about realizing that this is just an alien form of the actual architecture which is how people relate to each other, and you note that when I am saying people, I mean not just human people but all different types of people. It's literally how we dance together, with dance partners and the moves and how not to step on too many people's toes when we are doing it. It's like how trauma is a form of dancing. In a way it's also like how actions, and molecules, and things in our world are high energetic, sped up versions of this quantum thing.

The ultimate form of movement isn't going from A to B, or mechanical motion, the ultimate movement is this kind of shimmering, without any mechanical anything. So when you isolate, when you do social distancing of particles or very small things, when you put them in a vacuum close to absolute zero, when you put the particle or the tiny thing into quarantine, you see it sort of shimmering. It's like when you meditate you are putting yourself into quarantine, or you are putting yourself in a vacuum, and it's not that there's nothing or that it's still or flat or static, it's that actually everything has its own way of **vooom-voom-voom** vibrating like this. And somehow everyone on Earth got to see, just for a moment, what it's like, the ground state, to use that word, of being a human being or being a sentient being, or maybe just being a being at all, I don't know, I'm just a human being. I'm not a bottle of Pellegrino, I don't know if bottles of Pellegrino have this experience happening too, being able to get to the feeling of just shimmering. What we call this sometimes is anxiety—this kind of **voom-voom-voom**—and we are always trying to discharge it and, in a way, fear of something is a fear of absolute nothing. The horror movie fear is like "oh my god there's something behind the door," but the fear of something behind the door is covering up the fear of, "it's just a door." And in a way, column, door, ceiling, everything is door, everything is threshold, talking architecturally, everything is in between. My work is trying to translate the fear that something is coming, this big disaster.

The fear could kill you, the fear could create fascism, it could create these walls, whereas the anxiety is more like a creepy *doppelgänger* version of yourself, it's always there: "oh my god not you again." No matter what I try, I smoke the drugs, I take a bath, I thrash around, I try to destroy the planet, everything, nothing works to discharge this feeling of being sentient. Okay I get it, so I'm just going to co-exist with this anxious feeling, which is the ultimate dancing, is just trembling in place. I'm sorry to be talking on so many different levels but I find this 'ness' concept extremely resonant, and I think we are living through this moment where we realize that we don't have to put up with the mechanical, mechanized world that we have inherited, we can make it quiver and shimmer and voom. We don't have to have this statue, why do we even have to have it in a museum?

FR

I'm very grateful that you are speaking on so many levels in a moment such as this one. I was thinking that the city is one reflection of that system that is collapsing as a form of representation. And that old architecture made of stone, the institutions it stood for, understood closure and canons as something essential to their definitions. With that in mind, if we want to imagine or vibrate into that future that we cannot touch yet but that is already here, how do we need to change? What can we do? Of course I'm not interested in recipes or in foreseeing something closed. I'm also very happy that we are getting into some interpretations of landscape architecture and architecture as it used to be defined. But the substance of design is what has changed. How can you imagine change, or what do you see in the cities after the protests? I hope this can lead us to new ways in which different kinds of people can live together.

TM

This interview, the way it is happening, is why I've been looking forward to it. I knew it was going to be great, just from the title of the journal. Perhaps the first thing to say is as precisely as you point out, offering another recipe is already paying too much lip service to this idea that if we could just get the past right, the future would be ok. But on the other hand, and this is what I like about architecture, you have to work with what you've got. You can't just beam it down from another dimension because it isn't another dimension, it's this one, there's no other world, we have what we have, bricks and stones and stupid statues of people, and we have racism and misogyny. This is what we have, so how do we take these things apart and how do we dismantle as a form of building? Right now, I feel like the world pendulum is a little bit leaning more towards the iconoclasm than towards the icons. I'm a fan of the poetry of John Milton. Milton wrote his poems against what he called the "modern bondage of rhyming," where the next line relates to the previous line and you know what it's going to do in a prefabricated way, you know that line is going to rhyme with this one. And against this he has this concept of rhythm, and rhythm is movement, it's constantly disrupting, and when you think about the word rhythm, what is it really? I mean it's these funny questions that no one thinks to ask, like what is rhythm? It's the measurement... of rhythm? And then you're like: no, that's a recursive definition, that rhythm is the measurement of rhythm. No, if you look at the word rhythm you find that it's made of two words. The '-thm' is from the Greek word *thymos* and it means life. And when people say this word in Greek philosophy, in legend, it's pulsation, it's the fact that your heart or whatever is pulsating all by itself **thump thump thump thump** without being measured by anything, it's doing its own thing. And the 'rhy-' bit means the body fluids, as in diarrhea or snot or whatever. So rhythm intrinsically is the autonomous pulsation of body fluids and then it gets measured and distributed according to some other kind of rhythm process, some other kind of measurement process. So somebody comes along and says, we have the most accurate measuring device in the world therefore we are in charge of you, we are the druids, this is Stonehenge, you are now our slaves, you have to now be sacrificed in this massive clock that we just made because this is now called patriarchy. I feel like that confusion of rhythm with its measurement, or time with its measurement, are deeply part of how patriarchy and ending up with white supremacy has almost successfully carried out its unconscious and not-so-unconscious mission of destroying Earth, really, really well. And if we just keep going a little more, it's going to do it. The current form this takes is neo-liberal capitalism, but it could be other formats that have also sucked for people. Just look around, simple quick check, is there bad stuff in your world, okay good yes, that means that the past was not good. One thing people like me can do, and I think also as an architectural project, is that iconoclasm, a.k.a. the rhythmical breaking up of these calcified statues of racism and misogyny. That would be the mission right now, I think. So how to connect to non-human beings, because right now non-human beings are seen as statues, they are not uncanny, they are different enough from us to appreciate them and this is precisely because of all these beings in between who have become invisible, they have been disappeared into the uncanny valley. There's sub-human, in-human, so that Hitler can stand on one side of the uncanny valley and see Blondi the alsatian on the other side and be kind of fascist. You know people are like "oh well there's a problem with white supremacy in ecological politics," and there is, because of this issue. And real, genuine ecological politics, of which architecture would be a subset, would be a lot more like a feeling of being haunted by uncanny versions of myself to the point where I realize that I'm also an uncanny version of myself. So maybe to break this down a little a bit architecturally, it might feel a little bit like the

View of *Olafur Eliasson: In Real Life*, 2019. Ph. Pablo Gerson notion of prototype never went away, the final version is just the prototype that everybody agrees on right now. You have to make a deal somewhere, somebody has to stop the machine and be like "this is the one we are going to go with," but it still has this feeling of a toy. There's no difference between the final one, the official one, and all of the toy versions. Everything was a toy and somehow this idea of a toy would then affect how the things were made at all. And so a basic playfulness could enter into architectural design. I'm thinking about, again, stone circles, because I was in these stone circles last year, and I had this very strong feeling about the difference between Stonehenge, which is very size-ist, and Avebury. Like the Spinal Tap thing about Stonehenge is absolutely perfect because it's really about that we have the biggest measuring device in the world, and then there's this other one called Avebury. Avebury is made of these found objects, it's older, it's not stones that have been carved out of the mountainside, it's just these rough and ready things that go into this village and surround this village and it's really different. It's more playful. As my daughter said, maybe it's profound or maybe it's just a gigantic boob joke because this is how it looks and it's sort of like the difference between seriousness and play. Genuinely playful would mean playful and serious overlap, and seriousness is deployed in a playful way. Playful seriousness would be the feeling. I can't tell you what to design but I can tell you what it would feel like. I think playful seriousness as opposed to serious playfulness, which would be Google using play as another way to make cooperation more omnipotent. I could tell you what it would feel like to inhabit a kind of space that was more politically progressive, it would be a feeling of serious but playful. Another axis would be enjoyment and disgust. It would be weirdly gross because you would be like "oh my god other lifeforms are enjoying, like algae growing on Brutalist architecture," "oh my god that's gross but in a way it's kind of weirdly cool." It's weirdly gross that I like that, but it's cool that it's gross that I like that, and there's this oscillation again. We know what this is actually, it's this chemical invented by Charles Baudelaire in eighteen-whatever: *ennui,* which is precisely the feeling of being a scientist. It's like, wow, this world is different from how I thought but that's kind of cool, it's weird that I like that, and there's this oscillation. So a world that is more attuned to caring about lots of different lifeforms and a world that was more attuned to being scientific as opposed to just believing the authority figure, would feel not like an automated Kraftwerk video but more like The Smiths, more like The Cure, it would be like being inside of a Goth kind of feeling where there is this kind of playful yet serious yet sad yet happy yet disgusting yet enjoyable, and the beauty of this is that we have this, we know the future chemical, we know it, we've been making it for two hundred years, it's called Goth. How come scientists always wear white sneakers and blue jeans? It's like they got stuck in a little place in the gameboard. And how come they don't just come to work with mascara and big hair? The same with design with architecture, it got stuck in expressing corporate power and whiteness and maleness and a world where that was being dismantled. Maybe the point is that you could never stop the dismantling. The way for me to be sane is to think that I could become insane at any moment, I could become really violent to myself. I'm a depression sufferer and depression can turn anything into a weapon. So maybe the future world isn't that we know we are perfect, it's that we know we can't be. One person's functioning is another person's horrible malfunction and so this world will seem weirdly always a little bit broken and always a little bit strange and uncanny but with a huge smile, like comedy.

FR

I can't avoid thinking about ruins right now, but maybe this time ruins seem polished, shiny, and perfect. They are not something that looks exploited, dirty, or destroyed. That's why it is tricky, things seem like what they used to be physically—or at least that is what we can see—but they are absolutely transformed, and there's something monstrous, almost sublime about it...

I feel like the Romantic period is still happening, and the Romantic period is where the fragment becomes the thing that you can make. And maybe the only problem is that the thing gets made by very rich people who can make these gothic follies on their land. But the whole point of the Romantic period is that it is a reaction to an age of sensibility where everything is supposed to be immediate. It's called Facebook, it's like the person who has the strongest, most immediate reaction, who cries the hardest the first is the winner, therefore, the person with the most leisure time is the winner: therefore the most privileged person is the winner. And you go back to sentimental design—like my ancestor, funnily enough, Josiah Wedgwood. He has this medallion, "Am I Not a Man and a Brother?" with a slave who is on his knees and the white guy is looking down, and the implication is you're looking down at someone, there's a power relation there. That is not what encountering someone equally really feels like; real democracy is weird. You don't know who people are, you don't even know who you are, there's kind of uncanniness and it's also this science feeling, it's not a feeling of disenchantment it's more like I'm enchanted, I'm fascinated, I actually can't believe what I'm seeing here. There's no normal, everything is a different kind of fascination all the time. And so somehow at the very beginning of industrial capitalism, artists already saw a lot of moves that you could make in this space, and part of the moves is the way that you are immersed, of being in the story, or in the art, or looking at the art, is part of the art. This idea that you are outside looking in is the problem, and you're always in, there's no outside. Absolutely, everything is at some point a ruin. At some point everything sucks, at some point everything I say at some perspective, twenty million years from now, or tomorrow, or some other part of the world, what I'm saying is crap. It's just a feature of things that they always have an intrinsic flaw to them, and that trying to avoid that quality is the violence. Knowing that your project is never going to be perfect, knowing that at some point your design will hurt more lifeforms than it's helping, that part of ecological practice is realizing that everything in the end has some hypocrisy to it, that there's never a way to get it perfect.

The real difference between the Bill Murray in "Groundhog Day" at the end is when he's playing as opposed to the Bill Murray trying to be perfect. It's the difference between the nature of Nietzsche's Superman and the Ultimate Man, the big strong buff six-pack abs perfect. And I feel like trying to do ecological design perfectly will result in incredible violence at some scale, whereas it should be about realizing that it's not about getting it perfect, it's not about finding the perfect recipe, it's more about connecting to the very idea of being connected at all, that actually what's the most important is that I'm already in a biosphere, I'm already in a relationship with all kinds of human and non-human beings. Because I'm finite, I'm flawed just like them, and funnily enough, we are all like these slightly malfunctioning toys in J.F. Sebastian's workshop in "Blade Runner." The whole world is that, the whole biosphere is like that scene in "Blade Runner." We're not trying to express an idea anymore. There are some architects out there that are like let's make an OOO (Object Oriented Ontology) building. How can you make a building that illustrates the idea that you can't illustrate ideas? How can you do that? It's more like, you are liberated now to realize that you can make political relationships with whoever you want and it's your choice now, it's up to you. Politics and art, in a way, are the same, but not in that fascist way. Fascism is like there's one special way of doing it and we are going to make it great, which is aesthetically great as well as mighty great, it's like we are going to make you feel great and here's how to do it, we are going to exclude all these people.

Politics is fundamentally aesthetic, it's not that it needs to be decorated with this fascist greatness, it is about that I'm going to talk to you now, I'm going to have you in my group, I'm going to include this dolphin and this cloud of bacteria and these human beings and we are going to make this little group, and who knows what will happen next.

FR

Probably, when thinking about an architecture that could be OOO, the problem is that architects, and designers in general, are used to working with form and this is not about form. We could rethink the same space that we are already inhabiting and see that it's already different. That's what I have been thinking about during this isolation, this sheltering-in-place. What changes every time is the dancing. I have been supposedly in the same house for months right now, but very different things and feelings happened every day. Each space has not been the same each time. And I think there's the actual thing. Between rhythm, emotions, and the dancing...

TM

I'm so sorry, I got excited, forgive me for interrupting. Utopia isn't impossible, it's that actually the future is perfectly, totally there. As they say the Situationist slogan, that the beach is beneath street. It's right there, all you have to do is slightly move, just put this thing on, six feet two meters, it's not a million miles, it's this slight difference. It's also what they say in esoteric meditation instructions: stop trying to be really different, because that's the whole problem. Trying to get more of good stuff and push away the bad stuff that's the problem. Instead, you could just make this tiny little slight adjustment, to slightly, slightly, slightly, like messing with the key in lock... oh my god I can open the door, wow!

I love Yoko Ono's Fluxus piece "This is Not Here" and it's above the door in the video of "Imagine." And I really feel like "Imagine" is the song for now, and it's funny how all these stupid corny actors did "Imagine" when this all started because, funnily enough, it's like what Lennon says to Neil Young when Neil Young says "I'd rather burn out than fade away." Well this is why we have been destroying Earth actually. Let's look at the idea of fading away, what if human beings just quietly, quietly, quietly, without hurting too many other lifeforms, just went extinct over millions of years, thousands of years, it doesn't matter. That kind of death, just dissolving into your environment. When all the chemicals in here become the same as the chemicals there, it's called Tim is dead, instead of burning Tim. And what we see out of the window because of the churning death drive basically that we are living in, the machinery, is another kind of dead which is quietly dead. Life doesn't mean the opposite of dead—that's survival mode, and as a survivor I know this mode. "I don't care if other beings suffer, I have to live." Whereas, actually alive means quivering in between this mechanical turning and not existing at all.

And what we see out of the window, from a certain position of privilege because we don't have to go to work, is how much we have in common with people who work in the supermarket and people who work in the hospital and pigeons who work in their own way in the street, on the telephone line, and little four-legged animals who walk about. Suddenly we feel this feeling of solidarity, which is not just a chosen political state, it's a feeling, it's just a feeling of being weirdly connected to things. It's the 'ness' of symbiosis, solidarity-ness. Imagine a single-celled organism and they're going blumb blumb blumb through the ocean, and then suddenly gulp, like "Oh my god, did I just swallow poison? Did I just swallow something that could kill me?" That's the fundamental symbiosis feeling. Maybe this interaction is toxic, maybe this other person is the bad person—but that's how you can be friendly to people.

Rather than knowing in advance who is the friend and who is the enemy, the fundamental symbiosis feeling is that maybe I poisoned myself, I don't know yet. Two million years later, no! No I didn't because now I'm an animal and that was an anaerobic bacterium and now I have this energy cell inside of me. You know that looking backwards, but looking forwards, it's like "could this kill me?"

And that's the feeling in that song. Imagine there's no heaven, it means imagine there's only this life which means you could die. And it's in the sound, it's in that kind of cold, calm sound of the piano. Yoko and John are walking through the cool mist to the mansion in the film. I saw this when I was twelve because Lennon was assassinated. I saw the video when it went to number one, and above the door of their mansion, towards which they're walking, the first piece of art that really haunted me was the Yoko piece: "This is Not Here!" But it's there! It is there! It's on the freaking door and it's what you see out of the window during so-called lockdown. You see utopia, literally this no-place that is also the good place, and it's 'not here,' but you can see it. So it's not impossible, you can do it, with a very slight adjustment of social relations, just stop being racist, just police officers stop hurting Black people! In a way it's that utopia is too easy, that's the problem, for intellectuals like me. We want to make it look really difficult and complicated: "I can solve this Rubik's Cube and you can't."

But what if it was too easy to just to stop the churning, just stop doing the harmful thing, and see what happens next. Instead of making it into this big complicated twisted thing, I'm looking at you Slavoj Žižek, I'm sorry dude, this performance of "I have the solution and it's really complicated and you couldn't possibly understand it..." yes you could, it's really easy. Maybe that's the problem: what if it's too easy to slip into the future? That we are making it look too hard is part of the problem.

FR

Or fear is part of the problem.

TM

Yeah, what would happen if we stopped. Oh my god there's a huge global colossal depression. Well, but, now we remembered lifeforms or why you can make money.

FR

Yeah, I'm in Argentina right now, in Buenos Aires, and the growing poverty here is a very sad and complicated issue. Developing countries are more fragile than others when confronting such an extreme crisis, so this situation of stopping the world is generating a huge emergency to think of other ways of doing things.

TM

I suddenly remembered this thing of Walter Benjamin, where he says socialism isn't progress, it isn't moving forward. What it is actually, is pulling the emergency brake, stop the world, stop it, I want to get off, I want to get off this train, and so finally, finally white guys finally noticing that is what we are going through right now and some of them freaking out. I'm hoping that it's just the Anglos, it's just Trump and Boris Johnson, and that they represent the end of something rather than the beginning of something that everybody else has to go through. I'm hoping it's just Anglos freaking out, Anglo white boys like me, suddenly experiencing what everyone else gets to experience every day, in some degree or other.

FR

It's been super inspiring and I would keep on talking for hours but I think we have covered so much already. Thank you.

TM

I'm so honored that you would interview me and listen. For me, thinking is a team sport and it's like I can't have thoughts without this. And this is my favorite way which is interviews, dialogue.

View of "Beauty," *Olafur Eliasson: In Real Life*, 2019. The exhibition was on view until the beginning of January 2020 at the Tate Modern in London and traveled afterwards to the Guggenheim Bilbao where it can be visited until April 2021. Ph. Pablo Gerson

POLOCHON: A PIG'S TALE

Dead Things (and Zoological Life) in Lina Bo Bardi's *Casa de Vidro*[1]

MARTIN COBAS

The famous *Casa de Vidro* close to São Paulo, Brazil, is not just another glasshouse but rather a cabinet of curiosities, Martin Cobas argues. He narrates the scenes in which architect Lina Bo Bardi started her very own collection of plants, animals, and creatures and how these objects are entangled with her architectural projects.

It all began inside a chicken (not a pig). Yet, this might not be the most promising beginning. Let me begin inside 'another' cabinet. A miscellany of decorative arts and wondrous objects, baroque sculpture, innumerous ex-votos (or votive offerings) of exquisite workmanship, Emile Galle's vases, Baccarat pedestals, life-like dolls, byzantine mosaics, reflecting spheres (too many of them), ethnographica, and a puzzling zoological menagerie, real and fantastic: two Paris-born Birman cats: Eos de Borobourdour and Elfe D'Irraouda;[2] a tortoise, an inventory of cockroaches and other taxonomical oddities, a mechanical cow, a *bode expiatório* (or scapegoat), a *polochon* (or bigger-than-life double-headed, or double butt, pig sculpted in *papier mâché*), a parade of animals exiting a circus...[3] In Lina Bo Bardi's work, animals, creatures, and architecture are enigmatically interlocked. But consider the animal: why so many animals? Why so many creatures cannibalizing architecture?

Although often referred to as a paradigm of 'modern transparency,' the *Casa de Vidro* (Glass House) designed by Italian-born Brazilian architect Lina Bo Bardi (1914-1992) in 1951 and located in the outskirts of the city of São Paulo is in fact several houses atop of a tea *façenda* overlooking the *Mata Atlántica* (Atlantic Rainforest) and the city. This paper analyzes the *Casa de Vidro* as a *Wunderkammer* or 'cabinet of curiosities,' and hypothesizes that Bo Bardi's work derives from a highly rhetorical handling of all things collected (and collectible),[4] investigating how the forces of collecting delineate a 'liminal topography' of 'multiple others'—humans and non-humans, often articulated in creaturely or cannibal form. Yet it is not only their rhetorical function that interests here but also their capacity to work as ontological markers of variation, difference, and proliferation. To paraphrase Bruno Latour, Bo Bardi took "the wrong side of the modernizing frontier" seriously.[5] These creatures eloquently display the unsettling antinomies and thresholds that Bo Bardi's topical modernity had to negotiate in the aftermath of the 'discovery' of the Brazilian Northeast (and its visual allure), and predating art critic Mário Pedrosa's proclamation—apropos to the inauguration of Brasilia—that Brazil was "condemned to be modern,"[6] a formulation that could be rewritten as 'condemned to be other' or, rather, 'multiple others.'

ONE OR SEVERAL HOUSES

Lina Bo Bardi's *Casa de Vidro* has often been presented as part of the modern lineage of glass houses, alongside Charles and Ray Eames's House (1949), Phillip Johnson's Glass House (1949) and Mies van der Rohe's Fansworth House (1951),[7] partially rehearsing a trajectory initiated by Philip L. Goodwin's "Brazil Builds, Architecture New and Old" (1943), an 'a-la-Wölfflin' comparative method. In Goodwin's narrative, between the "charming" old and the "inspiring" new;[8] are the glass houses, implicitly, between the vernacular and the transparent modern. Yet the *Casa de Vidro* is in fact several houses at once: the glass house (the pavilion), the vernacular house (with its patios and rooms in enfilade), the 'primitive hut' (a *studiolo* of sorts), the meandering Portuguese tiled paths and, even, the historical tea *façenda* upon which these houses were built. There, where Goodwin saw apparently irreconcilable oppositions, Bo Bardi saw continuities and exchanges.

Although the collections are primarily displayed in the 'modern pavilion,' they inhabit all the houses (the 'hut' included). A case in point is the master bedroom, a space that performs at the juncture of the real, the fantastic and the theatrical, as it could be seen in a rare drawing made by Bo Bardi in the late 50s that resonates with the chamber in several ways: exposing elements of the baroque and the magical, overloading the space with characteristically grotesque tropes such as the negation of space, the weightlessness of forms, and the presence of hybrids. In the drawing, anthropomorphic figures (real and reflected) coexist in continuity with baroque ornamentation and subtle zoomorphic descendants. The theatrical element in the master bedroom comes upon the shimmering blue curtain, a motif Bo Bardi takes from British modernist theater theorist and director Edward Gordon Craig.[9] It stages architecture and advances a communal space of the real and the theatrical.[10] Walter Benjamin famously argued that collecting is a relationship to objects in which the collector "studies and loves them as the scene, the stage of their fate."[11]

The *Casa de Vidro* therefore articulates multiple temporalities in a series of spaces in which the collections contribute co-present geometries (and geographies), defining a new temporal threshold that overrules every niche of time-determination or spatial-temporal stability. In this space of translation, multiple topographies intersect; this translation is both geometric and linguistic: it does not only happen at a rhetorical level (to which I will return briefly) but also at a geometric one, i.e. a properly architectural one. This geometric translation could be thought of as a series of visual and spatial operations: lines of fugue, projections, transpositions, in a game commanded by the several reflective spheres in the collection, which introduce a series of unmistakably baroque effects, from the *mise-en-abyme* of infinite reflections to the *trompe-l'œil* and anamorphism of distorted and fragmentary narra-

Turtles in the courtyard of *Casa de Vidro*, São Paulo, 2017. Ph. Martin Cobas

tives. The house becomes a multilingual space where 'multiple others' are given a provisional (symbolic) wholeness (or order) and the possibility to constellate. It is in this sense that the *Casa de Vidro* becomes a *Wunderkammer*, a kind of collection that, as Lorraine Daston and Katharine Park noted in reference to the *Wunderkammern* of the Renaissance, "challenged the metaphysical opposition of art and nature," and in which the wondrous and extravagant (or creaturely deviant) speak to the ritual and the mundane.[12] Continuities partake the inside and the outside—the territorial *Wunderkammer* of tiled paths and epiphytes, brick-ovens, and dazzling zoology, the living and the dead.

To stylize the house as a *Casa de Vidro* reduces it to a *mise-en-scene* of modernity, a tension that becomes even more evident when considering it *vis-à-vis* the collections, complicating the notion of display: the *Casa de Vidro* becomes an architectural form both 'of' and 'on' display, an expressive accumulation that reminds of Sigmund Freud's description of Charcot's house as a "magic castle," a repository of all the fantasies (and fears) of the owner.[13] It is this doubleness between the self and its projection that is at stake in the *Casa de Vidro*,[14] in which spatial and semantic continuities are mediated, interfered, and distorted, sometimes exalted through theatrical effect; often in the disarming anamorphosis of the reflecting spheres. We will see how these co-present time-topographies integrate the geological, botanical, and zoological (you might wonder, in particular, about the *polochon*). And their creaturely afterlife, the ever-proliferating collection that colonizes the outside world; de-territorializing (collecting) and re-territorializing.[15]

STONE: *BAROCCA*

Yet, how did it all begin? And how did it travel to architecture? It all began inside a chicken. Bo Bardi's first scene of collecting took place in her childhood, chronicled in a short piece written in 1947 (originally in Italian), "Stones Against Diamonds:"

While I was still very young, I remember something momentous happened in the form of a chicken my mother was preparing for our Sunday roast. In its stomach was a collection of glass and pebbles worn smooth by water [gizzard stones, or gastroliths], in shades of green, pink, black, brown, and white. My mother gave them to me, and that was the start of my collection, which I kept in a little powder compact, a present from my Aunt Esterina... I was six years old.[16]

Recollection (and recursivity) are characteristically baroque tropes (the Portuguese word *barroca*, indeed, means "an odd and irregular-shaped pearl," the *pérola barroca*), and "Stones Against Diamonds" offers the cue to the baroque's multiple temporalities and folding time. The sort of agency and affective liaison that Bo Bardi projects into all things collected help elaborate on the vegetal and zoological life (and afterlife) that too often accompanied the collections well beyond the *Casa de Vidro*.

Drawing and architecture became entangled scenes of collecting. To begin with stones, for instance, in the almost prelapsarian rocks of the *cavaletes de vidro* (glass easels) for the project for the Museum of Modern Art (MAM) or the Museum at the Oceanside, (São Vicente, 1951), like ontological eggs at the threshold of architecture and the sea. Or the *barroca*, often in the form of encrustation, as in the *Casa de Vidro*, where the motif operates as a tectonic connective tissue between the several houses, an inter-

Monkey or *macaco* in Lina Bo Bardi's *Casa de Vidro*, São Paulo, 2017. Ph. Martin Cobas face between wilderness and domesticated nature in the form of retention walls covered by local washed stones with tile encrustations and orifices from which epiphytes could grow, a gesture of roughness and geological impetus that became a trademark of Bo Bardi's architectural work and that predated her most radical 'green walls' in houses and museums alike.[17]

Whereas thus far I have focused on encrusted continuities and topographic performativity on what the Brazilians call *terreo* (with far more complex cultural implications than 'ground floor'), I will now move to the subterranean currents of nature.

ROOT: *APUIZEIRO*

Here the space of geological recollection soon approaches the botanical world. Geology becomes botany, as in the façades and rootless epiphytes that grow in the above-mentioned projects. It is, however, in Bo Bardi's "*Contribuição propedêutica ao ensino da teoria de arquitetura* (Propaedeutic Contribution to the Teaching of Architectural Theory)"—an essay on architectural theory written in 1957—that her most comprehensive approach to the question of nature is to be found.[18] "Propaedeutic Contribution" is set up as a montage in which text and images are juxtaposed to create an idiosyncratic texture deliberately detached from scholarly rigor. It is escorted by two other texts that also touch upon the question of nature; the last one suggests an analysis nourished and mediated by her first encounters with the peoples and cultures of the Brazilian Northeast (from 1958 on), which she described as a synthesis of "Portuguese baroque, African erotic mysticism, and the bare tragedy of the backlands."[19]

Nature is frequently the trope that commands the subtle interplay between text and image. Consider, for instance, the opening: a quote from the Brazilian romantic writer and painter Manuel de Araújo Porto-Alegre (1806-1879) and a reproduction of Leonardo Da Vinci's "Deluge."[20] While Porto-Alegre's quote does not speak directly to his output as a visual artist and dwells instead on a romantic approach to architecture, its pairing with Da Vinci's drawing immediately elicits a crossed-complementary analysis, recalling Porto-Alegre's *Florestas* (Forests) and the long tradition codified by Alexander von Humboldt and the French travelers and painters that bridged romantic aesthetics and scientific curiosity in the tropical exuberance of the New World, here displayed *vis-à-vis* Da Vinci's cataclysmic prophesy.[21] There is both aesthetic pleasure and political urgency in this opening. This is also apparent in a spread in the first edition of the manuscript, illustrated with a series of eloquent images: Eugène Muller's "La Forêt" (1878), the interior (altar) of the São Francisco Church in Salvador, Bahia, and the Old Missionary Church in Pará in which the caption reads: "the roots of the apuizeiro [a type of fig tree characteristic of the Amazonia] interlacing the construction)." The *apuizeiro* passage, accompanied by Giambattista Piranesi's *Vedute*, takes the trope of ruination to its most vegetal and motile.

The image of the Pará church and the *apuizeiro* tree is also reprinted in the first number of the journal *Habitat*, published by the Bardis in 1951 (coinciding with the completion of the *Casa de Vidro*),[22] confirming both the interinstitutional circulation of images and a visual topography that, albeit conceived of in montage-like fashion, was nonetheless meticulously observed.[23] The *apuizeiro* tree, the king of vegetal canibalism, belongs to this tradition.

But let us return to the *Casa de Vidro*: in 1953, Bo Bardi published a short piece in Habitat 10 entitled

Roots of the figueira tree, *Casa de Vidro*, São Paulo, 2017.
Ph. Martin Cobas

"*Residência no Morumbi* (House in Morumbi)" in which the house is described as "an attempt to achieve a communion between nature and the natural order of things."[24] In characterizing that communion in nearly ontological fashion—a significant step forward in relation to her previous iterations of the natural—Bo Bardi deliberately avoids any sense of the 'exterior' and exacerbates an imaginary continuity that makes the house inhabit an exteriority, as if occupying the place of the outside, of the non-architectural, in a paradigmatic gesture that is both romantic and cannibal. This symbiosis is achieved (not only rhetorically) through what Bo Bardi calls a "sort of suspended patio,"[25] an unlikely (and un-rooted) aerial tropical garden 'rooted' in a *figueira* (fig tree) planted by Bo Bardi when the house was completed, a questionable decision by any architectural standards, insofar as the *figueira*—a close relative of the *apuizeiro*—is a particularly voracious tree. Like a displaced or misplaced envelope, the patio extrudes the *figueira* towards the sky and exposes its roots. The *pátio suspenso* dwells on a kind of suspended ontology and suggests that the unrooted levitation of the 'modern pavilion' is in fact achieved and exacerbated through the rooted gravitas of the tree.

In similar fashion, in a "little stroll on the forest" in Rio de Janeiro's Parque Lage (for which Bo Bardi designed an unbuilt exhibition pavilion in 1965),[26] Georges Didi-Huberman evokes Glauber Rocha's 1967 film "*Terra em Transe* (Entranced Earth)" through the radical and *radiculaire* root. Didi-Hubermann deems this root just as radical as Rocha's political exegesis or as the great Amazonian Forest, also "alive and monstrous:"

I have the impression that if I pool very strongly from one root, only one of that bunch, it is all the forest, as well as all the mountain, that I will be pooling from.[27]

In Bo Bardi's discourse, the rooting of the *pátio suspenso* parallels (literally and metaphorically) the ever-proliferating collection that runs aloft, underdetermined and rhlzomatic, across the circumstances (aesthetic, social, political) of the *terreo*. Objects (and images) travel—not quite rootless, and yet with a crucial openness—residing only temporarily in one place or the other.

Detail of the 'modern pavilion,' *Casa de Vidro*, São Paulo, 2018.
Ph. Martin Cobas

This is, for instance, the fate of the pebbles and little stones of Bo Bardi's collection; its territorialization.

Bo Bardi's reference to the *apuizeiro* enters a cultural lineage in Brazilian art and literature that begins with Euclides da Cunha's *Os Sertãos* (*Rebellion in the Backlands*, 1902), the canonical non-fictional account of the War of Canudos, a key historical event that epitomizes what Bo Bardi described as "the bare tragedy of the backlands."[28] But also in Alberto Rangel's *Inferno verde: cenas e cenários do Amazonas (Green Hell: Scenes and Scenarios of the Amazonia*, 1908), which offers one of the most enthralling narrative images of the *apuizeiro*.

The apuizeiro is a vegetal octopus. It embraces the sacrificed body, extending upon him a thousand tentacles... It is a colony, not a single animal; generations live in one body, in one part, in a fragment of bone. It is irreducible to one individual. It is the solidarity of the infinitely small, essential, elemental, inseparable in the republic of synergic embryos... it reproduces easily, in the latent and unstoppable precipitation of eternal procreation.[29]

Or, contemporary to Bo Bardi, with María Martins, who she knew through Pietro Bardi's work on Brazilian art and whose sculpture revisits the anthropophagic rhetoric of the *apuizeiro* presented as a sort of "vegetal octopus," as described by Rangel.

The *apuizeiro*, in sum, strategizes Bo Bardi's account of nature at various levels: as a common-ground of political and social resistance, as a metaphorical cannibal-monster, as the symbolic presence of the tropical forest, as the actual deadly embrace of nature in the "vegetal octopus," and Didi-Huberman's 'continuous root,' i.e. nature at its most vegetal, nature (and life) 'in' the plant, suggesting that Bo Bardi's understanding of nature was as universal (i.e. as an ontology) as it was topical, an element also at stake in the array of references that illustrate "Propaedeutic Contribution." It is indeed the *apuizeiro*, the rizomer-rhizome, that is both topical and universal; it complies with what Lorraine Daston defined in a recent book as "specific," "local," and "universal" natures.[30]

The subterranean "rule of continuity" invoked in Didi-Huberman's image of territorialization (and potential deter-

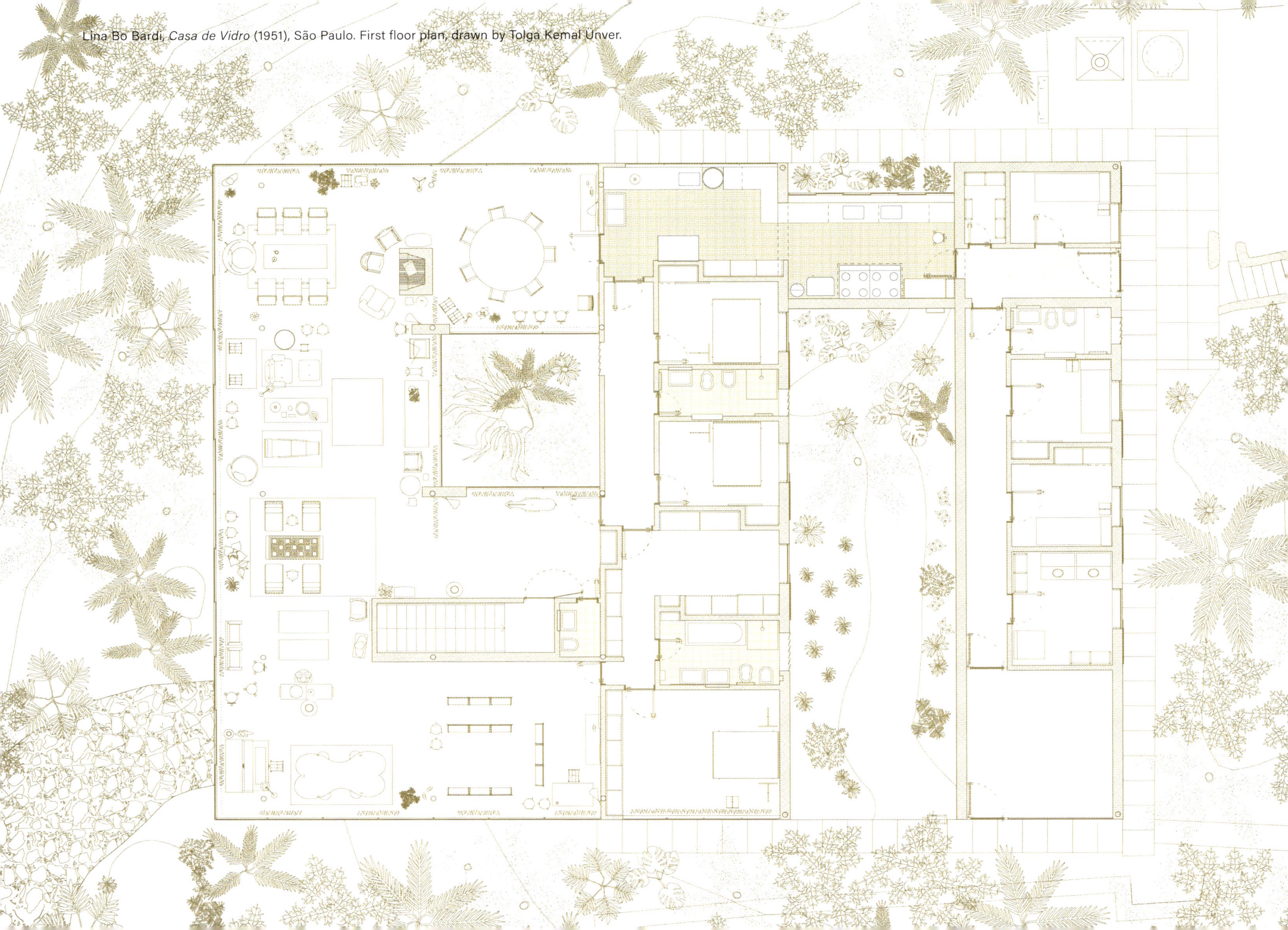

Lina Bo Bardi, *Casa de Vidro* (1951), São Paulo. First floor plan, drawn by Tolga Kemal Ünver.

ritorialization) has significant resonances with the so-called ontological turn in anthropology—whether in the work of Philipe Descola, Bruno Latour, and Eduardo Kohn or, in its Brazilian lineage, Eduardo Viveiros de Castro.[31] In *The Life of Plants: A Metaphysics of Mixture*, Emanuele Coccia suggests that "plant life is life as complete exposure, in absolute continuity and total communion with the environment."[32] This total exposure, unlike that of most higher animals, speaks of a complete, almost anarchist receptivity towards the 'other,' whether subject or milieu. Coccia further asserts that the plant "melts in the world to the point of coinciding with its very substance," and reads this effect as a form of cannibalism, indeed, as an "immense cosmic tautology."[33] The plant signals downward.

In line with Coccia, Bo Bardi's crucial insistence on the vegetal world—both as instrument of topical determination and universal signification, could be read as a form of 'universal cannibalism,' advancing a communion with others (whether human or non-human) accomplished through 'provisional enchantments.' Hence nature is here not a constant universal against which the theater of bodies and cultures is displayed but rather multiple, affective, and reactive.

Bo Bardi therefore advances what Brazilian anthropologist Eduardo Viveiros de Castro defines as "multinaturalism," which implies the coexistence of different natures.[34] Differences, even micro-differences, create a form of (non-linguistic) communication that Bo Bardi took seriously: with plants, animals, and creatures alike.

POLOCHON: A PIG'S TALE

Vegetation very easily turns into animation. Among Bo Bardi's library holdings there is a seminal essay by Brazilian botanist Frederico Carlos Hoehne, "*Da sensibilidade e motilidade dos vegetais* (On sensibility and motility in plants)," which testifies that Bo Bardi was well acquainted with the relevant scientific achievements of the time, particularly that which was produced in Brazil. Notably, Bo Bardi's most relevant architectural flirting with scientific nature was the unrealized project for the Instituto Butantã (1964), a major Brazilian research institution. One of Bo Bardi's designs depicts a fragment of the live reptile diorama with native Brazilian flora, in there is a striking continuity between the animal (snakes) and the vegetal (cacti). Butantã's unrealized project stands as Bo Bardi's closest examination of nature as proper scientific display (although too often display appears in disguise). The topicality of Butantã contrasts with a plethora of drawings produced by Bo Bardi between her arrival to Brazil and the late 1980s, a true cabinet of curiosities or, yet once again, in the tradition of the New World Baroque and its Borgean codification, a *Book of Imaginary Beings*. This series of drawings could be characterized as fantastical or "*imaginaria* (imaginary)." Most of them either possess man-like features or gestures or hybridizing human-animal bodies: the child plays 'on' a butterfly, a woman dressed in red 'becomes' a bird, the cow 'is' in love (the "*Mucca Inamorata*"), or men battling 'with' serpents, in the aftermath of the Butantã's project. Arguably, none of Bo Bardi's imaginary beings is as strikingly original as the *Polochon*: a bigger-than-life double-headed (or double-butt?) pig sculpted in *papier mâché*. Finally, the *polochon*. Very likely, an elegant addition to Borges's book.

Fragments of tiles in pavement, entrance, *Casa de Vidro*, São Paulo, 2018. Ph. Martin Cobas

The *patio suspenso* with the *figueira* tree, *Casa de Vidro*, São Paulo, 2015. Ph. Martin Cobas

Georges Bataille laughs, staring at a pig held by the tail.[35] Bataille wrote in *Madame Edwarda*: "If God really existed, he'd be a pig."[36] Bataille's provocation was inspired, as much of his work was, by Alfred Jarry's absurdism.[37]

The *polochon* built a properly *Paulista* ecology, a topical exercise in continuity, variation, and 'creaturely invention' that eventually became Bo Bardi's most enduring 'animal act.' It was created in 1985 as part of the set design for the play "*UBU, Folias Physicas, Pataphysicas e Musicaes*," an adaptation of Jarry's *Ubu Roi* (*King Ubu*, 1896) made for the *Teatro do Ornitorrinco* (Ornitorrinco [Plathypus] Theatre), an experimental theatre company of São Paulo.[38] The play, whose main character is a monstrous and scandalous man, Ubu, was a critique of the bourgeoisie written as a burlesque or parody. Although the *polochon*-as-creature was Bo Bardi's own invention, the word (neither a noun nor a creature) had been introduced by Jarry near the end of the play in one of Mère Ubu's inventive word plays: "*Tiens, capon, cochon, félon, histrion, fripon, souillon, polochon.*"[39]

Bo Bardi presented polochon as "*le polochon*," nicknamed "*o porco de duas cabeças* (two-headed pig)," "*o porquinho* (the little pig)," "*porco travesseiro* (pillow pig)," and, finally, in an effort to name the creature's offspring, "*filhotes* (puppy pigs)." The *polochon* was designed not exclusively as part of the set design for "*Ubu's Folias*," but also as a sculptural piece to be displayed at the lobby of the theatre; indeed, the *polochon* played the clerk. It was designed (drawn) in the *Casa de Vidro*, it was built in the *Teatro do Ornitorrinco*'s workshops, it clerked Ubu's audiences, and then returned to the *Casa de Vidro* in family fashion. There is an ecology of the *polochon*, a sort of virtuous circle of design, atelier-made collective sculpture, performative creature, misplaced sculpture (the pig traveled the world), and *pater familias*...

There are yet more pigs, such as the ones pictured by Abelardo da Hora in a series of engravings entitled *Meninos do Recife* (Boys from Recife), in the footsteps of Cândido Portinari's neo-realism, or Pierre Verger's Mexican pigs.[40] And finally, there is the peccary, the anthropologist's pig. In a passage from "The Relative Native," Viveiros de Castro confronts the anthropologist with a question: "Are peccaries human?"[41] The author goes further to ask how to take that question "seriously," not by assimilating it as real or false, but by reading it "empathically:"

I am an anthropologist, not a swinologist. Peccaries are of no special interest to me, humans are. But peccaries are of enormous interest to those humans who say that peccaries are human... the indigenous concept of sociality include peccaries in their extensions... The native's belief or the anthropologist's disbelief has nothing to do with this. To ask (oneself) whether the anthropologist ought to believe the native is a category mistake... What is indeed worth knowing is: what are the Indians saying when they say that peccaries are human?[42]

Peccaries and humans are "inseparable variations of a single concept." Thus, Viveiros de Castro continues, "If we conceive of humans as somehow composed of a cultural clothing that hides and controls an essentially animal nature, Amazonians have it the other way around: animals have a human, sociocultural inner aspect that is 'disguised' by an ostensibly bestial bodily form."[43] Viveiros de Castro inaugurates a space between animals and humans that had been traditionally explored through the creaturely, a concept with a long and complex genealogy that touches upon the philosophical, the theological as well as the literary.[44]

Bo Bardi's tropical creature operates precisely in this direction: it reflects upon the non-human animal as constitutive of our own human ontology, that is, in continuity with us. This entanglement between humans and non-humans creates a 'liminal topography,' a malleable and plastic milieu in which Bo Bardi thought to operate and display a social, political, and ethical critical agenda through which to reconcile apparently irreconcilable ethical conundrums between cultures and, more fundamentally, between bodies (human and non-human). In so doing Bo Bardi triggered unprecedented affective and cognitive responses. To reframe the question of the creaturely alongside a non-Western ontology—i.e. including Amerindian communities of the Amazonia, Afro-Brazilian cultures of the Northeast, etc., Bo Bardi shows, implies, subversive and provocative 'animal acts,' and also the engagement with "the wrong side of the modernizing frontier," as I suggested at the beginning of this essay. Implied in this is Bo Bardi's systematic rejection of a machinic functionalism in favor of a re-enchanted world in which there is room for invention, provocation, and

View of the 'modern pavilion,' *Casa de Vidro*, São Paulo, 2018. Ph. Martin Cobas

magic. For instance, think of the *polochon* as a double-headed pig (and therefore an only-eating creature; possibly autophagic) or, in a discrete variation, as a double-butt pig (an only-evacuating creature, the anti-cannibal). Think, then, of the *polochon* as a dual citizen: of the kingdom of scarcity and the kingdom of excess.

In the sometimes complementing and sometimes competing realms of representation, architecture, and display, Bo Bardi makes the animal (or imaginary creature) 'communicate.' Even though the worlds of the animal and of the creature are neither symbolic nor linguistic (as we read in Heidegger, Lacan, or Levinas), they are certainly communicative; there is, as Diane Davis suggested, a "creaturely rhetorics."[45] This non-linguistic status makes the animal simultaneously untranslatable and readily available for 'conversation' (in a non-verbal communication). Animals are co-constitutive of the topographies we inhabit, and in this way social relationality is extended to non-humans. The animal therefore occupies a place beyond language in the city of all possible languages.

EXODUS: SUNDAY FUGUES

By way of conclusion, I would like to briefly dwell on a painting Enrico Bo dedicated to her daughter Lina in 1952. The oil painting, entitled "*Domenica, fuga dal circo* (Sunday, scape from the circus)"—a fatherly attempt at remediating his daughter's Sunday blues—portrays a parade of animals exiting a circus. Guided by the bandicoot, the troupe made a properly architectural exit, escaping through an opening in a massive brick wall, and thus laying bare the dialectics of confinement and escape. The animals cannot be contained in, nor constrained to, the confines of the cabinet; they are eager to explore the world outside. And so is the collector—as in the *Caixote de arte popular*.[46] The bandicoot points to multiple escapes: architectural, museographic, curatorial, editorial, social.[47]

Bo Bardi sought to mobilize the collections and expose its 'multiple others' (creatures included) to a critical cultural agenda, addressing the forces that regulate the affective liaisons between drawings, objects, and spaces, and that facilitate the transitions between the collector's introspection, the house as a 'space of translation,' and the outside, i.e. between the collections and the city, between drawing and its architectural afterlife. It is in these transitions that Bo Bardi finally met an "ecology of others" and Brazil the 'creaturely modern.'

In the last decades the creaturely has emerged as a ubiquitous trope in post-humanist discourses and the so-called ontological turn. Albeit often disguised in a series of sister concepts (e.g. the hybrid, the mutant, miscegenation), it came to the fore as a revision of what had often been regarded as scientifically and/or ethically aberrant, notably the human-animal divide. The history of the 'creaturely modern' foreshadows this path. Remember the *polochon*.

1 The essay was included in mine dissertation "Liminal Creatures/Liminal Topographies: Rhetoric of Excess in the New World." I thank Beatriz Colomina and Anthony Vidler, my advisors, for important suggestions regarding this argument. Thanks are also due to Sol Camacho, Marcella Carvallo, and Carolina Tatani at the *Instituto Bardi, Casa de Vidro*, Bruno Mezquita at the MASP Archives, Joanna Barbosa at the *Instituto Moreira Salles* (IMS), as well as Renato Anelli, José Lira, Lilia Moritz Schwarcz, Alvaro Puntoni and Fernando Viegas. Special thanks goes to Marcelo Ferraz.

2 On December 9, 1955, Eos de Borobourdour and Elfe D'Irraouda crossed the ocean from Le Bourget airport in Paris to Rio de Janeiro and then São Paulo. "Cats very fragile"—so read the box in which the two creatures completed their transatlantic journey. The sender: Germain Bazin, then Director of the Louvre Museum. The addressee: Lina Bo Bardi. Between tropical intestinal diseases and crystal-like fragility, the cats became more and less than animals.

3 This partial listing is based on the cataloguing of the *Casa de Vidro* collections elaborated by the *Instituto do Patrimônio Histórico e Artístico Nacional* (National Institute of Historic and Artistic Heritage, IPHAN) and on a photographic survey performed by the author during a series of visits to the house in 2017, 2018 and 2019.

4 The Bardis' journey to Brazil was a journey of collectors. Lina Bo Bardi and Pietro Bardi arrived in Brazil on October 17, 1946, onboard the *Almirante Jaceguay*.

5 See Bruno Latour, "Anthropology at the Time of the Anthropocene," Distinguished Lecture delivered at the American Association of Anthropologists, Washington, December 2014.

6 Mário Pedrosa, "Brasília, a cidade nova" [paper delivered to the Congrès international des critiques d'art], *Jornal do Brasil*, 19 Sept. 1959. Republished in: Mário Pedrosa, *Dos murais de portinari aos espaços de Brasília* (São Paulo: Perspectiva, 1981), pp. 345-353.

7 See, for instance, Renato Anelli and Sol Camacho, editors, *Casas de Vidro/Glass Houses* (São Paulo: Romano Guerra, 2018).

8 Philip L. Goodwin, *Brazil Builds, Architecture New and Old 1652-1942*, photographs by G. E. Kidder Smith (New York: The Museum of Modern Art, 1943), p. 9. Goodwin's book accompanied the Bardis on their transatlantic trip.

9 The blue curtain reappears in the form of a clothesline structure in the *Bahia no Ibirapuera* Exhibition (São Paulo, 1959). The exhibition was held in parallel to the *5th Bienal Internacional de Arte de São Paulo* in the famous marquee of the Ibirapuera Park, and was designed by Lina Bo Bardi in collaboration with Martim Gonçalves. Later, the 'shimmering blue' reappears in the 'blue hall' for the São Paulo City Hall.

10 This *Wunderkammer* has an important precedent in Bo Bardi's drawing "*Camera dell'architetto* (Architect's room, 1943)," in which the architect is confronted with history—and its potential intimation—to rehearse a 'historical present.' With this term Bo Bardi designates, both rhetorically and philosophically (via Antonio Gramsci's writings), a history that draws from narrative and from Benedetto Croce's philosophy of history, for which it is the interest in 'present life' that incites an inquiry into the past.

11 Walter Benjamin, *Selected Writings*, Volume 2, 1927-1934, edited by Michael W. Jennings (Cambridge, MA: Belknap Press of Harvard, 1999), p. 487.

12 Lorraine Daston and Katharine Park, *Wonders and the Order of Nature, 1150-1750* (New York: Zone Books, 2001), p. 253.

13 Sigmund Freud, "Charcot," in *The Freud Reader*, edited by Peter Gay (New York: W. W. Norton & Company, 1989), pp. 48-54.

14 In an earlier and longer version of this essay I explored the psychological elements at work in the act of collecting, drawing on Freud's work, Donald Winnicott's object relations theory, and Werner Muensterberger's

study on collecting. See, for instance, Werner Muensterberger, *Collecting: An Unruly Passion, Psychological Perspectives* (Princeton: Princeton Univesity Press, 1994).

15 The dissemination of the collection could be characterized as a 'sociology of the collection,' i.e. a series of operations that facilitate the transition from the psychological to the sociological dimension of collecting and that include curating, exhibiting, circulating, and several other modalities.

16 Lina Bo Bardi, "Stones Against Diamonds," in Marcelo Carvalho Ferraz, editor, *Lina Bo Bardi* (São Paulo: Instituto Lina Bo Bardi, 1993). Reprinted in Lina Bo Bardi, *Stones Against Diamonds*, Architecture Words 12, translated by Anthony Doyle and Pamela Johnston (London: Architectural Association, 2013), pp. 35-36.

17 In particular, the Valéria Cirell House (São Paulo, 1958) and Chame-Chame House (Salvador, 1958), the first iterations for the façade of the *Museu de Arte de São Paulo* (MASP, 1957-1968), and in the tropical exuberance of the 'vertical garden' in the façade for the project for the São Paulo City Hall (1990).

18 Lina Bo Bardi, *Contribuição propedêutica ao ensino da teoria de arquitetura* (São Paulo: 1957). Reprinted in 2002 by *Instituto Lina Bo e P. M. Bardi*. For an English translation see Cathrine Veikos, *Lina Bo Bardi: The Theory of Architectural Practice*, translated by Cathrine Veikos (London: Routledge, 2014).

19 Lina Bo Bardi, in flyer for the *Museu de Arte Moderna da Bahía* (MAM), 1959. *Instituto Bardi, Casa de Vidro*.

20 Beatriz Colomina and Mark Wigley made an important argument in this respect. See Beatriz Colomina and Mark Wigley, "A de Angústia: A Guerra de Lina Bo," in *Habitat: Lina Bo Bardi*, edited by Adriano Pedrosa, José Esparza Chong Cuy, Julieta González and Tomás Toledo (São Paulo: Museu de Arte de São Paulo Assis Chateaubriand, 2019), pp. 58-71.

21 On Manuel de Araújo Porto-Alegre see, for instance, Julia Kovensky and Leticia Squeff, editors, *Araújo Porto-Alegre: singular & plural* (São Paulo: Instituto Moreira Salles, IMS, 2014). In particular, the sections "A floresta brasileira" and "O álbum de Araújo Porto-Alegre," 32-24 and pp. 43-51.

22 See *Habitat: revista das artes no Brasil*, No. 1 (Oct.-Dec. 1950).

23 This tradition could be credited with facilitating (if not inaugurating) a powerful iconography that reminds us of the *Brasiliana* iconographic tradition and explains much of Brazilian contemporary art. A case in point is the work of Adriana Varejão. See, for example, Lilia Moritz Schwarcz and Adriana Varejão, *Perola Imperfeieta: A Historia e as Historias na Obra de Adriana Varejão* (São Paulo: Cobogo, 2014).

24 Lina Bo Bardi, "Residência no Morumbi," in *Habitat* 10 (January-March 1953), 31-40. Reprinted in Lina Bo Bardi, *Lina por escrito: Textos Escolhidos de Lina Bo Bardi* (São Paulo, Cosac Naify, 2009), pp. 79-81. Translated by the author.

25 Ibid., p. 81.

26 Georges Didi-Huberman, "Images Terre à Terre," in *La besogne des images: art, littérature, philosophie*, ed. by Léa Bismuth (Paris: Filigranes Éditions, 2019), pp. 50-61.

27 Ibid., p. 53.

28 Euclides da Cunha's *Os Sertões, campanha de Canudos* (1902) narrates the War of Canudos led by Antônio Conselheiro in the village of Canudos, in the Northeast, between 1896 and 1897. The deadliest civil war in Brazilian history, the episode came to symbolize the irreconcilable distance between the modernizing metropoles and the hinterland or backland, the state apparatus, and the *sertõe*.

29 Alberto Rangel, *Inferno verde: cenas e cenários do* Amazonas (São Paulo: 2001), p. 108. Translated by the author.

30 See Lorraine Daston, *Against Nature* (Cambridge: The MIT Press, 2019).

31 For a general definition of the turn to ontology see, for instance, Eduardo Kohn, "Anthropology of Ontologies," in *Annual Review of Anthropology*, vol. 44 (2015), pp. 1-35.

32 Emanuele Coccia, *The Life of Plants: A Metaphysics of Mixture*, trans. by Dylan J. Montanari (Cambridge: Polity Press, 2019), p. 5.

33 Ibid., p. 7.

34 Viveiros de Castro developed the notion of 'multinaturalism' over a series of papers, some of which are compiled in *The Relative Native*. See Eduardo Viveiros de Castro, *The Relative Native: Essays on Indigenous Conceptual Worlds*, translated by Julia Sauma and Martin Holbraad (Chicago: HAU Books, 2015).

35 This image has been published in *La besogne des images: art, littérature, philosophie*, edited by Léa Bismuth (Paris: Filigranes Éditions, 2019).

36 I quote Bataille from Yannick Haenel, *"Dieu, s'il 'savait,' serait un porc,"* in Léa Bismuth (editor), *La besogne des images: art, littérature, philosophie* (Paris: Filigranes Éditions, 2019), 202-205, 203. Bo Bardi quotes from Fedor Dostoievsky's *Brothers Karamasov* in her text *"O projeto arquitetônico* (The Architectural Project)," a propos the design of the *SESC Pompeia* (Pompeia Leisure Center): *"'Tout est permis, Dieu n'existe pas.' Mas o que existiu de verdade foi a Guerra..."* See Giancarlo Latorraca, *Cidade da Libertade* (São Paulo: Instituto Lina Bo e P. M. Bardi, 1999), 26-40. Reprinted in Lina Bo Bardi, *Lina por escrito: textos escolhidos de Lina Bo Bardi* (São Paulo: Cosac Naify, 2009), pp. 147-154, 151.

37 Alfred Jarry (1873-1907), the French proto-symbolist writer, founded Pataphysics as a branch of philosophy that studies imaginary phenomena beyond the metaphysical.

38 On the *Teatro do Ornitorrinco* see Christiane Tricerri, editor, *Teatro do Ornitorrinco, 1977-2007* (São Paulo: Imprensa Oficial, 2009).

39 Alfred Jarry, *Ubu Roi* (New York: New Directions Books, 1961)

40 Abelardo da Hora (1924-2014) was a prominent artist and social activist from the Northeast; Pierre Verger (1902-1996), the French-born Brazilian ethno-photographer, an important intellectual interlocutor of Bo Bardi and a regular guest at *Casa de Vidro*.

41 Viveiros de Castro's notion of perspectivism refers to the idea that subjects (human and non-human) are defined in a relational and therefore provisional way. See Eduardo Viveiros de Castro, *The Relative Native: Essays on Indigenous Conceptual Worlds*, translated by Julia Sauma and Martin Holbraad (Chicago: HAU Books, 2015). See also *Cannibal Metaphysics*, edited and translated by Peter Skafish (Minneapolis: Univocal Publishing, 2014).

42 Eduardo Viveiros de Castro, *The Relative Native*, p. 31.

43 Eduardo Viveiros de Castro, "Exchanging Perspectives: The Transformation of Objects into Subjects in Amerindian Ontologies," in *Common Knowledge*, Volume 25, Issues 1-3 (April 2019), pp. 21-42. 23.

44 Important sources in this respect are Walter Benjamin's essay "On Language as Such and the Language of Man" and *The Origin of German Tragic Drama*. Note the common root of the words *Kreatur* and creature/creation. This characteristically Western epistemology is substantially distinct to the one proposed by post-humanist discourses; it is precisely this divide that is interrogated in this essay.

45 See Diane Davis, "Creaturely Rhetorics," in *Philosophy and Rhetoric*, Volume 44; No.1(2011), pp. 88-94.

46 The *Caixote de arte popular*, or 'container' of popular art, was designed by Bo Bardi as a traveling *Wunderkammer*. It was first installed in 1978 at the SESC Pompeia Leisure Center in São Paulo.

47 Among Bo Bardi's multiple curatorial endeavors arguably none of them offer a more vivid sense of recollection than the exhibition *A Mão do Povo Brasileiro* (The Hand of Brazilian People), which opened in 1969 at the inauguration of the *Museu de Arte de São Paulo* in Avenida Paulista. The choral strategy and 'ethnographic curatorship' had become Bo Bardi's trademark and persisted until the last projects at SESC Pompeia Leisure Center in the 80s. See *A Mão do Povo Brasileiro, 1969/2016*, edited by Adriano Pedrosa, Julieta González and Tomás Toledo (São Paulo: Museu de Arte de São Paulo Assis Chateaubriand, 2016)

Cabinet in the master bedroom containing a small version of the *polochon*, sculptures, and *ex-votos*, *Casa de Vidro*, São Paulo, 2018. Ph. Martin Cobas

HOLDING THE EXIT DOOR

The Repair of the Bauhaus Masters' Houses

ISABELLA MORETTI

The architecture competitions for the new Masters' Houses ensemble in Dessau were framed as a story of destruction and repair, but the project to rebuild is also a story of institutional investment in cultural relevance. Between preservation and interpretation, Isabella Moretti retraces the controversies surrounding these objects.

Model of the ruins of the Sieben Säulen, Bauhaus Dessau Foundation, 2015.
Ph. Isabella Moretti

During the inauguration weekend of the new Masters' Houses designed by the Berlin-based studio Bruno Fioretti Márquez in May 2014, I could be found happily holding the exit door of House Gropius. I was working as a research intern at the Bauhaus Dessau Foundation in Germany. My assignment was simple: to keep the public from entering the house from the back door and to assure that visitors flowed in the right direction. The object, the house, came with a prescription—me—informing the public on its correct usage, preventing wrong-doings. This did not provoke any objections: visitors gazed at the unusual appearance of the box-like architecture, wandered in front of windows and doors that would not open, and enjoyed a lovely spring afternoon. Before groups of visitors arrived, the then-President of Germany, Joachim Gauck, gave a welcoming speech. He pointed to the "beauty in everyday life," the "democratization of aesthetics," and the going "beyond ornament" the bauhaus stands for.[1] It was a frictionless speech that, if uttered a century ago, would have doomed bauhaus's leading role in a modern design tradition that primordially valued innovation and confrontation. Over time, the school's thought and imaginary has been placed within different, sometimes contradictory, political ideologies, from Bolshevism to Imperialism or Corporatism.[2] Amid this evolving yet central debate, the bauhaus has retained its relevance in contemporary discussions, never really being relegated to an episode of the past.

The events of the following story unfold between 2002 and the inauguration. They deal with the 'urban repair' of the partial destruction of the Masters' Houses ensemble and the later demolition of its surrounding wall. The aim of this story is to comprehensively map the discursive, material, and symbolic references condensed in these architectural objects, illustrating the competing impulses between a preservation of the material remains and a symbolic continuation of bauhaus ideals. Either option responds to a modern project but their perspectives hardly coincide. Two models lay at the center of this debate. They engage in telling a story that moves between hopes, tests, and decisions impressed upon these objects in the quest for "updating modernism," which is, in fact, the name of the project where the first model is inscribed. In addition, the book *The New Masters' Houses in Dessau: Edition Bauhaus 46: Debates, Positions, Contexts* published by the Bauhaus Dessau Foundation in 2017 is a meticulous documentation of the debates and generously shares the different and sometimes opposing viewpoints held within the institution as well as other municipal and federal authorities. This book is also a key source for retracing the disagreements embedded in the design process.

THE TOURING MODEL

It was 1925 when Walter Gropius visited the *Kiefernwäldchen* lot for the first time; it was just minutes by foot from the main bauhaus building. One year later the settlement was built. It consisted of one villa with a car garage and three shared houses, each with a bicycle garage. When Mies van der Rohe became director in 1932, a perimeter wall and a corner kiosk were added. The addition generates debate on its own; historians do not agree on whether it is a design by Ludwig Mies van der Rohe or Eduard Ludwig, his closest assistant at the time, and whether it was actually a self-initiated project of the director or a programmatic necessity posed by city management.[3] Following that addition, the ensemble, as it stands today, was complete. However, since then and after the school was forced to move from Dessau to Berlin, the Masters' Houses were occupied in various ways and modified, either to resemble the neighboring aesthetics or to energetically optimize their performance by, for example, sizing down windows. In 1939 ownership was transferred to the Junkers Werke, a local firm that started off as a heating system business but then moved into the aviation and armament industry. On March 7, 1945 a bomb destroyed House Moholy Nagy completely and three-quarters of House Gropius, leaving only its basement and garage unharmed. House-half Feininger, which was left standing, was later occupied by a doctor and then transformed into a clinic during the 50s. After the war, the City Dessau took over the settlement's premises and sold the remains and the House Gropius lot to the Emmer family, who built on top of the basement. Roughly respecting the original layout, the design was crowned with a pitched roof. At some point after the Emmers moved in, the surrounding wall was suddenly demolished without notice overnight; in 1974 the ensemble was declared a monument. In 1996, House Muche-Schlemmer, House Feininger, and House Kandinsky-Klee entered the list of UNESCO's world heritage along the other bauhaus buildings both in Dessau and Weimar. However, it was not until 2002 that House Emmer was bought by the Bauhaus Dessau Foundation, opening a discussion on what to do with the 'interruptions' of the modern legacy.

First model. "UmBauhaus: Updating Modernism" was the name of an idea, a film, and a book conceived by Omar Akbar, Mathias Hollwich, and Rainer Weisbach in 2004. Hollwich and Weisbach travelled through Europe and the United States with a model of the Masters' Houses ensemble. Kept in a wooden box like a guitar bag, the model, which had been built in the foundation's carpentry workshop, toured the offices of well-known architects and historians. Hollwich and Weisbach collected thoughts on "what to do when something is missing?" as Francesco Bandarin posed it, or, in more pragmatic terms, what

Film stills of "UmBauhaus: Updating Modernism" by Matthias Hollwich and Rainer Weisbach. Available online at vimeo.com to do when something is not strictly missing but does not make sense with the historic and conceptual whole? The model had different tiny inserts for the vacant lot where the House Gropius used to stand: the 'original,' the House Emmer, and a Mickey Mouse-shaped house, among others. The imaginary replacements posed questions about reconstruction, preservation, and spectacularization.[4]

Bandarin called House Emmer a "deviation" and suggested installing a Gropius Museum instead; Rem Koolhaas was reluctant about the director's position and argued that the Masters' Houses were not actually that interesting; Donna Robertson speculated that Gropius himself would have replaced it. Oswald Matthias and Liselotte Ungers exposed a curious angle, arguing that reconstructions are generally absurd but only justifiable if they deal with an *Urtyp*—an original architecture type such as the skeleton frame of Schinkel's *Bauakademie*—because it has a structural relevance rather than an ideological one. Oscar Niemeyer was also categorical: "the bauhaus was an idea and had to die," he stated whilst looking at a drawing instead of holding the model. Christoph Ingenhoven disregarded House Emmer as a "horrible" sight; Peter Eisenman held the mini House Emmer in his hand and simply murmured "no, no, no;" Stanley Tigerman, on the other hand, recognized the house's potential to nurture debate. Jonathan Weber rejected the notion of a reenactment while Filip Noterdaeme proposed to repeat the same decision process and hold an event every hundred years in order to feed Gropius's spirit. All of the participants signed the box, it was exhibited, and then safely returned to the archive of the Bauhaus Dessau Foundation.

Some contributions pointed to the necessity of calling for an open and international competition, which as a matter of fact, followed after several consultations between the authorities of the City Dessau, the State Sachsen Anhalt, and the foundation. In retrospect, the main actors acknowledged four different positions: a true-to-the-original reconstruction of House Gropius and Moholy-Nagy; a contrasting new building in a contemporary fashion; the conservation of House Emmer and the space left by the decimated House Moholy-Nagy; or a complete intervention that was respectful of bauhaus' historical ideals and preservationist advice. Interests varied: some sought to boost tourism in a small and shrinking city in eastern Germany, others saw the possibility of revitalizing historical facilities through new spaces and programs, still others saw the potential of revamping bauhaus's ideas. It was thought that politicians would favor reconstruction, preservationists would argue for conservation, and the foundation would promote completion with a contemporary interpretation.

But it was the word 'reconstruction' that rang alarms. The experiences surrounding the reconstruction of the Braunschweiger Schloss in Berlin had been traumatic for the architecture scene and Philipp Oswalt, the director of the foundation at the time, was strictly against it. His aim was to develop a "new culture of reconstructing."[5] Compromises were made and a two-phase competition was held under the rubric of an "urban repair of the ensemble" and "the restoration of a fragmented site," but not without external and institutional pressure. The International Council on Monuments and Sites (ICOMOS) included the site on the list of World Heritage in Danger before the winners of the competition were announced. Ulrike Wendland, the conservationist in charge argued that the monument was the gap, that all traces were equally relevant, and that the final decision was inherently political. Out of 215 entries, 26 made it to the second phase of the competition held between 2007 and 2008. By then House Emmer had long been demolished. Two entries, by nijo architekten (Zürich) and Gnadler Meyn Woitassek (Stralsund), were awarded the second prize; first place remained vacant. The office nijo architekten was closer to meeting the clients' idea and was asked to develop the design further; they recovered the historic volumes but built them in black fiberglass as metaphoric shadows of the absent pieces. The relationship, however, did not last. The architects retired and new guidelines, incidentally based on nijo's design and decision process, were taken up for a second competition. The new instructions read: respect original volumes, maintain rhythm of windows and doors, be white, refuse the reconstruction of terraces and balconies, include fire protection and accessibility regulations.

Six nearby architecture offices were invited to present a comprehensive concept that would comply with the constraints: BFM (Berlin), Dressler Architekten (Halle/Saale), Jamie Fobert (London), Jabornegg Palffy (Vienna), Knerer & Lang (Dresden), and Kuehn Malvezzi (Berlin). BFM stood out with the notion of "architecture of imprecision;" the critic Florian Heilmeyer astonishingly accounts that the competition was, in the end, won by a story rather than a project. "We understand the house not as reconstruction but as interpretation," the architects insisted.[6] Again, that word 'reconstruction,' and, again, softened by 'interpretation.' Sigmund Freud preferred to talk about construction rather than interpretation because he regarded the latter as a mere association instead of a confrontation with the past, repressed or not.[7] Susan Sontag complain that interpretation was a strategy for the excessive conservation of outdated ideas, arguing that "[o]urs is a culture based on excess, on overproduction; the result is a steady loss of sharpness in our sensory experience."[8]

THE FROZEN MODEL

Another model. Actually, a photograph of the plaster model of the Director's house made by the Gropius Atelier in 1925. Strongly lit, almost burned cubic forms stand against a dark background, openings hardly differentiate in a bas-relief with only a thin shadow to cast their existence. This model more closely resembles the design for the new houses, which has also been related to works by Thomas Demand, short stories by Jorge Luis Borges, or photographs by Hiroshi Sugimoto. The architecture office BFM appreciated working with a concept of 'repair' rather than 'reconstruction,' because it favored an "unperfected, abstracted, and fragmented interpretation" of the object in a meditation either in vicinity to Eisenman's cardboard architecture or to Donald Judd's boxes. They argued that memories are defined by forgetting and that the careful exclusion of their specificities or details maintain the appearance worth remembering. In increasing abstraction, a hint, a wink, or a gesture to the former Masters' Houses and their masters is kept latent.

Since their conception, the Masters' Houses were meant to both display objects and be displayed as models for modern living, modern culture, and modern building.[9] Construction technology and style were forced to coincide in an industrial aesthetic and a strict dismissal of ornament. However, it is well known that bauhaus objects were framed as industrially produced for mass consumption but were actually handmade and only affordable for an elite. Historian Alina Payne shows how the bauhaus thought of objects as sculptures for the everyday and its masters as "inventor[s] of modernity"[10] that pushed the debate on objecthood (*Sachlichkeit*) but were nevertheless reluctant to grant the object proper agency or resign authorship. Her argument places the origin of the theorization of objects in Gottfried Semper's impressions after visiting the Great Exhibition of 1851, which triggered the rethinking of objects as organizing agents of life, where ornament and object were entangled rather than opposed. Semper transformed "the ornamental artefact into an experimental 'model,'"[11] thus the bases were set to move from an ornamental conception of architecture to the scale of the object.

The New Masters' Houses do look like models. They hide their constructive specificity in order to achieve a blurred appearance by abstraction. The new walls respect the old ones' thickness but they are poured concrete acting as structure, insulation, and finishing; a light monolith that does not compromise the basement's historical foundations. All windows and doors (except for exit and entrance) are fixed and closed. Their frames are kept minimal and the opaque glasses mounted in them were hand-painted by local craftsman specialized in the repair of gothic *vitrauxs*. One side was treated with white paint and the other with grey. From the inside, visitors hardly see what is happening outside, only the shadows thrown by the moving foliage of pine trees leave a subtly-moving trace on the surface. From the outside they are opaque. As buildings drift towards abstracted models, it is no surprise that, colloquially, the new Masters' Houses are referred to as ghosts.

Generally speaking, details are what hold the construction together, not only pragmatically but also, in this case, conceptually: the encounter between parts is to be reduced in order to achieve maximum signification by becoming imperceptible—like an ornament used to veil those encounters. "God is in the details" goes the famous phrase attributed to Aby Warburg, a phrase that has also been related to Mies van der Rohe.[12] The gods and figured details might differ in this case, but what the new Masters' Houses achieve in their magical act of dematerialization is an affirmation of their material technology. "Details are always vulgar," wrote Oscar Wilde in *The Picture of Dorian Gray*; details might be redundant or vulgar, but they are also inescapable. Thus, between model and appearance also lies the detail (or the pathos). That is the thing with architecture: the more you accelerate the interpretation machine, the blurrier the sight, but the detail must hold—rain cannot enter the house (or the museum).

Opposite the kiosk, on the *Gropiusallee* roundabout, lay the ruins of the *Sieben Säulen*, which is a copy of the Saturn Temple at the Forum Romanum in Rome. Like the ruins of House Moholy Nagy or the Gropius basement below House Emmer, which the new Masters' Houses were eager to fill in their targeted architecture of forgetting, the *Sieben Säulen* expose the drama behind the idea of urban repair. An idea that shows little tolerance to difference in the aim of restoring the ensemble's continuum from 1925 to the present. Whether the bauhaus be an institution, a school, a pedagogy, a style, an idea—utopian or failed, what is worth preserving, how or if it should be updated, and who is invited to comment or decide continues to be unclear and segmented. Having mentioned all these names and detailed facts that were already prefiguring the houses that now stand 'complete' in the *Kiefernwäldchen*, it becomes oddly difficult to withdraw them from that place, to not relate them to the ruin or the political expectation. But, at the same time, they become harder to traverse without being caught in the monolithic cycle of interpretation. If the design alludes to forgetting with the illusion of remembrance, has the debate not reached a dead end? Probably not yet. Until it does, the exit door remains open, waiting for the last 'master' to leave.

New Masters' Houses in Dessau, Bruno Fioretti Márquez Architekten, Berlin. Ph. Yvonne Tenschert, courtesy Bauhaus Dessau Foundation

1 The speech is available online on the Bauhaus Dessau Foundation's Youtube channel.
2 Alina Payne, "Bauhaus Endgame: Ambiguity, Anxiety, and Discomfort" in *Bauhaus Construct: Fashioning Identity, Discourse, and Modernism*, edited by Jeffrey Saletnik and Robin Schuldenfrei (London, New York: Routledge, 2009), p. 257.
3 See Ingolf Kern and Werner Möller, "Das graue Etwas," in *Neue Meisterhäuser in Dessau, 1925-2014*, edited by the Bauhaus Dessau Foundation (Leipzig: Spector Books, 2017).
4 The project was a collaboration between the Bauhaus Dessau Foundation and the PVCplus Bonn initiative. Contributors to the film were: Francesco Bandarin, Rem Koolhaas, Donna Robertson, Oswald Mathias Ungers, Liselotte Ungers, Hans Kollhoff, Chris Bangle, Oscar Niemeyer, Peter Ellis, Fillip Noterdaeme, Tyler Brulé, Christoph Ingenhoven, Stanley Tigerman, Peter Eisenman, Carlo Weber, Anna Klingmann, Jonathan Park, Dan Wieden, Andreas Möhn, René Bouman, Walter de'Silva, Adriaan Geuze, Matthias Sauerbruch, Hinnerk Wehberg, Meinhard von Gerken, Winka Dubbeldam, Xonis Balbes, and Jürgen Mayer. The book in a German and an English edition was published by the Jovis Verlag in 2004.
5 Philipp Oswalt in response to Günter Kowa in *Bauwelt*. Available online: schlossdebatte.de
6 Architects Donatella Fioretti and José Márquez in conversation with Philip Oswalt, Olaf Nicolai, Ulrike Wendland, and Florian Heilmeyer, "Die unscharfe Moderne," in *Neue Meisterhäuser in Dessau, 1925-2014*, edited by the Bauhaus Dessau Foundation (Leipzig: Spector Books, 2017). For a complete and comprehensible timeline of the arguments, resolutions, and phases of the debate, see "Chronik Meisterhäuser" by Monika Lüttich in the same publication.
7 Sigmund Freud, "Construcciones en el análisis," 1937. Available online.
8 Susan Sontag, "Against Interpretation," 1964. Available online.
9 For more information on the houses as *Muster* (models) see writings by Regina Bittner or Anna-Maria Meister.
10 Alina Payne, "The Agency of Objects: From Semper to the Bauhaus and Beyond," in: *Dust & Data: Traces of the Bauhaus across 100 years*, edited by Ines Weizman (Leipzig, Spector Books, 2020), p. 37.
11 Spyros Papapetros, "Ornament and object—ornament as object. Review of: Alina Payne, *From Ornament to Object: Genealogies of Architectural Modernity*." Available online: arthistoriography.files.wordpress.com
12 Ibid.

TABLE MANNERISMS

PENELOPE DEAN

Architecture critic Penelope Dean examines the tables in Hideyuki Nakayama's 004 House in Matsumoto, Junya Ishigami's Tables for a Restaurant, and Go Hasegawa's House in Sakuradai to explore the act of becoming something else. What happens when tables are not only suited for sitting at? Dean explores how functional excesses suggest the end of the object.

table (ta•ble)

a piece of furniture consisting of a smooth flat slab fixed on legs

Mirriam-Webster Dictionary

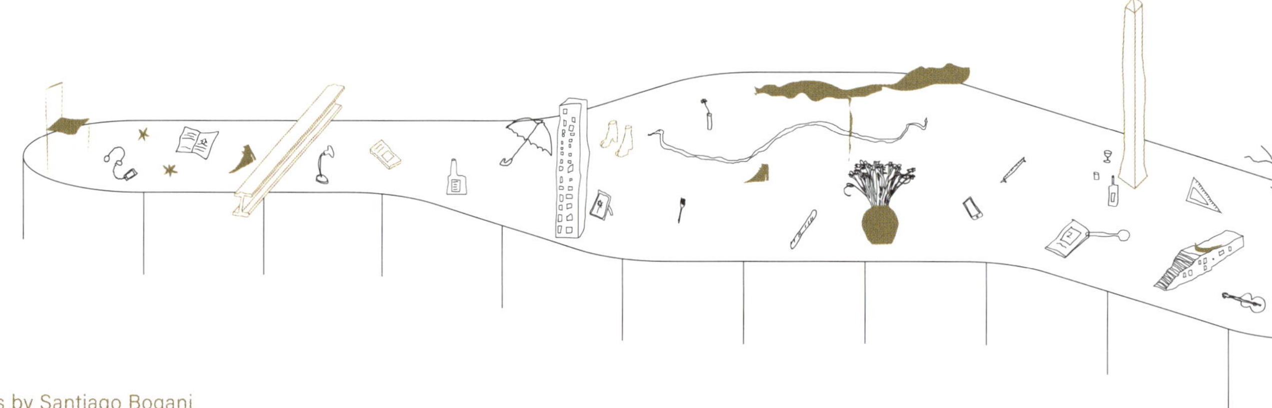

Illustrations by Santiago Bogani

There is no more ubiquitous piece of furniture in architectural culture than the table. Practically, tables perform as objects of convenience. Conventionally, they serve to establish scale for the plan and represent the function of a space: coffee table, dining table, drafting table, occasional table, offering table, operating table, side table, work table. Historically, they have inspired integrated-tables (floors and walls that absorb tables), macro-tables (buildings that look like tables), and micro-architectures (tables that look like buildings).[1] Occasionally, they disappear as one thing, and reappear as something else.

I can think of eight tables in three recent projects that exceed themselves in this last way: Hideyuki Nakayama's 004 House (2006), Junya Ishigami's Tables for a Restaurant (2008), and Go Hasegawa's Sakuradai House (2006). Each table exhibits the characteristics of neutrality and minimal form. Each exaggerates a flat rectangular surface, adding a degree of excess or redundancy. And each goes beyond mere utilization and materialization to assert a super-cultural surprise. All at once, each becomes a thing that seems to name the table, just as it names something else.[2]

To write about such tables from the West is no easy task. From here, criticism usually entails stripping away noise to uncover the significance of something. However, these Japanese projects are already so succinct, so flatly present, that there is little left to subtract. As Roland Barthes writes in *Empire of Signs*, "there is nothing there to read."[3] The labor of criticism here, then, is to add: to expound on how and why something does what it does. What follows is an attempt to elaborate an answer to a straightforward question: what is that other thing, that super thing, these tables do?

MAGIC MAT

The long table in Hideyuki Nakayama's 004 House in Matsumoto, Nagano, Japan, offers an excellent opening into the question, because it hosts un-table-like functions. The table is expediently constructed from two identical tables (with flat tops and rectilinear legs, the most generic of table constructions[4]) crudely bolted to each other and into the floor. Centered like a fashion runway on the first floor, or an enlarged diving board, the table proportionally duplicates the tiny house's plan. It is less something that occupies the house than something the house is built around. It is almost as though the table wears the house while it also constructs it.

The tabletop organizes domestic inhabitation along two axes. Table one (west) works horizontally, serving as a normative dining and work table—one eats and works at the table. Drawings and film show it sprinkled with domestic objects—tableware, potted plants, laptops, lamps, vases, and place mats—and surrounded by four chairs at one end. Encircled with circulation space, it obliges sedentary activity. Table two (east) activates vertically, producing an unlikely bridge between a second-floor bedroom and a sunken study—here one resides either above or below the table. Like scaffolding on a construction site, it spans a large hole that extends beyond its southern edge. There is another opening above it. Also encircled with circulation space, though this time in section, the table becomes circulation as it stages a vertical movement through the double-height void. It is an expedient device for transportation impossible to sit at.

Significantly, this device is not always drawn as a conventional piece of furniture. In one set of sections published in *Japan Architect*, the table 'disappears.'[5] Less object than a line, it emerges like Aladdin's magic carpet: a mat levitating between two floors with a figure standing on it. This two-dimensional delineation contrasts with the three-dimensional depictions of all other furniture (chair, sink, toilet, kitchen cabinetry, closet) in the same drawing. Why is the heaviest piece of furniture represented as the lightest? In other published drawings, the table is drawn with thickness, but a chair sits on top of it, while interior photographs

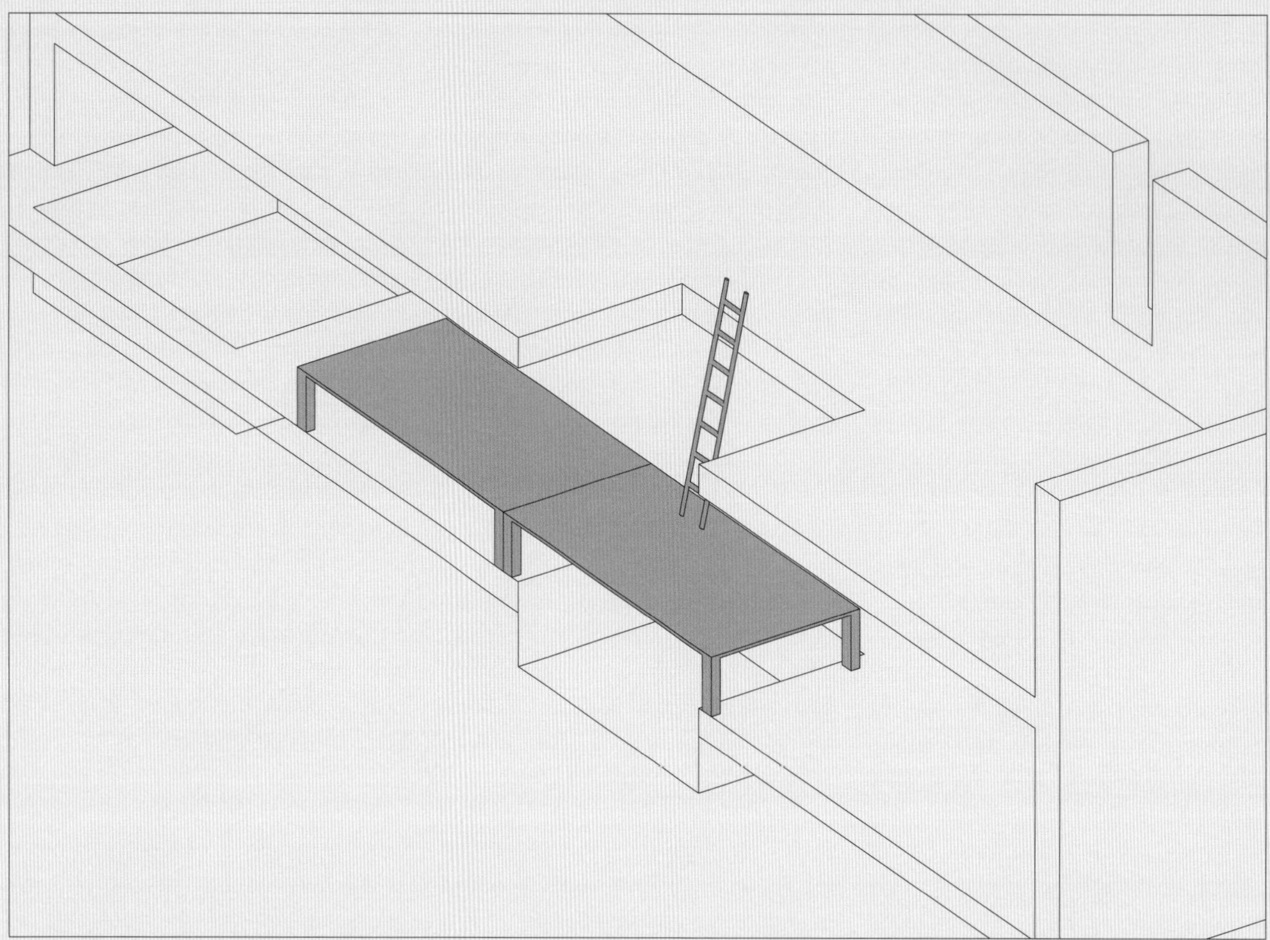

Axonometric section of the table in Hideyuki Nakayama's 004 House in Matsumoto, Nagano, Japan

show a ladder propped up on it. All of these representations accentuate the table as something in excess of merely floor or furniture; they give emphasis to a removal of the table's functional specificity in its eastward progression.

This removal is literally enabled by the rearrangement of space above and below the table. For example, the 'under the table' space that typically belongs between two parallel planes—the floor and the table underside—is here transferred into the study below, as the expected floor drops out into the void increasing the rooms floor to ceiling height so that adults can now play under the table. Without a floor to accommodate the placement of chairs, the table loses its primary reason for existence. Through subtraction and displacement, the table is stripped of its table-ness. As one traditional table function (sitting at) is replaced by others (climbing on, standing on, hiding under), table talk fades into table walk.

Once liberated from its table-ness, the tabletop can perform other functions. In addition to providing a ceiling to the sunken study, it visually screens the second-floor bedroom from the study. It acts as a landing in an exploded stair sequence that progresses from a concrete ledge in the study, to cedar board stair object, urethane resin painted floor, more cedar board steps, the tabletop, wooden ladder, to the rattan lined second floor. It collaborates with a double height void to yield continuous space around, over, and under. In all these ways, the tabletop is liberated from object to architecture.

In Nakayama's example, the table's quality leads to a grasping of it as an event rather than an object, an occurrence that entails inhabitants putting back together a shattered stair sequence from ad hoc furniture parts: stepstool, chair, table, ladder. Like a fixed elevator caught between two floors, the table provides a center of gravity, but without delimited prescriptions: inhabitants need to learn how to use the table; how to get to the table.

Long table in Hideyuki Nakayama's 004 House in Matsumoto, Nagano, Japan

In this way, the table deterritorializes a fixed architectural element—the staircase—into a novel assemblage of elements perpetually subject to reconfiguration. It conjures the super-cultural idea of architecture lifting up and setting down inhabitants without machinery: the fiction of a magic mat.

GREEN CLOUD

Junya Ishigami's Tables for a Restaurant advances another flatly fictional possibility. Inside a fifty-square meter room, five differently sized tables are arranged in two rows with circulation space between them. Their surfaces horizontally divide the interior into five private dining areas—five 'tables for two'—in lieu of vertical walls, yielding an alignment that is both confined and open. An imaginary rectangle, offset from the restaurant's interior walls, determines and limits the arrangement. Tables are held in place by the circulation that surrounds them; they absorb leftover space to expand horizontally. Tabletops act, as Ishigami puts it, as "gentle separators of the space" and "a space in its own right."[6]

The tables, which are too large for the program despite relatively small dimensions (from 2 x 2 m to 2 x 0.6 m), operate as a set. Relationships between seats, sightlines, and plants unify the five into a single, yet abstruse, composition. Pairs of seats huddle at table extremities—at a corner, side-by-side along an edge, directly opposite one another—to allow intimate propinquity. Potted plants, positioned on surplus surface areas, provide garden-like scenery that envelops diners. Seating positions alternate in plan to provide physical distance between pairs of diners throughout the room, and eye-level foliage obscures one table from another while serving as *petite shakkei* (borrowed scenery) for other tables. Each table plays a role in a system entirely established by dependent interactions. Each offers proximity and distance.

Photographs show the surreal visual effects of this coordinated effort on the interior: what is usually on the ground—potted plants—now float on a line. The table's wafer-thin profile allows for this optical illusion. Like Ishigami's earlier Table (2006)—a 9.5 x 2.6 x 1.1 m table unrolled from a single 3 mm thick aluminum sheet—the tables achieve their paper-like-quality through an excision of material thickness and detail. And like Table, each presents a scaleless image: tabletops—here 4.5 mm thick steel sheets finished with a 0.3 mm thick wood veneer—seamlessly fold down at ninety degrees into legs. In profile, the tables become drawings: thin black lines from one side; beige infills sans outline from the other. The overall effect diminishes the tables in perspectival depth: five tables become one; five become a 'single line.'

This is not any kind of line. It is a ground line without mass; a horizon line that separates earth from sky; a base line from which the tables emulate their surroundings. Below the line, dark undersides, edges, and legs recede into the polished, dark grey, concrete floor. A forest of slender furniture legs (chairs and tables) conjure an imaginary earth striated with columns. Above the line, the table's beige veneer surface disappears into the restaurant's off-white walls and ceiling. Bulbous white pots spouting stems, sprigs, fronds, leaves, and flowers invoke an imaginary sky populated with solid balloons and green feathers. And projected back from the line, the tabletops assume the role of backgrounds: a blank canvas; a rectangular frame from which other things can emerge.

Between five or ten species of plants populate each tabletop—winter jasmine, flowering currant, white mustard, clover, geraniums, maidenhair

Junya Ishigami's Tables for a Restaurant

to name a few species—in differently shaped pots. The loosely arranged objects, leaves, flowers, and stems, affectionately drawn by hand in green, pink, purple, orange, blue, and yellow colored pencils, are intricate figures that advance from their backgrounds. Their casual arrangements contrast with the formal table layout. Indeed, each tabletop has its own plan. Plants are set inside rectangles like elements of a still life painting: in and on the plane simultaneously. Collectively they act as spatial counterpoints to empty areas left aside for eating. They connote that the conventional use of the table occurs at a single corner, an end, a side. The combination of table and objects yields an atmosphere with an "indistinct aesthetic"[7]: a foliated *stratus opacus*; a vegetal mist made of tiny vol-

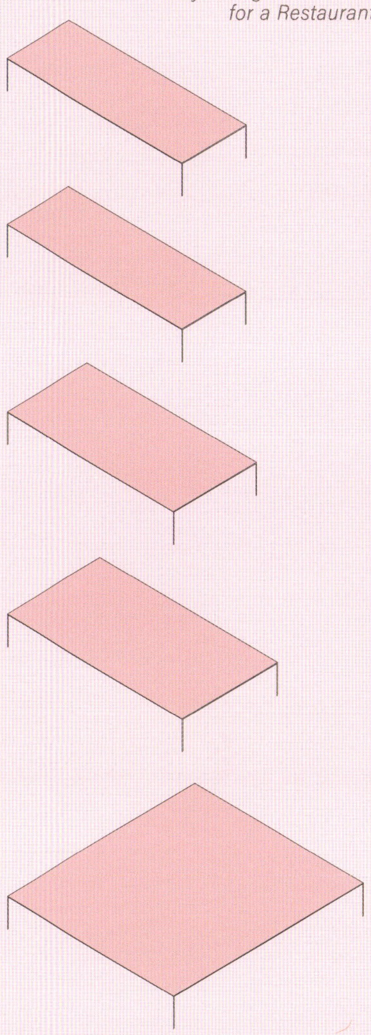

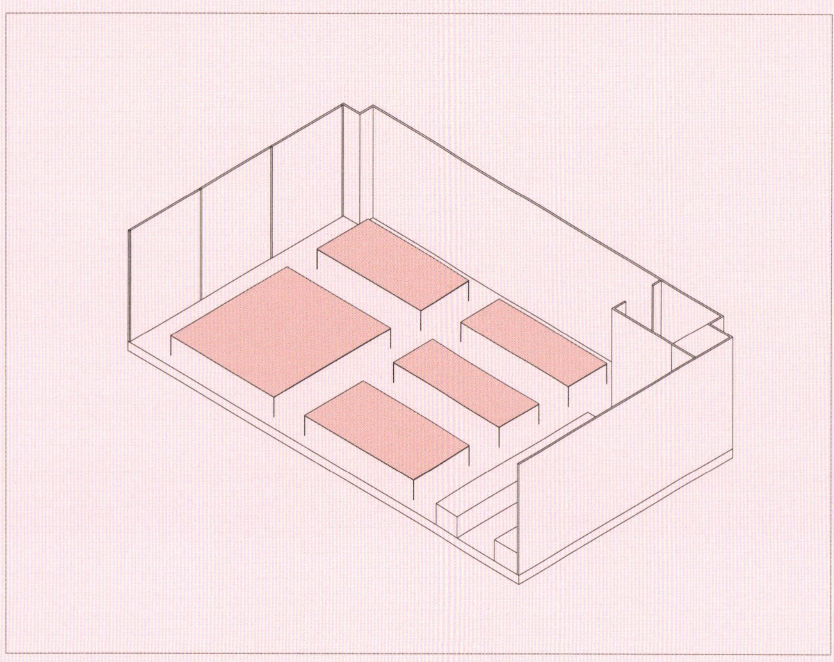

Axonometric view of Junya Ishigami's Tables for a Restaurant

umes unified in color, shape, texture, and form; a 'green cloud'. This allusive midriff-like figure plays the same role in the interior as the monochromatic white and grey mist in a Japanese screen print: both occlude information and allow scope for imagination.[8] Yet it achieves its effects through an extraordinary visual inversion: if the white clouds of Japanese screen prints obstruct through their blank emptiness, the green cloud in Tables for Restaurant obscures through 'articulated fullness.' Everything else is drained.

SUSPENDED ROOM

The large table at the epicenter of Go Hasegawa's House in Sakuradai offers a third super-cultural surprise. At just over 4 x 4 m, it fills an entire room—the central hole in a two-story donut plan—as private bedrooms encircle it at ground level and an open dining/kitchen/living space at an upper level. A double height void with a glass ceiling soars immediately above; painted plywood walls with clerestory windows define its edges. As an object, the table elides easy categorization: instead of designating a specific kind of activity, it multiplies new descriptions for rooms—"void room," "floor space/table," "yard-like table," and "second living room"—even though the architectural drawings consistently label it, simply, if mysteriously, as "table."[9]

This descriptive ambivalence can be attributed to the fact that the table holds more to a space, than to people or objects. It is, more accurately, a gigantic plain without legs: a vast birch paneled surface built like a floor. Indeed, a system of 60 x 60 mm floor joists spaced at 800 mm centers support it. Closed off by stud walls veneered in plywood, the table's section is thick, more of the ground than the sky, lying somewhere between a raised landform, a mesa, and an earth sculpture—a distant reprise of Walter De Maria's "The Earth Room" (1977). At the same time, it exhibits what artist Donald Judd once referred to as "reasonableness, usefulness and scale" as a table.[10]

This reasonableness can be found in its height and in how it performs as a desk. Desk-ness occurs at three locations: where the table meets the children's bedrooms at two corners, and where it connects with the study on one side. Through an unlikely Venn diagram of room and table, the overlap yields a pocket of space for a chair (or two), and leads to a curious suspension of rooms on either side of it. On the one hand, surface area is subtracted from the top to allow peripheral rooms to be 'brought to the table.' The indented shape of the tabletop accommodates the room; plywood sides, which mimic surrounding walls, complete the room. On the other hand, pairs of sliding doors extend from walls on either side of the table to inversely close off the central atrium, effectively 'tabling the room.' Here, the table reinstates itself as a square space in plan by imposing its orthogonal shape onto its periphery.

Largely defined in relation to what is "slightly outside of it," the table structures visual relationships at its edges and provides the possibility for an inhabitant to be in two places at once.[11] Visual opulence radiates from inward facing chairs: sightlines diffuse through rooms and atrium to outside. When seated at the table, one can select framed scenery—trees, street, neighboring houses, sky—through large, strategically positioned openings in walls and glass ceiling and along horizontal or diagonal lines. Simultaneously, the body divides at the table's boundary. As Hasagawa describes, when seated at the table, the body is present in two kinds of space: the lower part in a chair in an

Table at the epicenter of Go Hasegawa's House in Sakuradai

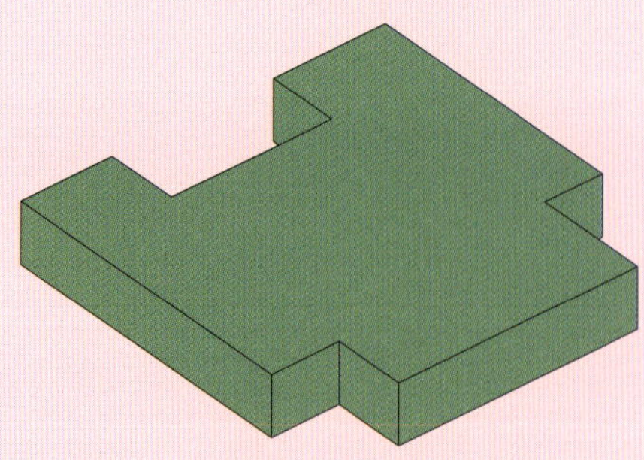

intimate private room; the upper part in a "magnificent table space."[12]

This highly programmed perimeter yields an unoccupied center: an empty middle, an external zone free from planned activities, an ambiguous space without fixed purpose.[13] Indeed, interior photographs evidence this divergence between purpose and non-purpose: embedded electrical outlets, plants, cards, pencils, papers, and toys aggregate at table corners and edges while a largely vacant middle exudes in between. In this regard, the table's outline and size is more important than its infill: everything that falls beyond reach from a chair becomes superfluous, residual, and free. From periphery to center, table-ness gradates into floor-ness.

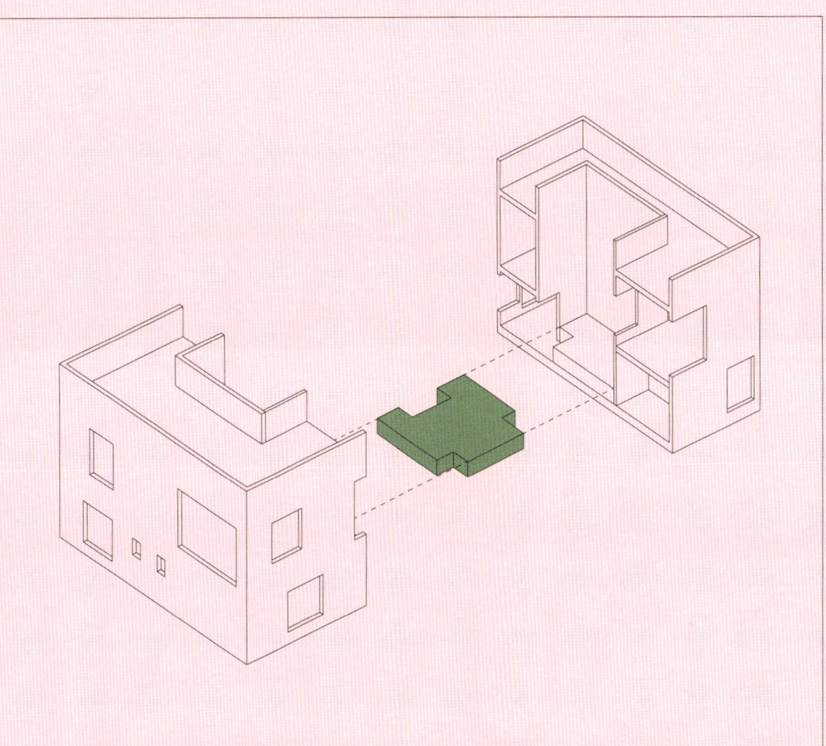

Axonometric exploded view of Go Hasegawa's House in Sakuradai

Yet in all of its orchestrations and accommodations, perhaps the most intriguing thing Hasagawa's table invokes is the idea of a suspended room; the notion that space hovers above the table. Rather than space structuring the table, the table now makes possible the space in an inversion of mimicry.

* * *

The most extraordinary thing about Nakayama's, Ishigami's, and Hasagawa's tables is that all of their effects are asserted in a single form. In each project, tables disappear and reappear under different guises and relate to people, objects, and spaces in distinctive ways. In Nakayama's 004 House, table effects are achieved through the combination of person and table. The table disappears through a denial of functional use and reappears as a free landing. In Ishigami's Tables for a Restaurant, the tables relate to objects arranged on their surfaces. Tables disappear through their technical precision—their material reduction to a line—and reappear as the invisible scaffolding for a cloud of objects. In Hasagawa's House in Sakuradai, the table directly relates to space: it simultaneously fills and suspends a room, all the while disappearing into the background. All of this is possible because each table has something inherently superfluous about it—a mannerist strain, as Robert Venturi would call it—which allows for contradiction, paradox, and ambiguity, and which makes its effects inherently architectural.[14]

Furthermore, the architecture of these tables lies not in their resemblance to architecture, but in what can be done with a rectangular plane parallel to the ground. In other words, the architecture is conceived horizontality, not verticality. Like the shift from wall art to floor art in minimalist art, the tables activate floor architecture instead of wall architecture, even (or especially) as they all act in the new dimension of section. In their effects, they also leave the object behind, suggesting that the super-object is, in fact, a post-object, an object that ushers in the end of the object, along with all of its related orientations and ontologies.

1 For a historical overview of table types see Marc Dubois's excellent essay, "La dimensione del tavolo = The table Dimension," in *Lotus International*, (vol. 98, 1998), pp. 112-138.
2 Here I draw on Bill Brown's "thing theory." See Bill Brown, "Thing Theory," in *Critical Inquiry*, (Vol. 28, No. 1, Things, Autumn, 2001), p. 5.
3 Roland Barthes, *Empire of Signs*, Richard Howard, trans. (New York: Farrar, Strauss and Giroux, Inc., 1982), p. 62.
4 In this way the, tables resonate with Jean Nouvel's "Less" (1994), Philippe Alldeys "Table P010" (1994), and Maarten Van Severen, "Long Table" (1988).
5 See drawings in "Hideyuki Nakayama: 2004 Matsumoto, Nagano, Japan," in *GA Houses*, (vol. 93, 2006), p. 141.
6 Junya Ishigami, *Small Images* (Tokyo: LIXIL Publishing, 2008), pp. 7, 10.
7 Here I borrow from David E. Cooper's lucid analysis of Japanese "aesthetics of the indistinct" in "Cloud, Mist, Shadow, Shakuhachi: The Aesthetics of the Indistinct," in *New Essays in Japanese Aesthetics*, ed. Minh Nguyen Lanham, (MD: Lexington Books, 2017), pp. 17-31.
8 Ibid, p. 18.
9 See for example, Go Hasagawa, "Go Hasagawa," The Japan Architect,(vol. 70, 2008), pp. 40, 51; and Go Hasagawa: *El Croquis*, (no. 191, 2017), p. 46.
10 Judd was writing about a chair: "The art of a chair is not its resemblance to art, but is partly its reasonableness, usefulness, and scale as a chair." See Donald Judd, "It's Hard to Find a Good Lamp," 1993.
11 Go Hasagawa, "Go Hasagawa," in *The Japan Architect*, (vol. 70, 2008), p. 51.
12 *Go Hasagawa: El Croquis*, (no. 191, 2017), p. 46.
13 See Go Hasagawa conversation in Cathelijne Nuijsink, *How to Make a Japanese House* (Rotterdam: NAi Publishers, 2012), p. 226.
14 Robert Venturi, *Complexity and Contradiction* (New York: The Museum of Modern Art, 1977), p. 20.

OF RADIATING SAMPLES, SOUVENIRS, AND RELICS

LUDOVICO CENTIS

Somewhere in between the cities and monuments that once gave geographic continuity to the governmental program that developed the atomic bomb in the United States, architect and editor Ludovico Centis started a collection. Either found or gifted, these objects quickly become relics, presented in this article with photographs by Alberto Sinigaglia.

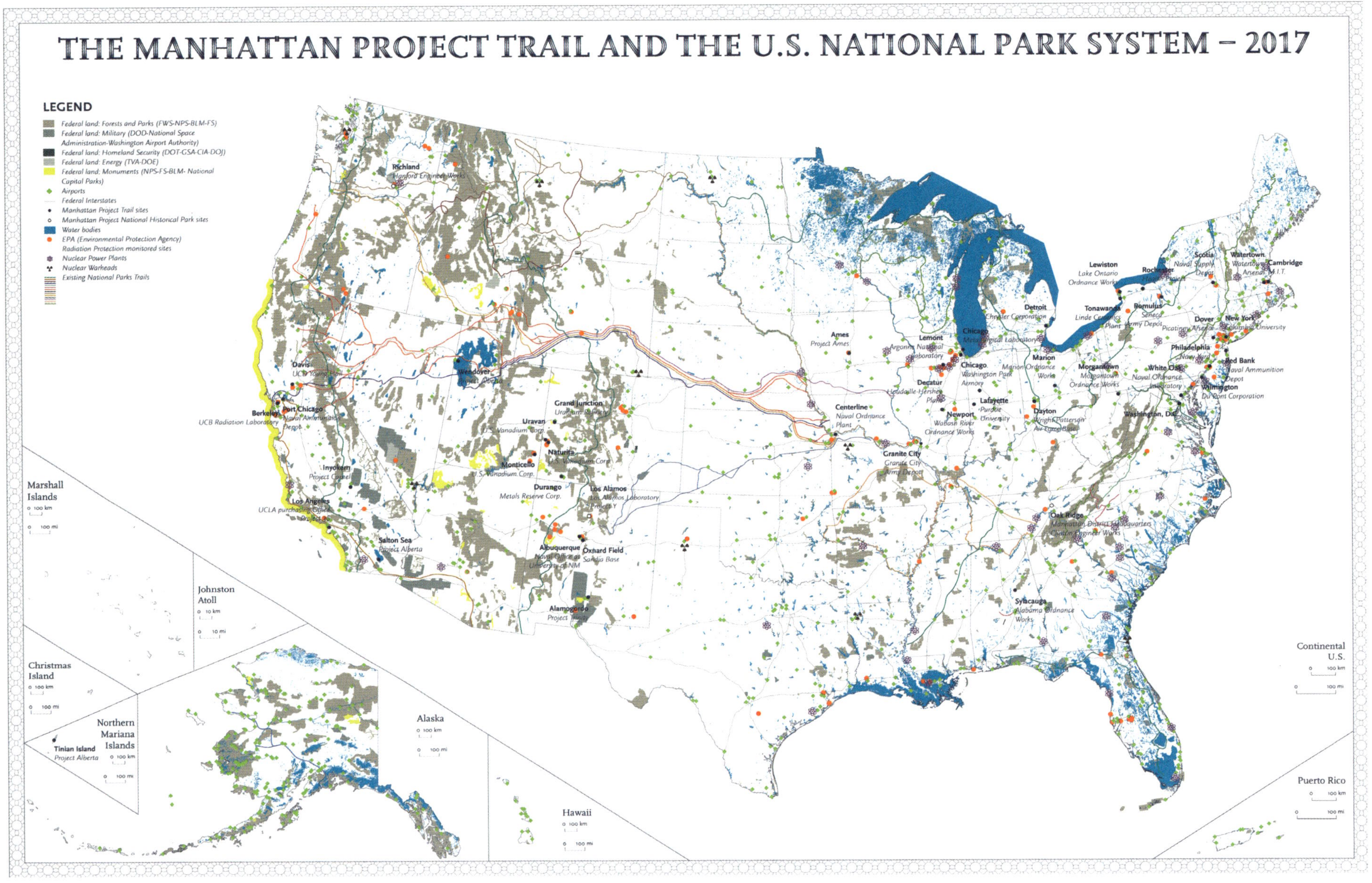

Ludovico Centis / The Empire, "The Manhattan Project Trail and the US National Park System," 2017.

During my fieldwork, as I traveled along the Manhattan Project Trail,[1] I collected objects that I considered as samples, souvenirs, and relics, and I had them photographed in Italy by Alberto Sinigaglia after my return. The large majority of these objects—badges, forms, maps, leaflets, stones, deer antlers, hats, commemorative coins, magazines, etc.—can be understood as samples or souvenirs. Collecting these types of commemorative objects is an ancient practice dating back at least to the first pilgrimages Christians made to the Holy Land, if not before, and more recently it has been embraced by such artists as Robert Smithson. In Smithson's works, such as the "Non-Sites" series,[2] it is, in fact, possible to recognize the connection between geological sites and a legendary dimension; the influence of the topographical reliquary tradition as well as strategies of displacement[3] that can be traced to early Christian examples such as the Jerusalem Chapel in the church of Santa Croce in Gerusalemme in Rome. Helen, the emperor Constantine's mother, brought relics—such as the fragments of the cross of The Crucifixion—as well as soil from Golgotha that was presumably soaked with the blood of Christ. During my time traveling the Manhattan Project Trail, I remember seeing several people—including kids—crouching down around the Trinity test site obelisk looking for remaining samples of Trinitite,[4] as well as more technologically equipped visitors wandering the site with detectors capable of tracing radioactive materials.

Three of the objects photographed here might be considered relics, rather than samples or souvenirs. The first object, a gift I received while I was in Buffalo, New York, from Lindsey Freeman—a sociologist interested in nuclear heritage and culture—is one of the many dosimeters that the civil defense administration distributed during the Cold War to workers in the nuclear industry so that they could measure their daily exposure to radiation.

The other two, a small case of pencil leads and a brick-shaped block, I received as gifts from Roger W. Tilbrook, a retired nuclear engineer who worked at the Argonne National Laboratory, and they share the same origin. In fact, they are both made from the original graphite bricks of Chicago Pile-1,[5] which were subsequently used for Chicago Pile-2[6] and then finally abandoned in a heap in a clearing during the clean-up work carried out by the Department of Energy on the occasion of the dismantling and remediation of the Argonne Site A in the 1970s. After verifying with Department of Energy technicians that the graphite was radiologically safe, Tilbrook preserved a considerable number of the graphite bricks that he later transformed into smaller blocks and pencil leads to give to friends who retired from the laboratory or, when the occasion presented itself, to researchers and visitors like myself.

While the dosimeter could be considered a kind of generic relic of the Cold War because it was one of thousands, which could make it seem like more of a sample than a relic, the graphite objects resulting from the original bricks of Chicago Pile-1 possess a much stronger aura. They are in all respects relics, for they are physical as well as conceptual things, ordinary looking objects charged with extraordinary meaning.

1 What I have conceived of as the "Manhattan Project Trail" is a collection of sites that extends from the federal capital to isolated towns in the South, expanding the network of locations included in the Manhattan Project National Historical Park and representing a richly meaningful cross section of the country. Washington, DC, New York City, Cambridge, Rochester, Lewiston, Oak Ridge, Chicago, Alamogordo, Los Alamos, Uravan, Wendover, Monticello, Inyokern, the Salton Sea, Berkeley, Richland... What at first glance seems like a random series of cities scattered across the US actually can be perceived as closely interconnected, and considered together, they constitute a trail that links all of the sites related to the Manhattan Project—the US government program that developed the first atomic bomb during World War II—and its legacy.

2 Robert Smithson, "A Provisional Theory of Non-Sites," in *Robert Smithson: The Collected Writings*. Ed. Jack Flam (Berkeley and Los Angeles: The Univ. of California Press, 1996 [1968]), p. 364.

3 Alexander Nagel, *Medieval Modern: Art Out of Time* (London: Thames & Hudson, 2012), pp. 97–133,151.

4 Trinitite is a kind of glass made of arkosic sand melted by the blast of the atomic device detonated during the Trinity test on July 16, 1945. Usually light green in color and mildly radioactive, it was sold to mineral collectors in 1940s and 50s. Today it is illegal to collect it from the site.

5 Chicago Pile-1 (CP-1) no longer exists. Built as part of the Manhattan Project, it allowed the initiation of the first man-made self-sustaining nuclear chain reaction on December 2, 1942. The head of the team who created it, Italian physicist Enrico Fermi, described it as "a crude pile of black bricks and wooden timbers" (See Enrico Fermi, "Fermi's Own Story," in *The First Reactor*, (Oak Ridge, TN: United States Atomic Energy Commission, Division of Technical Information, 1982), pp. 22-26. CP-1 was built at the University of Chicago on a squash court located under the western stands of old Stagg Field. The final iteration of the pile, made of AGOT graphite bricks arranged in a quasi-spherical form mounted on a 'cradle' of timbers and enclosed within a tent made of hot-air-balloon fabric, had an approximate width of 25 feet across the middle and 6 feet at the edges, and a height of 20 feet.

6 Chicago Pile-2 (CP-2), which was built in 1943 around thirty miles south-west of Chicago on what would become the Argonne National Laboratory's first campus, was the first nuclear reactor with a concrete shielding added. CP-2 has been dismantled and its parts buried following an environmental clean-up some decades ago, and now it is a forested area accessible to the public. Today's Argonne National Laboratory is situated a few miles north-west of the old campus.

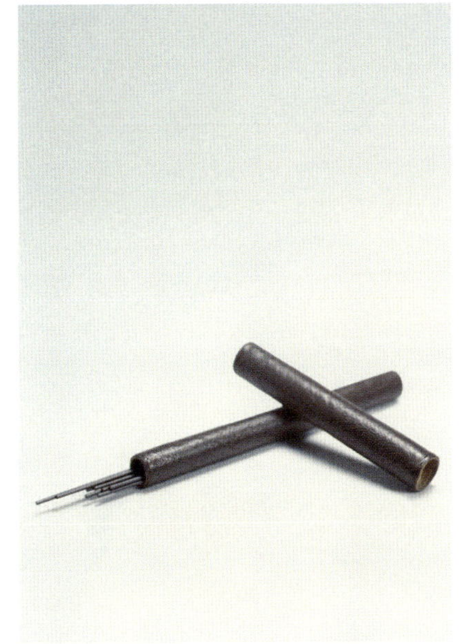

Ph. Alberto Sinigaglia

Georg Lippsmeier, *Midwifery School and Hospital Tripoli/Libya*, 1966, BIB 242123. African Architecture Matters Collection, CCA, Montreal.

VIVECA PATTISON ROBICHAUD, CURATOR, BOOKS, CCA

Ph. Matthieu Brouillard, CCA

Midwifery School and Hospital Tripoli/Libya, published by Georg Lippsmeier (1923-1991) in 1966, consists of thirty-nine leaves, twelve unnumbered, with illustrations and folded plans, all staple bound together in a beige, thirty-centimeter book with the office's original shelf mark of 727.4/612/ embossed onto a red sticker and affixed to the lower left corner of the cover. This object tells a story of the three locations it has inhabited: the site in Libya, documented within its pages, where this building was never built; its life as a volume in Lippsmeier's library in Starnberg, Bavaria; and its present location as part of the African Architecture Matters Collection in the below-ground vaults at the CCA.

Lippsmeier designed the Midwifery School in the Sykhel Guima suburb in Eastern Tripoli, Libya, next to the preexisting Mother and Child Welfare Center. The school would have served as a hospital and polyclinic with dormitories for doctors, nurses, midwives, and students. The building does not exist, but the building program does. It emphasizes a strong horizontal line to give a stable appearance and minimize its size relative to adjacent structures and the surrounding landscape, so as to not appear out of scale. The entrance is on a secondary road so as not to disturb traffic on the main thoroughfare. Additionally, the landscaping blends in with the existing area and includes planted ground cover to keep dust to a minimum. Integrated in the publication is a birds-eye perspective drawing of the entire complex of buildings, building plans, architectural and structural descriptions, mechanical and electrical installation guides, description of construction materials, and building cost estimates by volume.

The book was given a shelf mark by one of the secretaries in Lippsmeier's office. It would have been registered on three separate inventories, one arranged geographically, one by author, and one according to the German decimal classification, which is how it would have been shelved in the office. The book still has its former address on the cover: the red sticker with its embossed shelf mark. This research library, located in the entrance directly beside a world map covered in pins indicating where the firm had designed projects, was a prominent feature of Lippsmeier's practice. Shelved with research briefs, other design booklets produced by the firm, and research materials, this book was in conversation with its neighboring volumes, in dialogue with Lippsmeier's built and unbuilt work, and constantly engaging with architects and researchers employed in the practice who would consult it, along with its neighbors, for inspiration, practical design solutions, and a myriad of other reasons. Creases and bends in the cover serve as evidence to this use.

After Lippsmeier's death, his son continued his architectural practice but ceased the research arm of the agency, which set in motion this volume and its library's westward journey, ultimately ending in a cross-Atlantic trip to Canada. Lippsmeier's library first became part of ArchiAfrica, a non-profit research group of Dutch architects founded by Antoni Folkers and was moved to the Netherlands. It was then transferred to African Architecture Matters, a non-profit consultancy firm working in design, planning, and research of the African built environment. To increase the visibility, not only of Lippsmeier's library but also the other collections owned by African Architecture Matters, these volumes were donated to the CCA, where they reside today. Lippsmeier might not have envisioned such a move for his library or this publication, but he should take comfort knowing that they continue to serve a research agenda. They have all been catalogued and are discoverable not only through the CCA's website but also through World Cat, an online catalogue of more than 10,000 libraries with over two billion items available in libraries worldwide.

Visibility of collections is always tantamount, but even more so for little-known titles and architectural office-produced designs and research briefs. These volumes are often published in small print-runs and distributed ad hoc, so it can be a challenge to even generate awareness that these volumes exist. Assembling them at a location where they are attentively curated and catalogued is the first step to promoting and encouraging their use, in a research seminar, for example, in a master's student summer program, in design projects, or exhibitions that are still undetermined. The African Architecture Matters Collection in general and *Midwifery School and Hospital in Tripoli/Libya* in particular, live on and remain relevant to new generations of scholars, architects, and enthusiasts able to learn from the research Lippsmeier put into his design practice.

Gordon Matta-Clark's Wooden Pulley. Wood, iron, and plastic, before 1970s, PHCON2002:0016:070. CCA, Montreal. Gift of Estate of Gordon Matta-Clark. © Estate of Gordon Matta-Clark.

MEGAN MARIN, CURATORIAL COORDINATOR, CCA

Ph. Matthieu Brouillard, CCA

The CCA Collection is home to a fundamental repository of materials related to Gordon Matta-Clark's creative process—the sketches he made, the notes he kept, the books he read, the films he shot, the photographs he took, and the letters he sent and received. With a focus upon everything ancillary to his artistic output, this wealth of documentation offers insight into how and why he carried out each of his architectural interventions. Although Matta-Clark's work has been the focus of numerous exhibitions and publications in recent years, there are key objects from this collection that have seldom, if ever, been on view.

One such object is a pulley from the block and tackle set Matta-Clark used to move himself up and down the sites of his infamous "building cuts." More precisely, it is a double sheave wooden pulley block, with a small inset medallion that features a star encircled by the text BOSTON AND LOCKPORT BLOCK CO. Its rustic surfaces—wood, iron, and plastic—are marked with the scuffs and scrapes that tend to adorn any well-used tool. As the only three-dimensional artifact in the Matta-Clark collection, it could easily be overlooked as a small novelty amongst an archive of predominantly paper-based works. Upon closer consideration, however, it is an outlier that provides an additional perspective on Matta-Clark's spatial strategies.

The block and tackle set appears in archival film footage multiple times as both witness and accomplice to some of Matta-Clark's most ambitious acts. A closeup is seen as he uses it to hoist himself up the side of a tract house at 322 Humphrey Street in Englewood, New Jersey, while drafting plans for 'splitting' along the building's shingled exterior. It appears again above the sparks that fly as he cuts through the metal facade of Manhattan's Pier 52 to enact Day's End. And again, it appears, as he drifts along a five-story building in Antwerp to score the surface for Office Baroque. Although pulleys had recurring roles in several of Matta-Clark's major projects, they have received remarkably little recognition.

While the block and tackle set was a crucial part of the process in each of these building cuts, it was equally a part of the performance. As such, the remaining pulley is a piece of cinematic memorabilia as much as it is a vestige of invested physical labor. Although the pulleys never remain in focus in the films for very long, they are undeniable focal points, nonetheless. Each one is a nexus that maintains a delicate equilibrium amongst everything occurring in the frame. Equally important, however, is that they are part of a system that, at least conceptually, liberated Matta-Clark's movements from the limits of gravity. Simply put, the pulleys are what facilitated his interventions at the urban scale.

Given that Matta-Clark's building cuts offered critiques of social space, the tools he used in their realization were part of a political commentary on architecture and civic action. His inclination to intervene on sites that had otherwise been discarded, underutilized, or forgotten situates the block and tackle set as a grassroots mechanism used to re-establish the meaning, use, and value of a particular place. As such, Matta-Clark's pulley is a relevant reference amidst current forms of activism. As people attempt to reframe and replace outmoded monuments, it is a reminder that ordinary objects can be appropriated to realign architecture with a shared social mission.

The Canadian Centre for Architecture (CCA) is an international research institution and museum premised on the belief that architecture is a public concern. The CCA's collection is a repository of ideas, provocations, inspirations, and trials and errors. Made up of both archival holdings and the output of activities, the collection is both a base of materials for research and a body against which new readings and contexts are tested. Out of its extensive catalog, the CCA has selected a seldom tool and a book for this special collaboration with NESS.

CCA.QC.CA

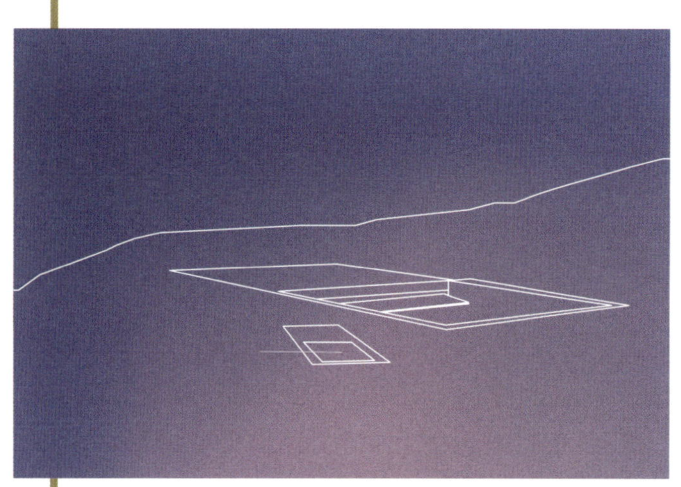

1

3

Reversed Animations

What if the architect actually becomes its design? What stories can architecture tell? Based on the answers of a questionnaire, we redrew the photographs, drawings, and sketches of each building and rearranged them into a graphic novel.

2

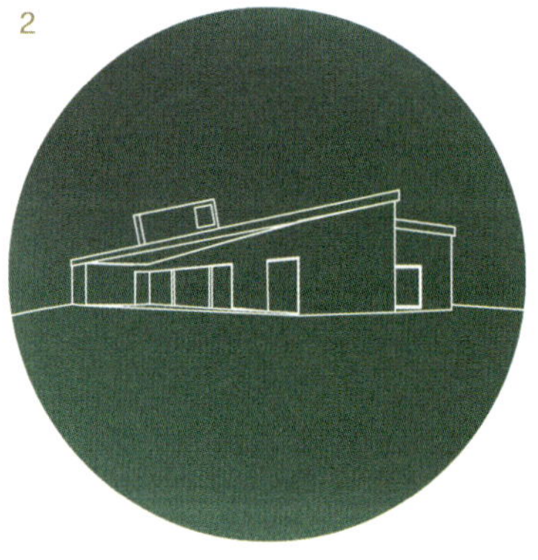

4

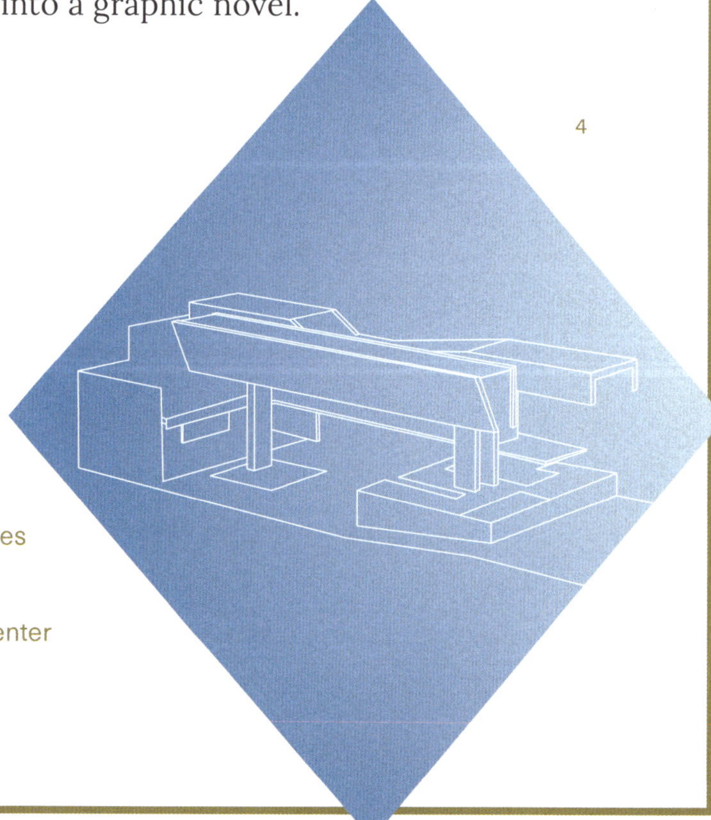

1 BCHO Architects's Earth House illustrated by Isabella Moretti

2 Diego Arraigada Arquitectos's House among Trees illustrated by Magdalena Tagliabue

3 Kéré Architecture's Surgical Clinic and Health Center illustrated by Magdalena Tagliabue

4 SPBR Arquitetos's Weekend House illustrated by Santiago Bogani

5

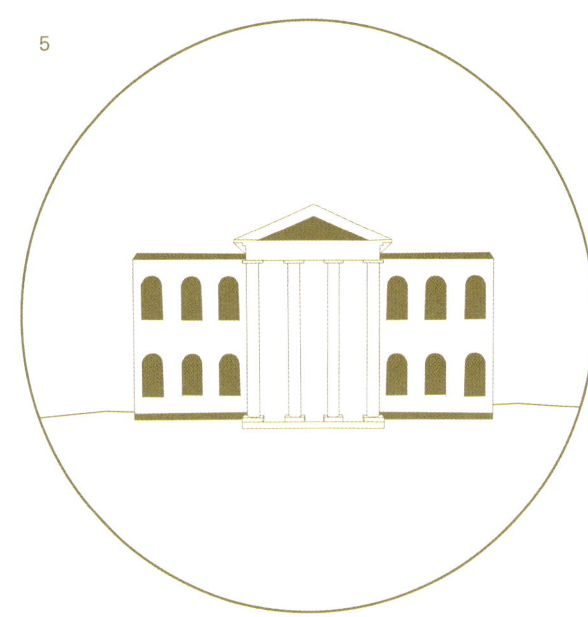

7

Playful Reenactments

What does the social network of a building look like? What contents and photos does it share, and with whom? We invited architecture critics to choose one building, ask questions, and speculate on its relations and orientations.

6

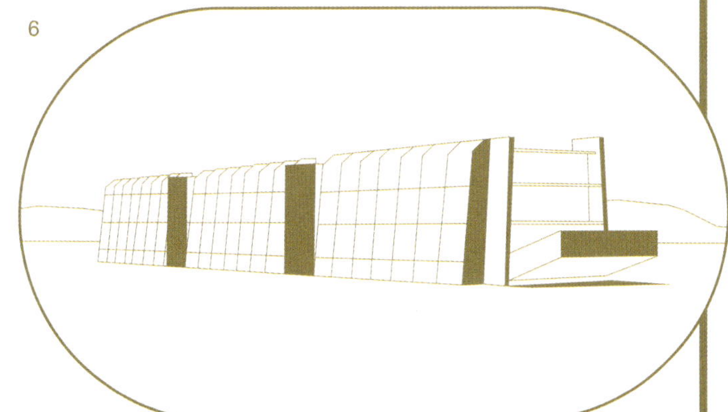

5 Jayne Kelley grooves to the Haunted Mansion in Disneyland

6 Laura González Fierro becomes the Vasconcelos Library by Alfredo Kallach

7 Ruth Estévez, Wonne Ickx, Otto and Lina Ickx Estévez play the Satélite Towers by Luis Barragán, Mathias Goeritz, and Jesús Reyes Ferreira

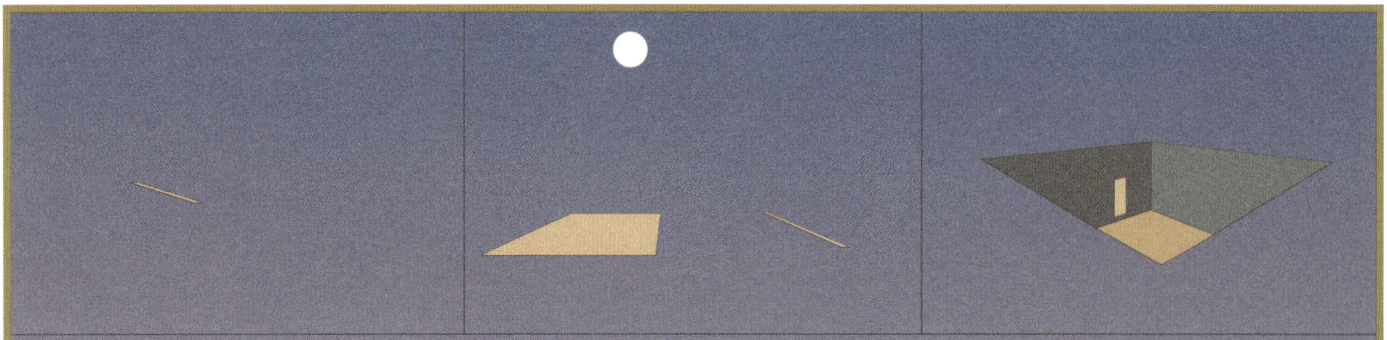

I stand under the surface of the earth.

I was built in honor of Yoon Dong-joo, a Korean poet who wrote beautiful poems about the earth, the stars, and the sky.

I am a house of the sky.

My walls are built with the same earth that was sitting here before I was born. The wood that was previously on the site was also incorporated to my construction. So, in a way, I have always been here.

A NIGHT COUNTING STARS,
by Yoon Dong-joo*

Longing for I know not what,
On this hill bathed in starlight
I have written his name
And covered it with earth.

Indeed, for I am like the insects crying through the night,
Bemoaning their shameful names.
But when the winter passes and to my star comes spring,

Thick grass will proudly grow on this hill
In which my name is buried
As green as it does on graves.

* Translation by David E. Shaffer

Earth House by BCHO Architects

DATE: 2009

LOCATION: Sugok-ri, Jipyeong-myeon, Yangpyeong-gun, Gyeonggi-do, South Korea

SITE AREA: 660 m^2 - 7104 sf

BUILT AREA: 32.49 m^2 – 350 sf

PROGRAM: Library, Meditation

STATUS: Completed

DESIGN: Byoungsoo Cho

TEAM: Hong-joon Yang, Woo-hyun Kang, Tae-hyun Nam

TEXT: BCHO Architects

ILLUSTRATION: Isabella Moretti, Santiago Bogani

A pine tree cut from the site was sliced into 80-millimeter thick discs and was cast into the concrete walls.

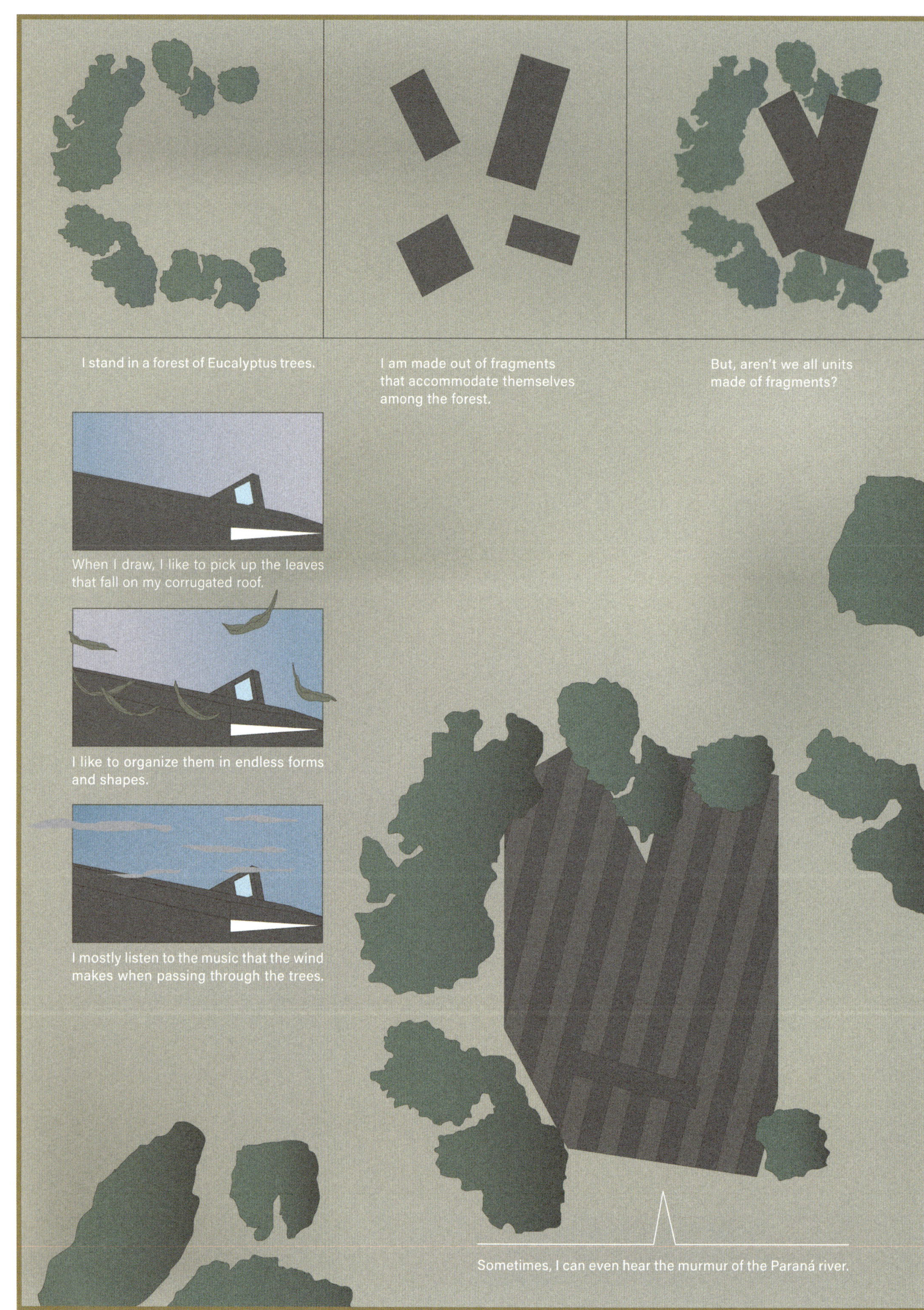
I stand in a forest of Eucalyptus trees.
I am made out of fragments that accommodate themselves among the forest.
But, aren't we all units made of fragments?
When I draw, I like to pick up the leaves that fall on my corrugated roof.
I like to organize them in endless forms and shapes.
I mostly listen to the music that the wind makes when passing through the trees.
Sometimes, I can even hear the murmur of the Paraná river.

House among Trees by Diego Arraigada Arquitectos

DATE: 2015-2017

LOCATION: General Lagos, Argentina

BUILT AREA: 269 m² - 2895 sf

PROGRAM: Single-family House

STATUS: Completed

DESIGN: Diego Arraigada Arquitectos

TEAM: María Emilia Bertero, Josefina Bilbao, Melanie Borbey, Agustina Coulleri, Victoria Fucksman, Pablo Gamba, Oscar Merle, Florencia Meucci, Luciano Navarini, Mercedes Paz, Sofía Rothman, Florencia Sobrero

ADVISORS: TEGGA Fernando Tettamanti, Matías Hagge, structural engineers. / CONSTRUCTION: Mahon (Diego Mancilla, Daniel Gauchat, architects).

TEXT: Diego Arraigada Arquitectos

ILLUSTRATION: Magdalena Tagliabue, Santiago Bogani

I stand on Léo, Burkina Faso, and I am five years old.
I have a structure that is open to everything and offers shade where needed. My walls are able to host all walks of life and all events that come with the human experience. From the birth of healthy children to everyday operations and more complex mishaps.
Even though I love to meet new people who I can grow fond of and then encourage to stay healthy, I am not one for reunions.
Once they have passed by, rested a little, and I have given them all I can, the best case scenario for all of us is that they won't have to return to me.
I am made of breathing, shade, Mother Earth, the essence of life, caring, and hope.

Surgical Clinic and Health Center by Kéré Architecture

DATE: 2014 Built / 2017 Extension completed

LOCATION: Léo, Burkina Faso

BUILT AREA: 1660 m^2 - 17,868 sf

PROGRAM: Surgical Clinic and Health Center

STATUS: Built

CLIENT: Operieren in Afrika e. V.

STATUS: Completed

DESIGN: Kéré Architecture (Diébédo Francis Kéré)

TEAM: Diébédo Francis Kéré, Pedro Montero Gosalbez, Emmanuel, Dorsaz, Jamie Keats, Dominique Mayer, Raquel Font, Diego Sologuren Martin, Yara Pavel, Jaime Herraiz

ADVISORS: EGC, Ouagadougou, structural engineer

TEXT: Kéré Architecture

ILLUSTRATION: Magdalena Tagliabue, Santiago Bogani

In the future I see myself as the manifold memory of the uncountable people that remember their time with me as testing but ultimately healing. I am a story around a dinner table, an anecdote between friends, a milestone in biographies.

I stand under the blazing sun of the city of São Paulo. My family is the green life that lives within my perimeters. This evergreen jungle that grows in harmony will always be a part of me.
Saturdays and Sundays are my favorite days of the week. I do my very best to give shadow, shelter, and fresh drinks to all of my guests.

I was built to embody the idea of shelter and joy, of comfort and rest. Green corridors and cold walls. I spend most of my time in silence, hearing the dissonant noises of the city that lives beyond my walls, as I patiently wait the arrival of my visitors.

Weekend House by SPBR Arquitetos

DATE: 2011 design – 2014 completed

LOCATION: São Paulo, Brazil

SITE AREA: 269.50 m^2 – 2901 sf

BUILT AREA: 183.40 m^2 – 1974 sf

PROGRAM: Weekend house

STATUS: Completed

DESIGN: Angelo Bucci

TEAM: Nilton Suenaga, Tatiana Ozzetti, Ciro Miguel, Eric Ennser, João Paulo Meirelles de Faria, Juliana Braga, Fernanda Cavallaro, Victor Próspero

ADVISORS: Raul Pereira, landscape architect; Ibsen Puleo Uvo, structural engineer; Apoio Assessoria e Projeto de Fundações - José Luiz de Paulo Eduardo, foundation engineer, Engesolos Engenharia de Solos e Fundações, geotechnical investigation; Reka - Ricardo Heder, lighting

CONSTRUCTION: José Antonio Queijo Felix, general contractor; Theobaldo Bremenkamp, Reinaldo Francisco Ramos, constructor; Móveis AEME - Agostinho Alves Moreir, woodwork; Carlos Augusto Stefani, steelwork.

TEXT: NESS

ILLUSTRATION: Santiago Bogani

In the future, I see myself unchanged, permanent: a summer breeze passing through some naked ankles and tingling the new leaves of the trees, taller than the year before.

Jayne Kelley Grooves to the Haunted Mansion in Disneyland

The Superobject Has Received Your Sympathetic Vibration

Haunted Mansion at Disneyland, Anaheim, California.
Illustrated by Santiago Bogani

In 1957, two years after Disneyland opened in Anaheim, California, Walt Disney spoke to the BBC about a new attraction he planned for the theme park: a haunted house. His purpose in discussing the project was less to inform potential visitors than to solicit full-time residents. Between the destruction of the war and the swathes of new housing that followed it, Disney explained, many of Britain's ghosts had been displaced from their ancestral haunting grounds—and his house could provide refuge. When it debuted in 1969, the Haunted Mansion claimed to have welcomed 999 ghosts from throughout space and time into happy retirement within its walls.

This origin story is well known among Disneyphiles, as is the fact that the mansion's 'exterior'—an imposing, ornate two-story structure modeled on an 1803 house in Baltimore that designers found in a Victorian sourcebook—was finished well before the ride itself. Disney doubled down on his call and turned the delay, largely the result of creative disputes, into a form of savvy advertising; the park installed a sign on the gates outside the building offering "post-lifetime leases" in a "country club atmosphere" for "ghosts trying to make a name for themselves...and ghosts afraid to live by themselves!" Over the six years it stood empty, the house collected rumors: that the ride was being retooled after frightening someone to death; that Disney himself was buried (or frozen) inside.

So already before it opened, the Haunted Mansion was not the unified stereotype it appeared to be—a forlorn house on a hill, tainted by a wronged or vengeful inhabitant. It was always intended to be animated by a collective; it was conceived as a kind of shared paradise. For its inhabitants, it is joyously "unlivable," the ride's disembodied narrator, the "ghost host," explains.

For us living guests, the experience of touring the Haunted Mansion is much more ambiguous. Its designers had trouble deciding: should the mansion be scary or funny? It ends up as both. What begins as purely creepy atmosphere layered with traces of the supernatural—an endless corridor, a piano played by a shadow—gives way, once the ghosts have vetted us and received our 'sympathetic vibrations,' to fanciful set pieces we witness and then move through: a booze-soaked ballroom party, attic storage (necessary even in the afterlife), a 'swinging wake' in a graveyard. The unfamiliar remains concealed until we have been fully absorbed inside it. The ride ends with a ghostly reflection jumping into our 'doom buggies,' in a facetious attempt to follow us home.

Charles Moore addressed exactly this aspect of the ride in his 1984 book on Los Angeles, *The City Observed*:

[The Haunted Mansion] is surely one of the most skillful, sophisticated, and engrossing spatial sequences on the planet. It is useful to see the ride as a progression from outside the event, where the observer and the observed are at some distance, to the inside, where the observer, mind and body, has entered into the observed, so that it finally envelops him and even at the end makes an attempt to enter him.

This outside-in fluidity is paralleled in the built form of the ride. Like many attractions at Disneyland, the mansion that visitors enter is only a portal; the rest of the house lies in a warehouse-like 'show' building beyond the bounds of the park, accessible through an elevator styled as a 'stretching' portrait gallery and an underground pathway. (The graveyard scene that appears to take riders outside is still inside.) The illusions it deploys mean that the Haunted Mansion both seems to and actually does expand to accommodate the activity inside, bulging to swallow those who enter it. "In no instance are these the cheap tricks of some tunnel of love," Umberto Eco once wrote of the ride. "The involvement (always tempered by the humor of the interventions) is total."

Whether it is desire or some unexplained obligation (a condition of the lease with Disney?) that compels the ghosts to open their community to visitors is also left ambiguous. Either way, it is clear that they are performing, for themselves as much as us. The humor of these performances is often boorish—despite Disney creating the Haunted Mansion explicitly for the ghosts, it can hardly be said to exhibit a respectful attitude toward its residents. Moore took issue with what he saw as the "smug and supercilious treatment [the ride] bestows on ghosts, just because they are dead." That haughtiness is there in Disney's BBC interview, too.

Still, the ride operates from the assumption that ghosts are scary, that we should be cautious in our approach. It squarely engages our preconceptions and then reworks them through a propulsive phasing of perspective. What it proposes is not the narrative of a safe encounter with death, reinforcing the importance of life, but a temporary and fundamental reconfiguration of reality that relegates the living to an ancillary role.

Since 1969, the Haunted Mansion's strange multiplicity has been multiplied successfully in other parks. The Walt Disney World and Tokyo Disneyland versions are almost identical to the California original. Paris and Hong Kong, however, required adjustments to the format; designers found that audiences in those cultures would not take to goofy ghosts. And it's true that the ride's 'grim grinning' inhabitants might leave us all more uneasy right now, with a kind of collective awareness of death more present than it has been in a long time. Today, the Haunted Mansion is still entertaining, but our own context reminds us that any reassurance it seems to offer has always been empty. It may be a paradise, but it's not an escape.

Laura González Fierro Becomes the Vasconcelos Library by Alberto Kalach

"I am a vessel of continental scale. The weight of my knowledge is real, people can feel it on their shoulders; when they walk through my aisles, when they read my stories, or when they stand on my grounds. I work against gravity—or at least I intend to do so—but my efforts are futile: my heaviness is felt in each moment of my existence, in every breath of life that comes into me. It is quite appealing to visualize an entire collection in a glimpse, especially when you can feel the heft of every word and comma in the room.

But perhaps it is that weight that makes me real, relevant, and alive; otherwise, where would I go? Who would I seductively dialogue with? Who would dance with me? Who would tell me stories at night? Who would quell my fears and reassure me that I will see another sunrise? Nobody will—but she would... she is always there, as my mother, my partner, my lover, my sister, my friend, my everything. She, who dresses in a beautiful historical gown, weaved in pre-hispanic tones, colonial whisperings, and modern desires. She lives far away and is always surrounded by attractive suitors; I get jealous sometimes, forgotten on this side of the city. Don't get me wrong, I value my close friendships enormously. I cherish my brothers from Tlatelolco but they have their own issues to deal with and I feel we come from different moments in history. There is empathy between us, nonetheless. I've certainly had some affairs. I always liked flirtatious situations—especially long strolls around La Ciudadela when we discuss the Popul Vuh or how we are trying to define our identities in a Labyrinth of Solitude—but nothing beats her experience; what she has seen, heard and hidden from humanity.

Sometimes when it gets dark, I feel my roots growing, as if they want to extend until they touch her feet. But there are too many layers of infrastructure and history to ignore and avoid. If my content can evoke many lives why can't I invent a romance that goes beyond my hanging bookshelves? I am an ark of knowledge; I have the most inventive stories within me and even so the more I know, the lonelier I feel. From Conquest and Colonialism to Independence and Revolution I became a modern ruin. I want to advance in time but I am just floating in oblivion.

Will I age as graciously as she did? It is uncertain, but my gardens will continue to grow and nature will eventually cover my bones, my skin. Maybe one day an anthropologist will discover me under the dense vegetation and reach the central nave, only to discover the whale skeleton suspended in time; they will know they have arrived at the forgotten Biblioteca Vasconcelos."

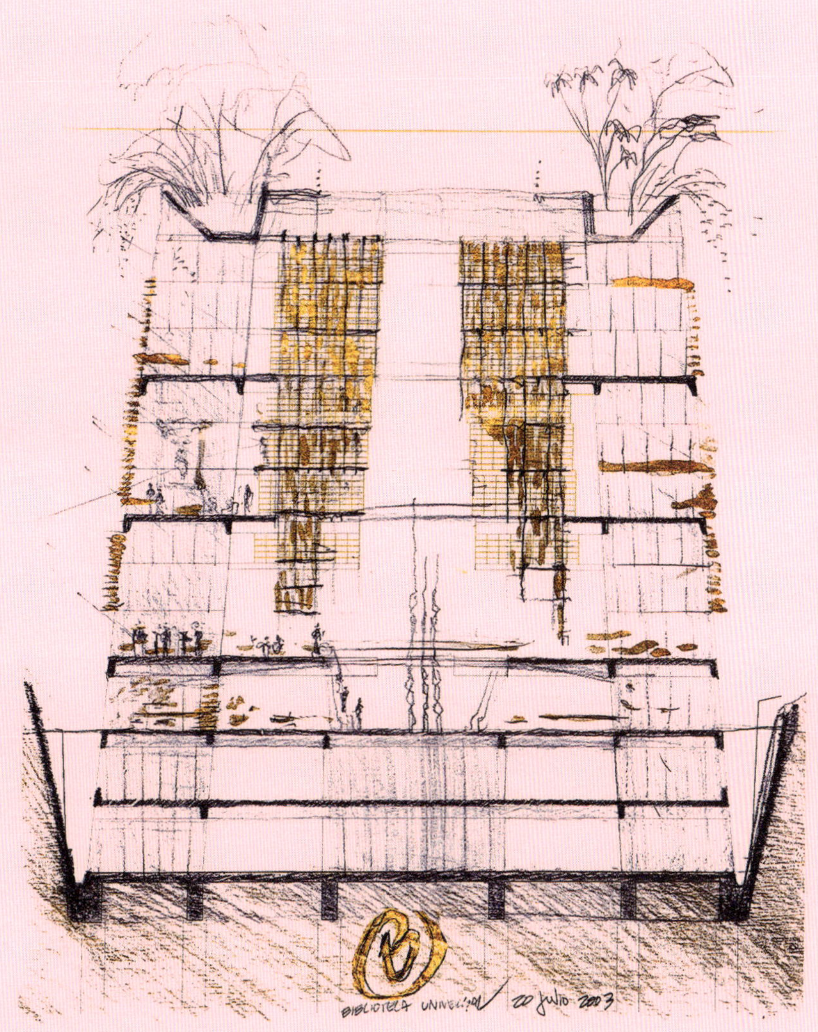

Biblioteca Vasconcelos, Mexico City, TAX, Alberto Kalach, Juan Palomar, Gustavo Lipkau. Courtesy TAX

This is about some towers in Mexico City that were very bored because they were always in the same place. They were uncomfortable because people started to put a lot of buildings and stores around them.

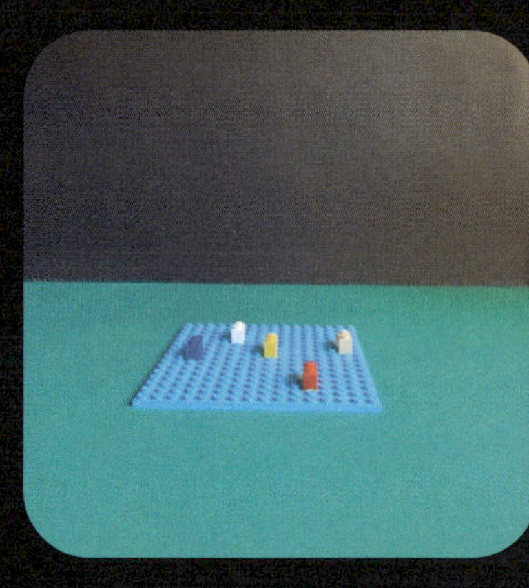

One day, they decided to leave their home behind to explore the world. The five towers decided to part ways, each travelling to different places...

The white tower went speeding at super gigantic supersonic speed through outer space: he wanted to go to the moon to explore the outside world. Zoooooom!!!!!!!!

The yellow tower decided to stroll into the woods, to enjoy the nature and the fresh air. He climbed onto some rocks to look at the view.

The blue dude decided that he wanted to be a lifeguard and rescue people that were drowning. And so, he jumped into the blue cool water and saved many people, even kids.

The red tower spent a week at the beach to sunbathe, relax, and be lazy. Later, the yellow tower convinced himself that he should be hanging out with his own colors and made a whole bunch of yellow friends.

The blue tower got bored of being a lifeguard and, while staring at the birds in the sky, he made up his mind to make some wings and learn to fly.

Sometimes, when all the towers were feeling lonely, the white tower would invite them to a party. It was a beautiful house with a pool, an art museum and a bed... and a cage with a giraffe.

And then the yellow tower fell in love with a wooden cone named Fernando. The red tower became jealous and flew away... (he asked the blue tower how to make wings).

They got sleepy and they all got in bed. When they woke up, they continued walking around the world together. They explored Africa, Latin America, Canada, Belgium, and Oceania. And they also explored the oceans and Tokyo.

Yellow and white became BFFs.

One day, they missed their homes and took their car back to where they came from. They settled back into their comfy sweet home... and talked about how they missed each other.

Back in Mexico City, they had the biggest, loudest, most fun party, ever.

The End

Models: Otto Ickx Estévez

Story & texts: Otto Ickx Estévez, Lina Ickx Estévez

Photo shoot: Ruth Estévez

Typing: Wonne Ickx

Archival Photo: Courtesy Ickx Estévez Collection of Postcards. Photographer unknown.

Documents

PRODUCTORA

MOS

PRODUCTORA is an architectural office based in Mexico City run by Abel Perles (Argentina), Carlos Bedoya (Mexico), Víctor Jaime (Mexico), and Wonne Ickx (Belgium). Their work is characterized by an emphasis on geometric rigor and a desire to generate simple and unique architectural vocabulary that relates to the context. They search for buildings that are timeless in their material and spatial resolutions. PRODUCTORA operates on different levels: from practice to developing critical discourses through numerous academic activities such as teaching architecture in Mexico and the United States. The office is currently working on projects in Mexico and abroad, ranging from residential to public buildings. Its work has been presented in the architectural biennials of Beijing (2006), Venice (2008, 2012, 2018), and Chicago (2015, 2017) as well as in the National Art Museum of China and in the Victoria and Albert Museum in London.

PRODUCTORA

Ph. Courtesy PRODUCTORA

CREATING CONTEXT

Approaching various topics related to their practice and academic activities, this conversation with PRODUCTORA allows us to cross several themes that reveal how the office looks at the discipline today. No matter the scale, their architecture dialogues with its context, always with ambivalence about a meticulous and precise reading of local traditions and formal abstractions.

PRODUCTORA Interviewed by Lisa Naudin

Lisa Naudin: How did you all decide to form PRODUCTORA, in what year, and why in Mexico?

Abel Perles: PRODUCTORA began in 2006 in Mexico. Víctor and Carlos are from Mexico, I arrived here in 2002 and Wonne arrived a bit later. We were work colleagues in other offices and we became friends. In 2006, we were collaborating informally until we decided to form what is now PRODUCTORA. The name, in a way, reflects our way of working through producing and generating work alternatives. We love the name, and it makes a lot of sense given the kind of office we are.

LN: How do your interests intersect at the office?

Wonne Ickx: It is interesting to connect this to the origin of PRODUCTORA because we got together in a pragmatic way. Our office was not grounded in an agreement around certain premises about architecture but rather through the practice and the creation of a shared vocabulary. It was about a language that arose in a very intuitive and natural way. Now that we have been together for fourteen years, I think that it is part of our success as well, which is to say that this group of four partners continues to work together. If an office is grounded in a set of established ideas of what architecture is, of what it means to do architecture, it becomes difficult to remain relevant as an office: these bases change over time. What unites us is this pragmatism, the methodology of work and the systems of collaboration and communication.

AP: In other words, we produce, we conduct trials in order to then evaluate; everything is put to review in a collective meeting. We attack a project from different points of view, from different personalities and knowledge bases... We basically work as a filter that allows us to put ideas to the test.

WI: I don't know if my partners agree with this, but I think that the formal discipline and geometric rigor of our work is in reality grounded in a system of communication. One can generate an architecture in decisions that are more intuitive, formal, and visceral. An example would be an architect like Frank Gehry—we talk about work that is intimately related to a single person, a unique creator. Between the four of us, we have to make decisions on concrete questions. Working with proportional systems, with modulations, with univocal descriptive geometries, allows us to clearly communicate our intentions. There exists a direct relationship between our system of internal communication, our methodology, and the results we formally produce.

Rehabilitation of an Old Textile Factory, Mexico City, Mexico (2018)

As a consequence of the 2018 earthquake, PRODUCTORA and LIGA installed their office in an old textile Factory that had been abandoned.

Ph. Courtesy LIGA

Víctor Jaime: We are interested in clear and legible gestures; we put in place systems in order to later break them; we visualize problems as opportunities. Rather than seeing these lines as rules of design, I think they define the personality that we have been developing as PRODUCTORA, where over time each of us has found his or her place and has been capable of developing personal interests. From this position, each individual brings their own talent to the project, which makes it so that we all partake in and feel part of each project.

LN: And how do you then convey this system of communication, either through teaching or through the dissemination of your work?

WI: As compared to other offices, one wouldn't say that our work is rooted in academic research. The academic work that we undertake is related to our personal interests. There are many offices or architects for whom teaching is really an essential counterpart to their design practice and they divide their time 50-50 between the university and the work at the office. In our case, it is different: the basic practice of the architect, to design and to build, is at the center of everything we do. In a way it is the reverse of other cases: our academic work often stems out of subjects that we work on in the studio. For example, two years ago we won a competition to develop housing and we thought a lot about Parisian living. We began to look at Henri Sauvage's work for the Rue de Amiraux, with its system of terraces, and that has become a central topic in my workshop at Rice University.

LN: We are interested in how his architecture dialogues with the environment in which it is developed, how geometry becomes a way of generating frictions or tensions with context and how this is worked on from the material and the programmatic, in relation to the form.

WI: Geometry is obviously a very important issue for us. I really like its direct relationship to context, or the idea of considering architecture as a formal object, or the idea of considering architecture as an object. It would seem that the idea of architecture as a formal object and the idea of taking care of the context have always existed as opposing visions. If we talk about the idea of the object, I would like to interpret it not just as that—which could be bigger and more powerful, more radical than other objects—but rather as something that is more than itself, in the sense that it overcomes its inherent formal composition. Instead of being content with the precise execution of the definition of geometry and taking delight in the radicalism of the formal gesture, what is valued is really seeing how those simple elements are connected to the context and are beginning to react to that. Wealth is often found in that friction. We are interested in thinking about how to insert a building so that it overcomes its value as a building, but also to re-write and redefine the context. More than concentrating our attention on what an object really generates *an sich*, our ambition as architects is to try to enrich the surrounding space.

LN: I would like to know a bit more about what kinds of preliminary readings you do regarding context.

WI: We don't. We almost never conduct an a priori reading or research before beginning to design. We explore the relevant conditions through the design itself, through multiple architectonic proposals. This does not mean that we aren't interested in context—to the contrary, context is what motivates and generates our work: preexistence and topography. Just recently we published a book, "Being the Mountain,"[1] which explores the relationship between modern architecture and topography. A preamble to that book was published not long ago in the OASE Journal[2] in the form of a short text that investigates the importance of the topography in the writings of Kenneth Frampton.

AP: We always attempt to have an intention that supports each context: we don't want to condition ourselves or have the context determine our work, but rather, we want our work to add to and to improve the context through a clear intention. For that reason, when someone sees one of our projects, from the first moment, they can detect a geometric simplicity while they are also visualizing a kind of power. Perhaps there, one can begin to read that specific object. Layers and interests begin to appear that enrich the apparent simplicity. It is in this combination of intentions that we always try to provide something more than context. We don't like to do very profound and widespread research at the gate because we do not want it to determine what we do... When I think of geometry, I just think in terms of forms, lines, in clear, convincing gestures... And again, there being four of us, we have to define these lines, these rules. I think that for that reason it is easy for us to focus on geometries to draw, to make models, to think of structures...

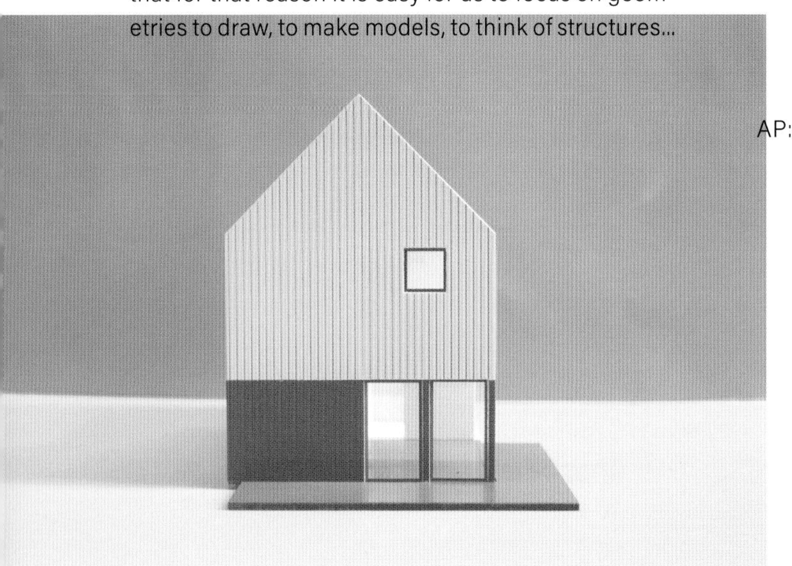

Housing Denver, Denver, Colorado, USA (2018)

For the set of four houses, the model was used as a processing and representation tool.

Ph. Courtesy LIGA

VJ: We have worked in very powerful sites: in front of the archeological ruins of Teopanzolco or in the plaza of a protected town at the entrance of the Oaxacan sierra called Teotitlán del Valle, where the selection of materials, the incorporation of certain urban gestures, or the act of hiding a large portion of the mass under the ground were strategies that responded to a respect for the site and its scale. We also worked on the roof of a very old house in the center of Mexico City, and it seemed to us almost logical to think of a very light and translucent object, or in the same way, of raising an ephemera pavilion in the Zócalo of Mexico City, we felt obligated to think in wood... Each

Being the Mountain, Chicago, USA (2020)

Being the Mountain examines the relationship between architecture and the ground it occupies, an interaction so obvious—a building must touch the ground—that it often remains underexplored.

Carlos Bedoya, Wonne Ickx, Víctor Jaime, Abel Perles. Being the Mountain (United States: Actar Publishers & the Illinois Institute of Technology College of Architecture Press, 2020)

site represents challenges and opportunities that we try to understand and add to our pallet of strategies. It is at times the climate, a neighboring building, or local technology that delineates our projects, this keeps our methodology open and undetermined.

LN: If we think of Donald Judd, Richard Serra, or Brancus—references you made in the "Specific Objects" conferences at Harvard Graduate School of Design in March of 2017; their work resonates with a way of working in space through repetition. How do they organize flow and invite people to use the building or the public space through that formal search?

AP: References are always on the table, they begin to be part of our history, of an internal language. Year after year, certain postures are added. This exchange begins to generate a combination of references that appear time and time again and more and more; they continue to grow... If someone saw our work overall, the geometric forms emphasized represent one of the many paths that we went about developing from the beginning. One would find ten years of trial of work with the triangle and perhaps ten years of experimentation with the circle. We were lucky in that the projects that made use of the triangle were materialized and thus contructed a visible sequence. Within the office, the different geometric forms—the rhythm, the sequences of columns, of points—have the same force. We continue our evolution of this combination of references in terms of lines of work and exploration with enthusiasm.

WI: I would like to take up the first part of your question again, when you mention Judd, Serra, and Lewitt. They are artists of great interest to us because they have been poorly interpreted and represented in history. From my point of view, in general, they are drawn as minimalists of little interest. What really interests us in Serra, Judd, and Lewitt or Carl André are not their pure formalism, but precisely those projects that speak explicitly to a relationship with space, be it in the context of the museum or the landscape. We think, for example, of Serra's piece "Sift" (1970), which evidences and even measures the topography of the landscape. Judd's boxes, which measure and divide in equal parts solid and hollow that are the same height as the gallery; or André's floor installations and the in-situ interventions of Buren or Lewitt. They are artists that put a very strong emphasis on the relationship between the objects and the spaces in which they are placed. Their sculptures look to question their positioning in their surroundings.

LN: To continue with this idea, I would like to expand on materiality: textures, colors, references, cultural references, landscape.

AP: When we began, being an office with many projects and few constructions, we had various works that remained in the white model stage. Timidly and with much precaution and even a bit of fear, we began to add color. After conducting some trials with materiality, we began to be able to construct projects. When one observes the different stages that the office went through, one can see the exploration of these subjects; and be there is still a great deal ahead of us.

With the most recent projects, like the Teopanzolco and Teotitlán del Valle cultural centers, when it came time to select materials, we chose concrete for its durability and its resistance. It is a material that could generate structure, closure, and finish. The need to get out of the gray of concrete and begin to discover alternative plays on tones associated with the site also began there. It was a rather natural process. The client of the Fleischmann house in Los Angeles is a graphic designer who works every day in color. Color is also, in that case, the possibility of differentiating what was pre-existing and what is new. The opportunties that the project itself granted allowed us to investigate and explore in order to know where we will take the project according to its site, its uses, and even its scale.

VJ: Materiality is defined from different points of view: there are times that it is defined by structure, or by how it is incorporated in a context by obeying a rule or a client. There are times in which the building has to appear light, closed, or take a prominent role; or there are simply cases in which it must evidence the interests of an office.

AP: In the case of Rooftop Prim what determined materiality was the structural premise through the basis of a repetition of two-inch by two-inch pieces. The rest of it was super light, transparent, translucent, synthetic material that was quick to mount. This sends us in a direction, and later, our intentions as architects ultimately define it. It has to do with the program and the use of the project.

WI: It is part of a narrative, a longer evolution. Perhaps conceptually, we are much more interested in a certain natural materiality in order to incorporate textures and colors in our architecture: a natural stone, different tones of wood, red clay, annealed tabique, etc. But, when we began to work on projects in the United States, where there are many more industrial products like PVC, polymers, vinyls, and fibrocement, we suddenly had to rely on paint in order to apply color; it was the first time we worked that way.

Not long ago we made a really interesting project in the South of Mexico, housing made completely of blue concrete, the Casa Bautista. All of a sudden, there, a space of exploration opened for us. At the same time, there are not only external motives for testing materials, textures, and new colors, but there is undoubtedly a sense of self-purpose, an ambition to continue renovating. After constructing two buildings in pigmented concrete, we had the opportunity to work on a light structure for the Rooftop Prim, which Abel mentioned, in which they asked us to come up with a cover for three patios in a historic mansion. We constructed with purely industrialized

New Headquarters of Houston Endowment, Houston, Texas, USA (2019)

The proposal is strongly connectec to the site and context: the landscape and history of Spotts Park. The new building, which is attuned to Houston's demanding climate, is intended to be "as welcoming as the shadow beneath a tree."

Ph. Courtesy LIGA

Teopanzolco Cultural Center Cuernavaca, Morelos, Mexico (2017)

The project for the new cultural center is located on a site opposite to the archeological zone of Teopanzolco, a situation that proposes two fundamental strategies: on the one hand to enhance the relationship with the archeological site and on the other to generate a significant public space. The horizontal platform surrounding the triangular building serves as a viewing area for the archeological zone and the city.

Ph. Courtesy Jaime Navarro

materials: a polycarbonate rooftop, a PVC deck, and handrails made of a plastic net. Experimenting with these synthetic materials is really refreshing for us.

VJ: We rethink and expand the pallet all the time; we have no formula. We are interested in understanding the possibilities of each thing and, in that way, selecting the materials for a constructive system, its appearance, local technology, costs, times, etc... It is always our goal to understand which tools best adapt to a project and then push them to their limit.

AP: And the possibility of expanding the pallet always represents a moment of enthusiasm. Also, in a way, we complete the cycle with a few paths and decide to change the types of resources we use in order to maintain interest without becoming repetitive. Now, with one of our current projects, La Laguna, we are playing a lot with the color green. It begins to become part of the identity of this project. Ten years ago everything was contemplated in white, today we have a lot of desire to work in color.

LN: For critics, for curators, or even for yourselves, one could say there are two interpretative genealogies in your work. The first stems from the LIGA[3] exhibitions, and the second involves constructing an international community and includes the work of PRODUCTORA together with, for example, Johnston Marklee, OFFICE Kersten Geers David Van Severen, architecten de vylder vinck taillieu, MOS, or Pezo Von Ellrichshausen. We would love to know how you see yourselves in regards to the categories that you are collectively included in: as a kind of determinism, a system of representation that works in collage with the idea of the naif, or with postmodern language, to give it a name. At the same time, in LIGA, you take up the role of curators and bring together the colleagues' work in the format of an exhibition.

AP: To begin, we have a direct relation with all of the entities you mentioned. With Johnston Marklee, with Pezo Von Ellrichshausen, with OFFICE Kersten Geers David Van Severen we have a history of being friends as well as having professional relationships. With MOS, we have collaborated on a few projects. We are from the same generation, we are exploring a few similar forms, we have similar stimuli that we have lived through.

With LIGA, we got in touch with Pezo Von Ellrichshausen from day one. LIGA transformed to become a source of references and a platform. It forced us to, in some way, be involved in what is happening and that made us aware of everything. In this sea of references, of interactions, I think that we ended up finding our place in what you describe. We also share some of the same problematics and uncertainties, despite not being in the same country or city.

"Layers and interests begin to appear that enrich that apparent simplicity. It is in this combination of intentions that we always try to provide something more than context. We don't like to do very profound and widespread research at the gate because we do not want it to determine what we do... When I think of geometry, I just think in terms of forms, lines, in clear, convincing gestures."

—AP

WI: It is an interesting question. Obviously, I like that you mention us alongside all of those offices because they are colleagues that I admire and appreciate a great deal. The process of categorization is always problematic and each attempt to analyze and simplify the current scene is ultimately a poor rendering, but it is nonetheless interesting. In March of 2018, there was an exhibit at Harvard[4] curated by Michael Hays and Andrew Holder that offered a very complex and obscure classification that I grasped very little of. I recall there being a diagram of a political compass made by Alejandro Zaera-Polo and Guillermo Fernández -Abascal in 2017 that offered a representation of the contemporary architectural landscape. In this circular diagram, PRODUCTORA was located in the middle and within various categories. And so, does this mean that we do not belong anywhere, we exist simply as a generation? The idea of "Low Resolution" utilized by Michael Meredith in the exposition of Low Resolution Houses[5] in Princeton University in 2018, is a generic term for an architecture that rejects a future in which technological bravado or formal expression are the only responses.

Even still, from within, it is much easier for me to see the differences between the offices than to find their similarities. For example, there are offices that work with historical references in a very cognizant manner;

there are offices that are very devoted to the intuitive idea of DIY, there are offices that are determined to generate geometric composition as a very formal exercise. We are in a moment in which the inherent ideological concerns of the projects of modernism and postmodernism, respectively, have lost their direct relevance. Now, the architects of our generation and of the following generations feel at liberty to work with the elements of both projects and to openly accept the premises of both ideologies. Instead of generating an eclectic architectural posture, rid of any political value, I think it could be a great opportunity to rescue what is interesting about the postmodern movement. I hope that it is not only the formal that provokes attention (which is a bit of the problem with what is happening). I hope that it can be a renovated perception toward popular culture and vernacular culture, a delicate attention towards social processes, a preoccupation for sustainability, a critique of an impoverished minimalism and thus a bit of "Complexity and Contradiction."

LN: At the same conference that we referenced earlier, Wonne explained that in the studio, they did not do collage, however they did have an uncertainty about how they communicate architecture: the collage was a system of communication and thus carries the notion of superimposition. Is this also connected to a kind of contemporary architecture?

WI: Yes, it is something that really interests us. In fact, the exposition, "Spaces without Drama"[6] that we made with LIGA at the Graham Foundation in Chicago in 2017 worked on that question. It spoke to the issue of representation, of collage, and of a certain kind of theatricality (or scenographic presence) in contemporary architectonic culture. We invited various architects to explore bidimensional surfaces to produce architectonic space as might occur in a collage or in the stage sets of classic theater. There were works by Johnston Marklee, OFFICE Kersten Geers David Van Severen, MOS, Pezo Von Ellrichshausen, Baukuh, Monadnock, etc., and also contributions by artists like David Hockney, Batia Suter, Pablo Bronstein and architects of other generations like Rossi or Ambasz. The collage, digital or not, took a central presence in the show despite the fact that in PRODUCTORA we rarely use collage as a design or representation technique. In our case, it is the model that is central to the process of research.

VJ: The tools of PRODUCTORA are those that each partner identifies and makes understood. For me, the model is like the task of the sculptor: when I work in the workshop I choose the material, the scale, and I make decisions with every cut I make. Many times they are just columetric sketches with very intuitive ideas that little by little become more polished when other partners engage with them, or they become diluted in the process of drawing. Further down the line, we change the scale, incorporate texture and color, etc, and we end up by exposing them to the camera to achieve an image that makes the project understood and communicates that which interests us, as if it was a three-dimensional collage.

WI: An office that really interests me is MOS: I really admire their graphic and representative quality, drawing after drawing, model after model. They have a very self-conscious and inquisitive production at a very high level.

"References are always on the table, they begin to be part of our history, of an internal language."

—AP

LN: I want to ask you about LIGA, how did that project begin?

AP: In 2010, we started to become aware that there was no regional platform for architecture. We were working, seeing what our young colleagues were doing at conferences. In 2007, we were selected to go to the Architectural League of New York. We realized that there was a lot more to say about our region. It began that way, as a question, as a space to share and circulate what was happening in the region. As there are four of us there was a lot of energy put into PRODUCTORA but there was room for more. I think that was the point of departure for LIGA. For us it was a source of energy, it opened the possibility for us to be involved in what is happening from another place. It is also the adventure of what it means to be part of a space of cultural diffusion. We have always been cultural consumers, we are very close to the local art world, and we thought why not do something simliar to what takes place in those arenas but for architecture.

WI: I loved what Mario Ballesteros wrote for our monograph in the magazine 2G,[7] in the annex or the dossier. It spoke of the relationship between PRODUCTORA and LIGA and in regards to himself as an editor. It concludes that our work in LIGA is very similar to that of an editor. In the end, an editor doesn't write a single text; rather he selects, corrects, invites, goes about moving pieces to finally generate his own voice. I like that analogy. From LIGA we define a position through the voice of others. In LIGA, we collaborate with the art curator Ruth Estévez, which permits us to go out and question our own media and the inherent traditions of our discipline.

AP: It is a voice that comes from the world of art, that adds to the voice of four architects. The decision to include Ruth Estévez really enriched the proposal. It integrated a very different perspective, making what is today LIGA.

LN: Where does PRODUCTORA find itself in today?

AP: We have been working for two years on a project we haven't released yet. We are excited. As a consequence of the 2018 earthquake, we had to leave the office we were in for nine years, but this created the opportunity to intervene in an old textile factory that had been abandoned. It is a half of a block; we are in charge of the master plan of rehabilitation, and we decided to bring our office and LIGA there. It is an interesting project with many edges, and it is in process. The first stage was dedicated to our offices and LIGA as a basic structure. It signified a big change in the physical space in that we had been working in from almost a decade, the area of the city it is located in generated new implications, like the kind of workshops that occupy the zone and the activities that take place within it. We had the opportunity to design our office to our liking and needs. It gave us oxygen and helped us to sow some new dynamics.

WI: We now have a number of projects in the United States, a co-housing experiment in Denver, and other residences in St. Louis together with Tatiana Bilbao, Macías Peredo, and MOS, among others. Not long ago, we won an international competition in Houston: new corporate offices of the Houston Endowment in collaboration with Kevin Daly Architects (KDA). It is really interesting to have a foot in the United States because the context is so different in terms of management and construction—it makes you think with different parts of your brain.

AP: We have a small office operating out of Los Angeles, where Wonne relocated seven years ago.

WI: Each time we work in bigger scales but we continue to make museographies and single-family homes. We have always had very unique projects to resolve. It is precisely that diversity that has made the work more interesting.

Alpes House, Mexico City, Mexico (2013)

This remodel of a 1950s house with a modular structure of steel columns and reinforced-concrete slabs restores a series of alterations that had wrecked the spatial qualities of the building.

Ph. Courtesy Cristobal Palma

1 Carlos Bedoya, Wonne Ickx, Víctor Jaime, Abel Perles. *Being the Mountain* (United States: Actar Publishers & the Illinois Institute of Technology College of Architecture Press, 2020)
2 Avermaete, T., Patteeuw, V., Teerds, H., Szacka, L. (2019). Critical Regionalism Revisited. OASE 103, Rotterdam, Paises Bajos: NAI Publishers
3 LIGA, Espacio para arquitectura is an independent initiative founded in Mexico City in 2011 that promotes contemporary Latin American architecture through expositions, publications, events, conferences, and workshops.
4 The exposition "Inscriptions: Architecture Before Speech" curated by Michael Hays and Andrew Holder, includes 400 images and 26 models that have as an objective revealing "shared cultural engagements agreements, and fantasies of the origins of architecture, offering a theory about the structural relations that unite and organize the aparent delirium of the contemporary countryside."
5 The exhibit "44 LOW RESOLUTION HOUSES" curated by Michael Meredith shows the house as a good and is a trial bench for architectonic arguments; it also constructs a new architecural category: the "low resolution house." According to Meredith, the forty-four houses on display fall in at least one of the following types of "low resolution" homes that are based on vernacular elements: homes that make construction visible or homes constructed out of geometric basics inclined towards a non-abstract compositional form.
6 The exhibit "Spaces Without Drama" curated by Ruth Estévez and Wonne Ickx challenges architects, artists, and a dramaturges to explore the connection between the arquitectonic collage and representations of the theatrical scene...
7 Jesús Vasallo. PRODUCTORA. 2G, 69 (Madrid: Editorial Gustavo Gili, 2014)

*

LIGA, Space for Architecture is an independent initiative founded in Mexico City in 2011 that promotes contemporary Latin American architecture through expositions, publications, events, conferences, and workshops. This initiative has rapidly evolved into a platform and a space for reflection on architecture as a discursive practice. Carlos Bedoya, Ruth Estévez, Wonne Ickx, Víctor Jaime, and Abel Perles seek to generate an archive of the offices of young creators from the region, recognizing the characteristics of architecture in Latin America without dwelling on styles or falling into generalizations.
LIGA tests new methodologies for using theoretical and factual tools to respond to the context in which we live.
In early April 2020, Guadalupe Tagliabue conducted an interview with LIGA members. You can find the entire conversation on our website at nessmagazine.com.

Ph. Arturo Arrieta

*

∗ Ph. Courtesy LIGA

*

"From the beginning LIGA proposed a particular way of exhibiting architecture, avoiding the typical exhibitions of drawings, photos, and models of an architect's work. From the first exhibition, we asked participants to create an original piece that reflects professional or personal concerns. This generated the identity of LIGA, it was a premise that stimulated other ways to talk about architecture..."

—Abel Perles

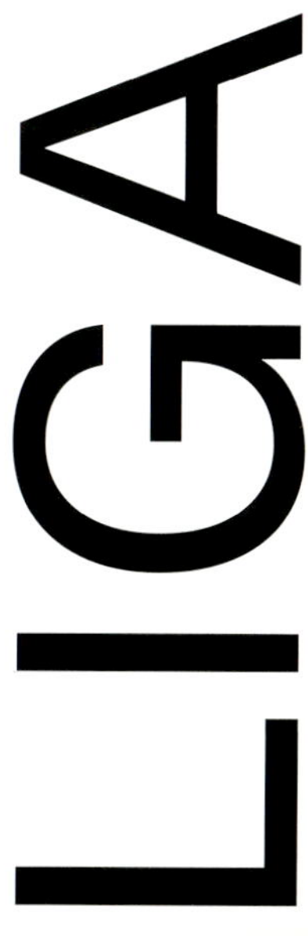

LIGA

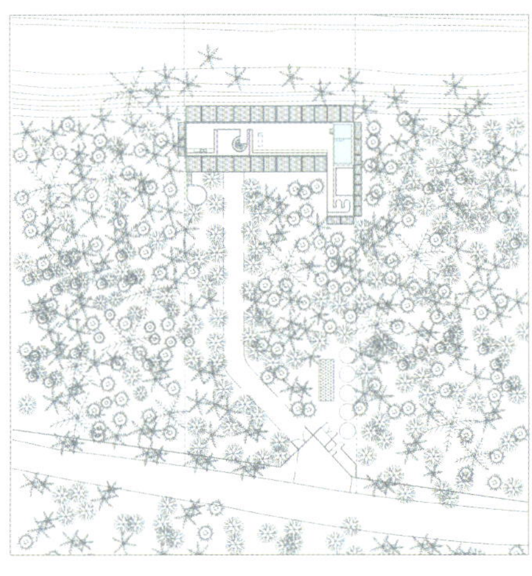

LOCATION: Quintana Roo, Mexico / DATE: 2019 / STATUS: Built / AREA: 3014 sf – 280 m^2 / PROGRAM: Residential / PROJECT TEAM: Carlos Bedoya, Víctor Jaime, Wonne Ickx, Abel Perles / COLLABORATORS: Alejandro Ordoñez, Josue Palma, Daniela Dusa, Antonio Espinoza, Gerardo Aguilar / STRUCTURAL ENGINEERING: Kaltia / MECHANICAL ENGINEERING SUSTAINABILITY: EOS / INTERIOR DESIGN: Pia Hagerman / LANDSCAPE: Planta / CLIENT: Ezequiel Ayarza / PHOTOS: Onnis Luque

The project was developed on a narrow beachfront lot on the Riviera Maya, near Tulum, in Quintana Roo and is fully powered by solar and wind energy. The entire project was cast in an organic blue color concrete, which reacts over time according to its exposure to the sun and its position in the house, creating tones that range from ocean blue to sunset pink.

Raising the house on cross-shaped columns reduces the impact on the environment and generates views over the dune that separates the property from the sea. The project is organized on three levels that are connected by a spiral staircase: the auxiliary ground floor below the house, the intermediate level containing all interior spaces, and a large roof terrace with a pool and an outdoor dining area presenting views of the Caribbean Sea, the jungle and the lagoon. Close to the master bedroom a distinct turret is situated: it works as a formal element that anchors the ensemble into place and doubles as a flexible space for work or meditation.

The intermediate L-shaped floor plan extends beyond the ground floor through large terraces and pergolas made with local wood. In this way, the interior spaces are enlarged and protected from the sun; it also creates a good cross ventilation (only the bedrooms have an air conditioning system). These terraces have a folding mechanism that protects the house in the event of hurricanes: by raising and lowering these heavy elements against the façade, the open and transparent residence is transformed into a robust closed box.

BAUTISTA HOUSE

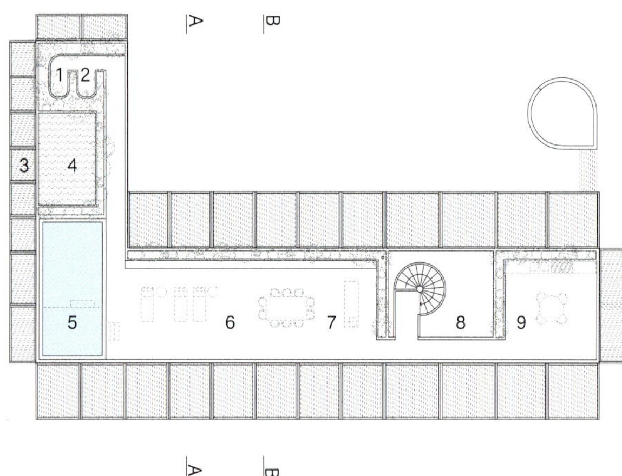

Roof Plan

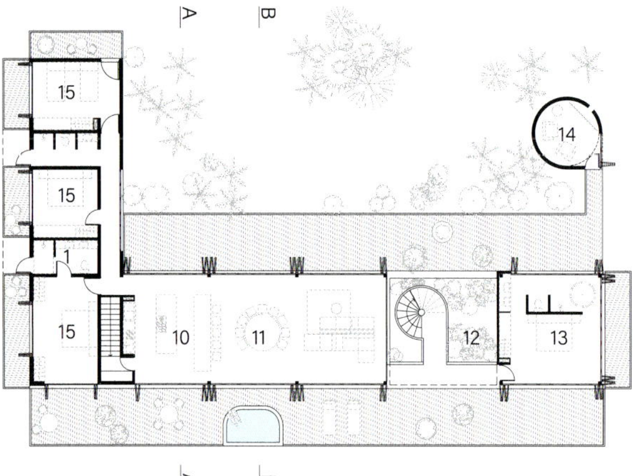

Second Floor

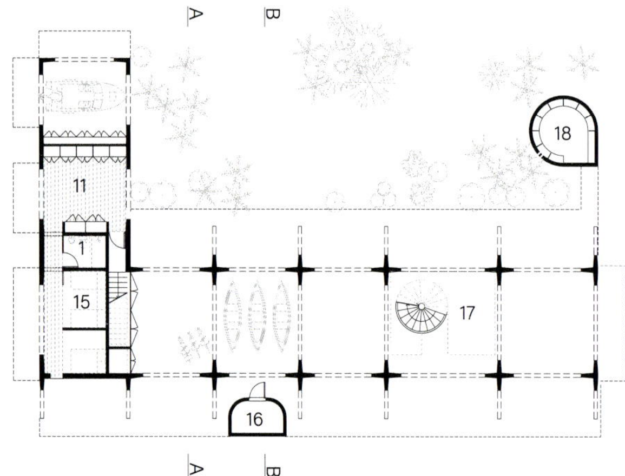

Ground Floor

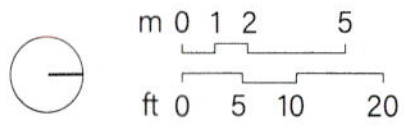

m 0 1 2 5

ft 0 5 10 20

1. Bathroom
2. Shower
3. Solar Panels
4. Water Heater
5. Swimming Pool
6. Sun Deck
7. Bar
8. Central Patio
9. Barbecue Area
10. Kitchen
11. Living
12. Central Patio
13. Master Bedroom
14. Studio
15. Bedroom
16. Machine Room
17. Access Stairway
18. Storage

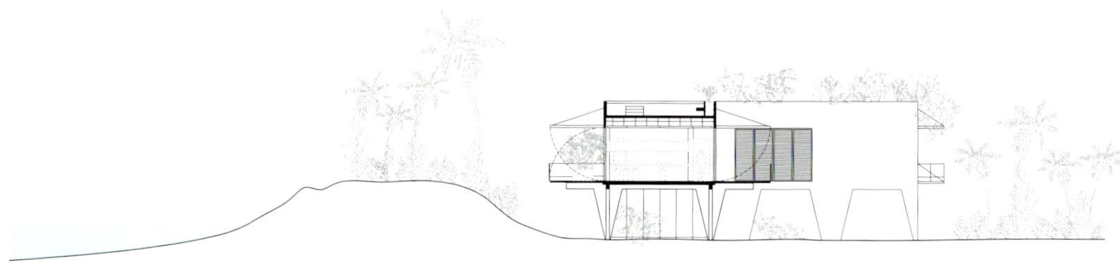

Section A-A

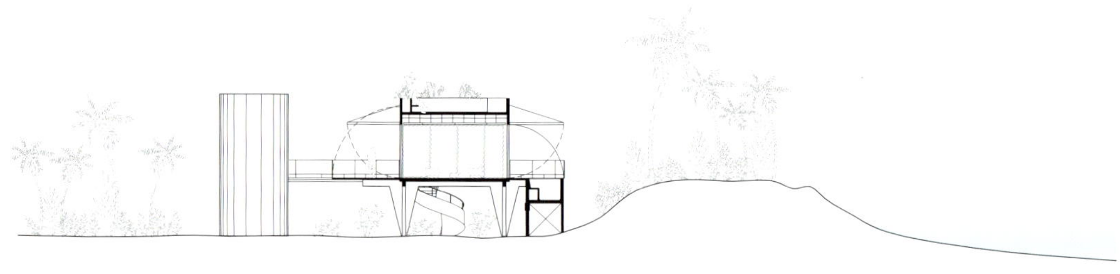

Section B-B

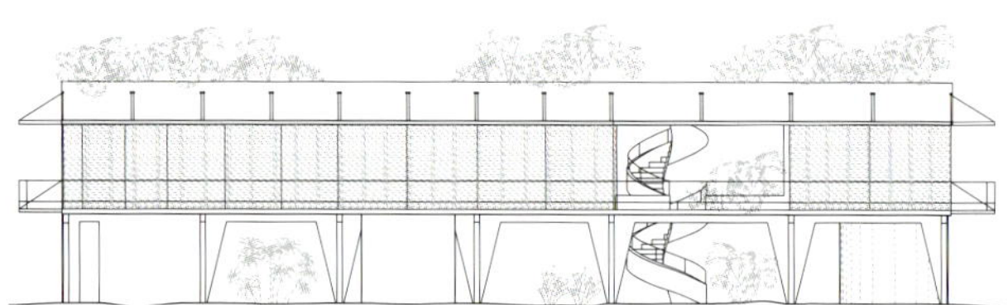

East Elevation

m 0 1 2 5

ft 0 5 10 20

Raising the house on cross-shaped columns reduces the impact on the environment and generates views over the dune that separates the property from the sea.

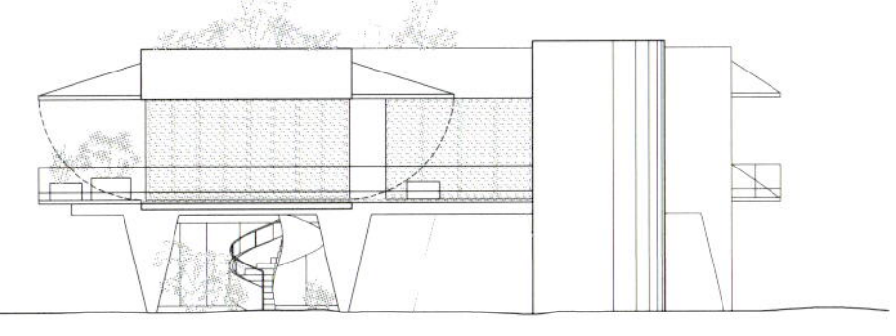

North Elevation

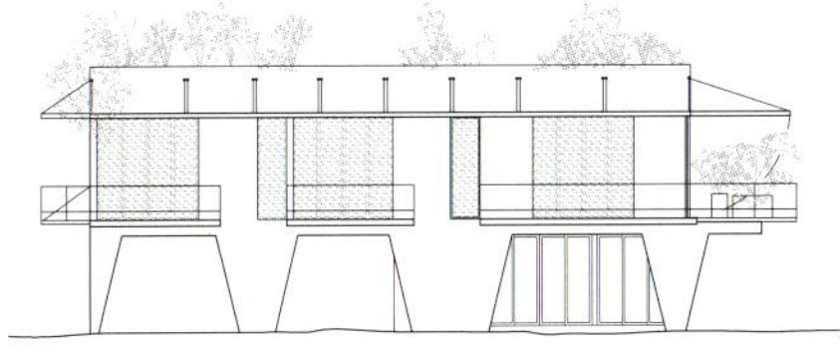

South Elevation

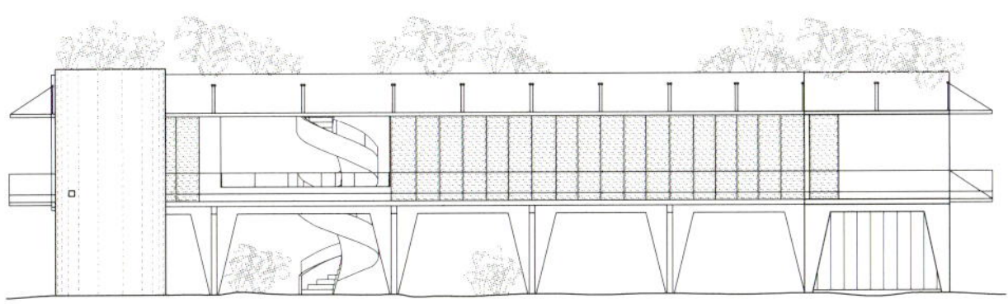

West Elevation

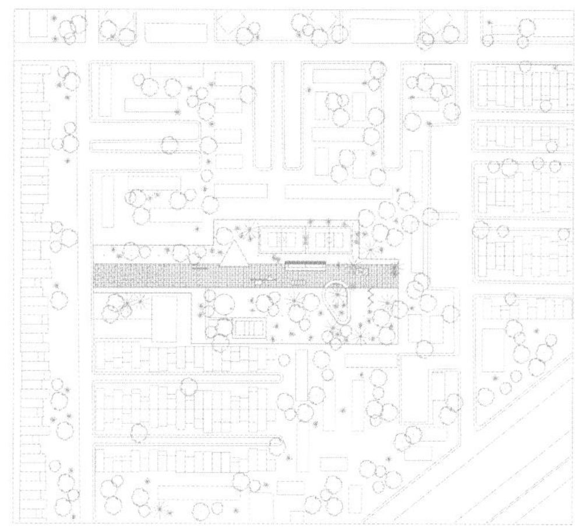

LOCATION: Housing Unit Hogares Castera, Municipality of Tultitlán, State of Mexico, Mexico / DATE: 2019 / STATUS: Built / AREA: 105,486 sf – 9800 m^2 / PROGRAM: Public Infrastructure / PROJECT TEAM: Carlos Bedoya, Víctor Jaime, Wonne Ickx, Abel Perles COLLABORATORS: Daniela Díaz, Natalia Echeverri, Alonso Sánchez, Diego Velázquez / CONSTRUCTOR: CRONOS / CLIENT: INFONAVIT / PHOTOS: Erick Méndez

This project is part of an initiative by INFONAVIT (Institute of the National Housing Fund for Workers) and CIDS (Research Center for Sustainable Development) to improve public spaces in residential complexes in the outskirts of Mexico City. The site is located within the Hogares Castera housing unit in the municipality of Tultitlán. The park consists of a large corridor—15 meters wide by 200 meters long—in which various recreational elements made of pigmented concrete are grouped together. The first element is a set of 50 by 50 cm concrete cubes spread regularly over the linear corridor. Inspired by Carl André's 'Spill' pieces, this grouping delimits the interior space of the park on the avenue and establishes a meeting point, a place of reunion and coexistence.

Next to a pair of remodeled bathrooms, there is a children's play area and an outdoor gym and volleyball court. A roofed pavilion and a platform for community events, with a flagpole and two multi-pitches, were also incorporated. More playful elements complete the corridor: a triangle game, stands and a climbing wall. In front of the courts there is a circuit for play composed of long strategically placed legs, a concrete bench and a circular platform. The corridor ends with a 6-meter-high wall that works as a frontenis.

PUBLIC PARK IN TULTITLÁN

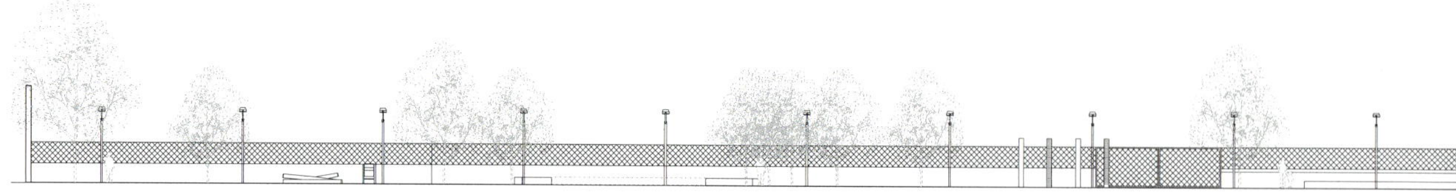

Longitudinal Section

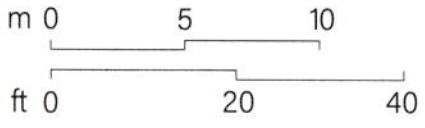

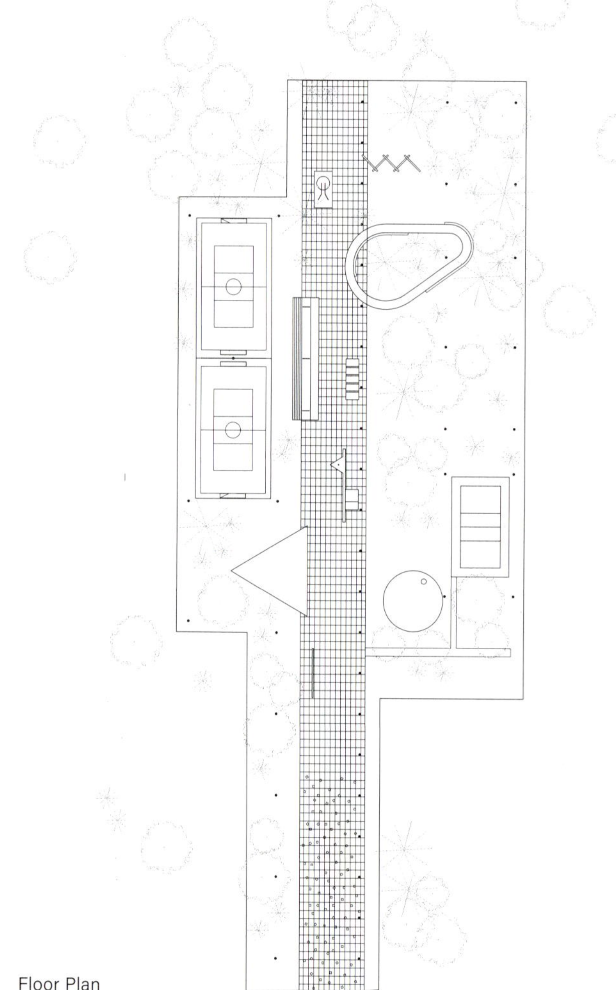

Floor Plan

m 0 10 20 50
ft 0 50 100 200

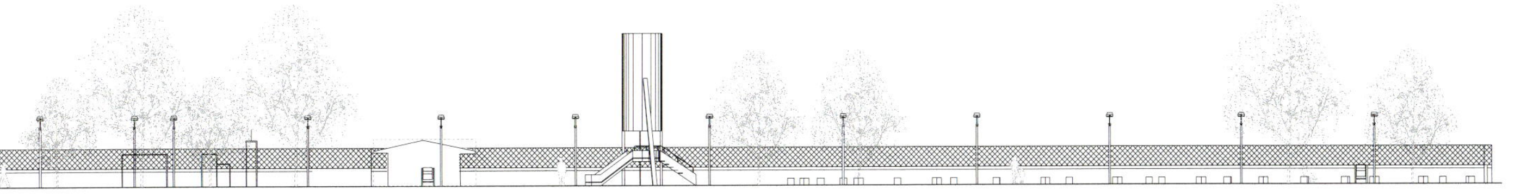

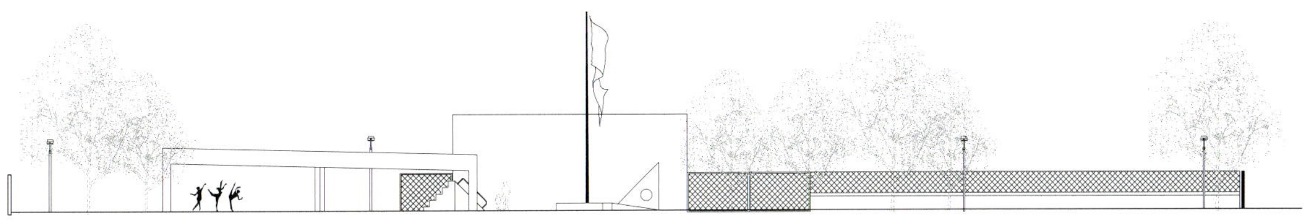

Cross Section

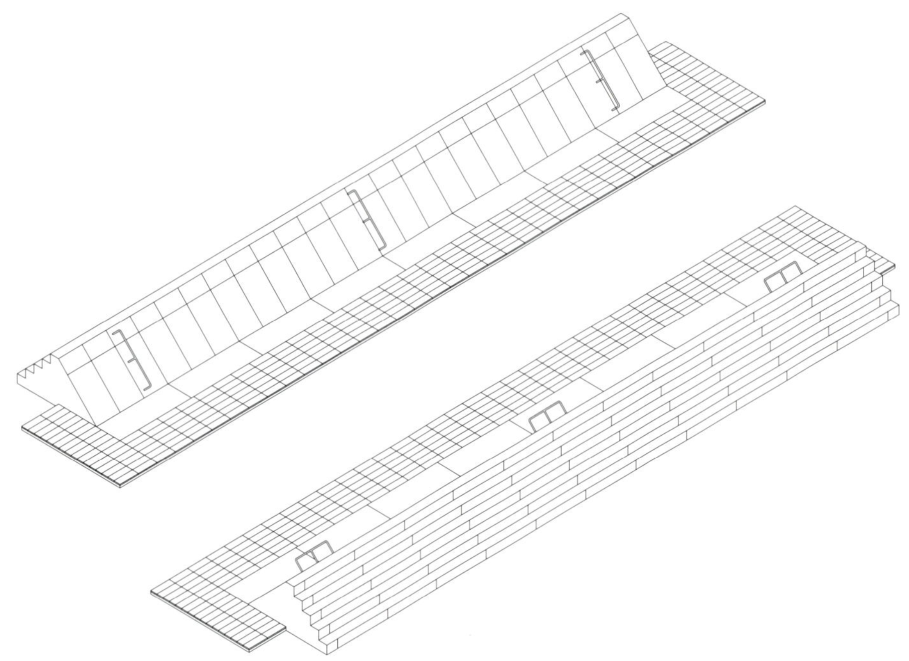

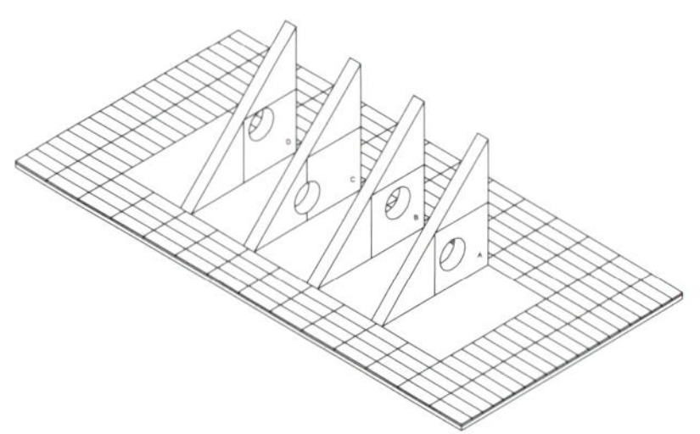

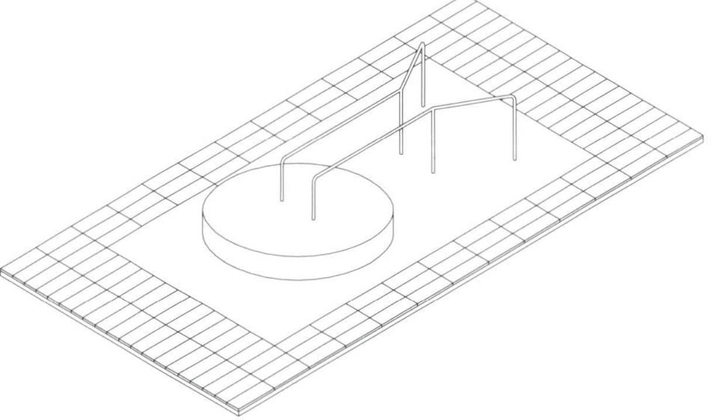

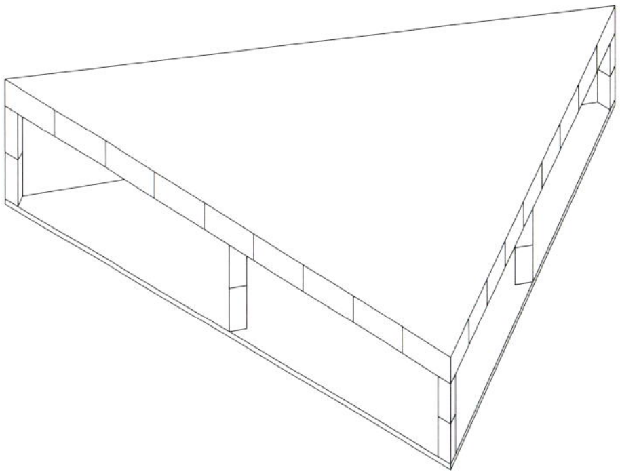

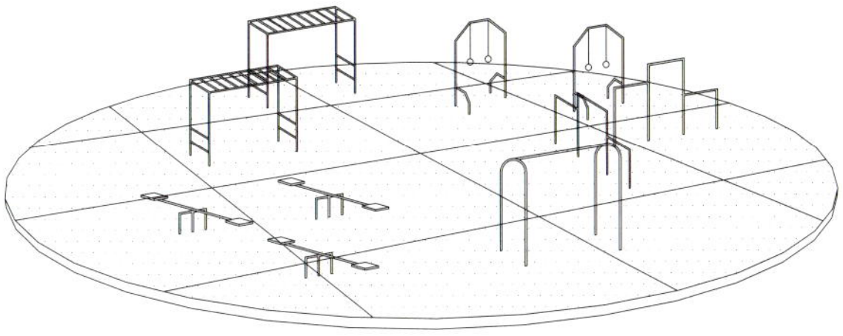

A platform made of pigmented concrete establishes a meeting point.

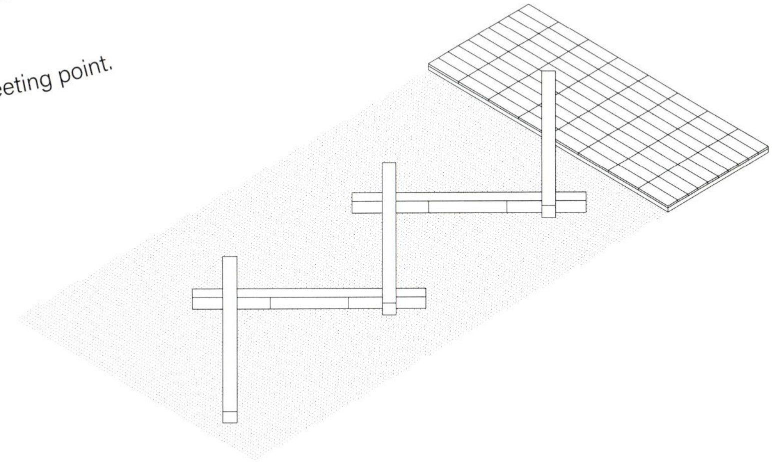

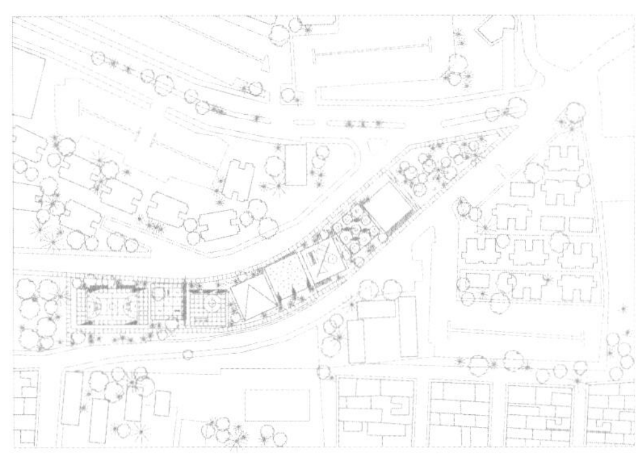

LOCATION: Housing Unit El Tenayo, Municipality Tlalnepantla de Baz, State of Mexico, Mexico / DATE: 2018 / STATUS: Built / AREA: 105,486 sf – 9800 m² / PROGRAM: Public Infrastructure / PROJECT TEAM: Carlos Bedoya, Víctor Jaime, Wonne Ickx, Abel Perles COLLABORATORS: Daniela Diaz, Natalia Echeverri, Alonso Sanchez, Diego Velazquez / CONSTRUCTOR: CRONOS / CLIENT: INFONAVIT / PHOTOS: Erick Méndez

This project is part of the same INFONAVIT and CIDS initiative as the Tultitlán Public Park (see p. 150). The proposal consists of the rehabilitation of a large pavilion that functioned as an open public space. The intervention proposes a group of nine 20-meter-squares that are arranged in the terrain following the topography. Each of the squares contains a specific program: a civic square with a flagpole, a tree-lined square, a children's playground, another one with square benches, a triangular multi-purpose pavilion, a skate park, an outdoor gym and two multi-pitches with bleachers. The whole property is delimited by a 2.5-meter-wide perimeter of sidewalk and jogging track. The connection between each of the squares and the walkway is made by means of stairs and ramps to comply with accessibility requirements. The intervention also includes the improvement of sidewalks, public lighting, gardening, and urban furniture.

PUBLIC PARK IN TLALNEPANTLA

Each of the squares contains a specific program: a civic square with a flagpole, a tree-lined square, a children's playground, another one with square benches, a triangular multi-purpose pavilion, a skate park, an outdoor gym and two multi-pitches with bleachers.

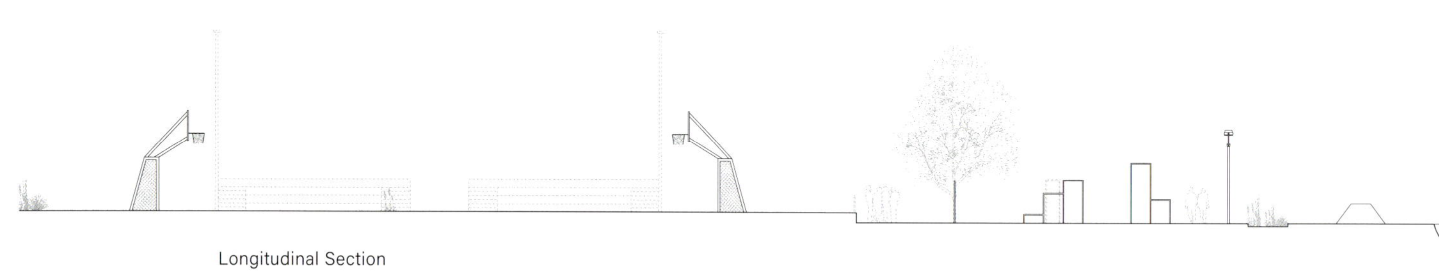

Longitudinal Section

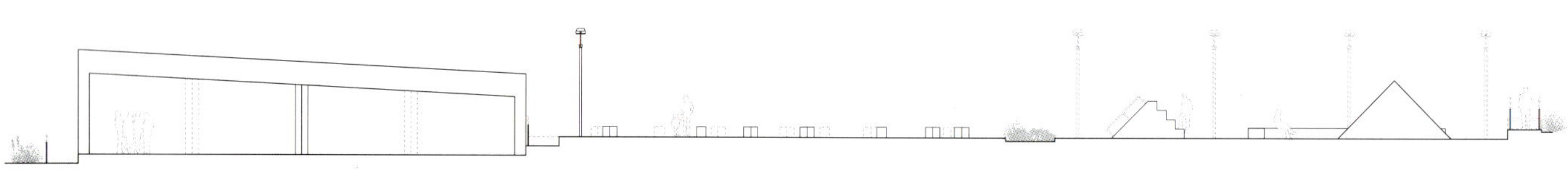

Cross Section

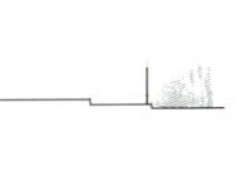

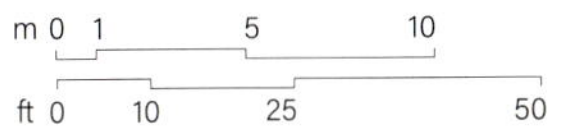
m 0 1 5 10
ft 0 10 25 50

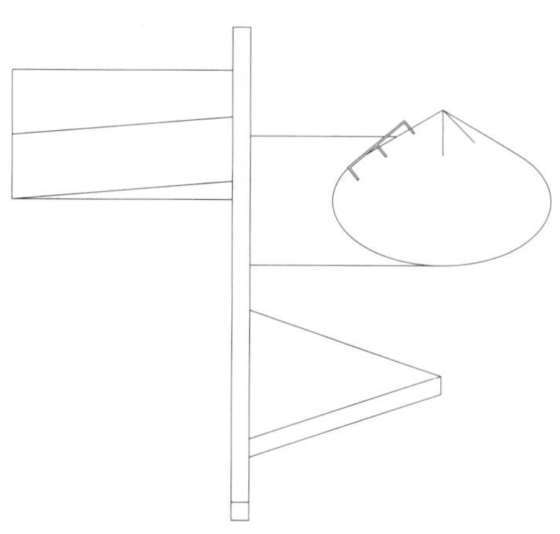

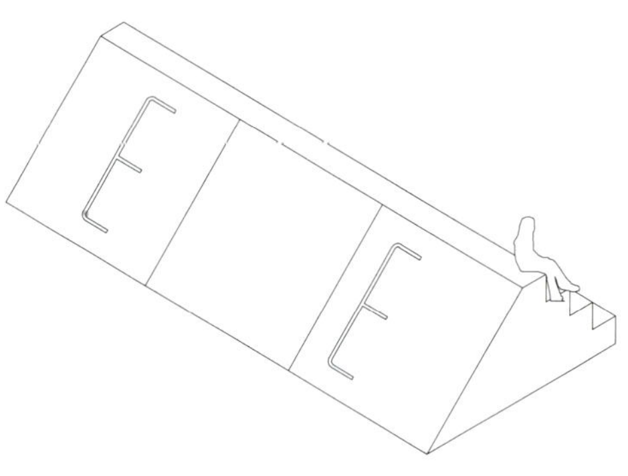

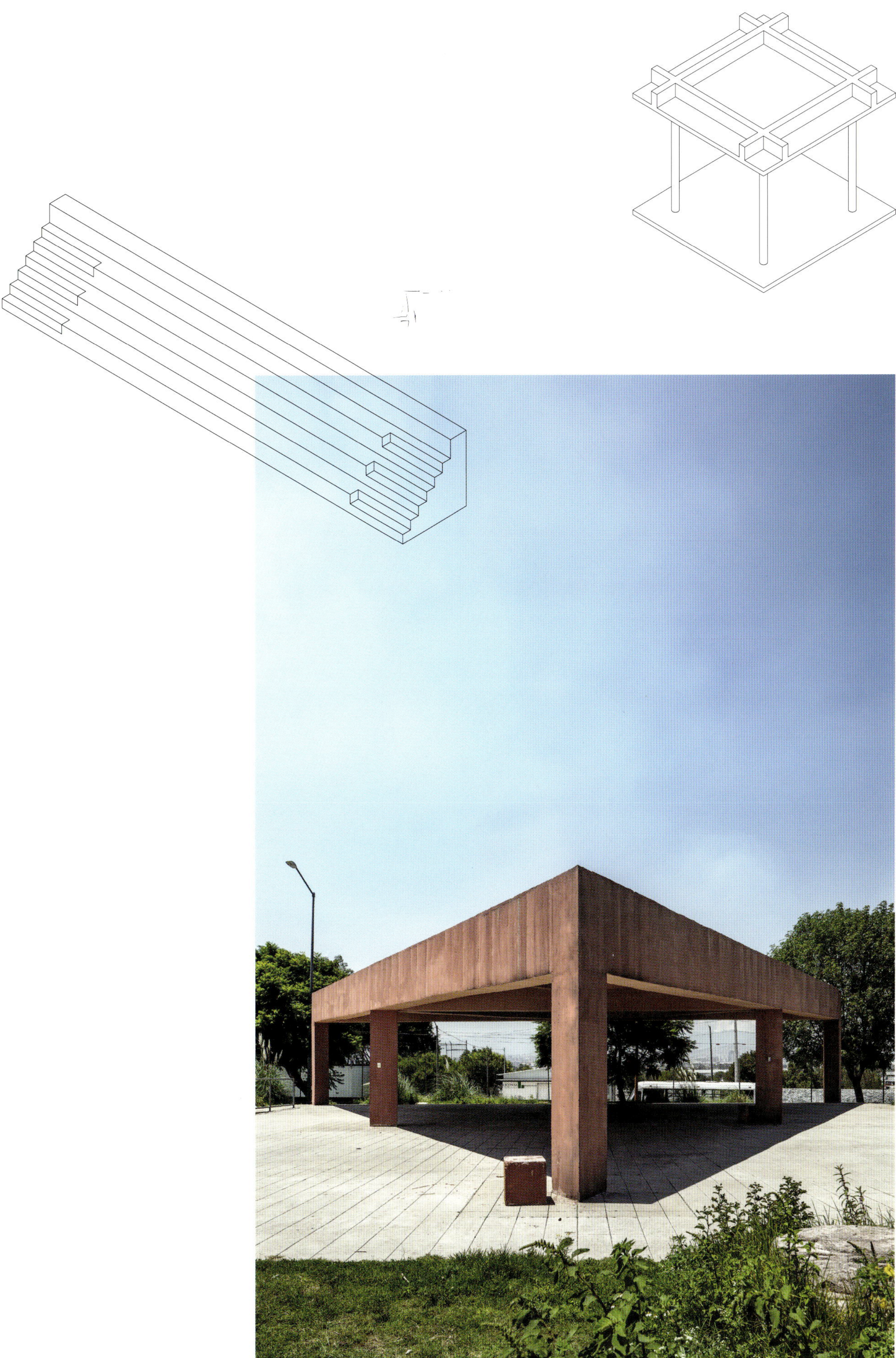

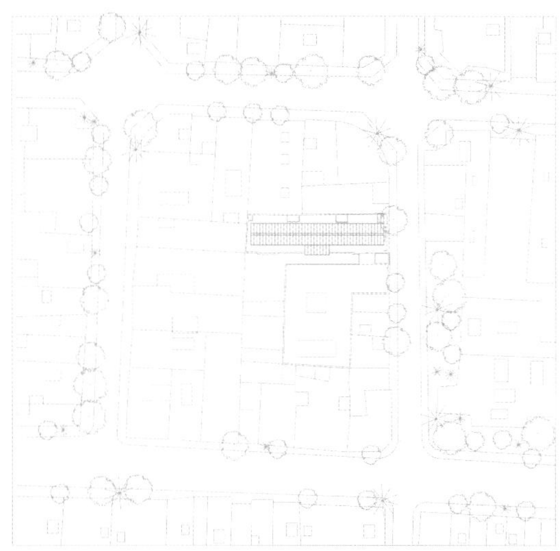

LOCATION: Colonia Juárez, Mexico City, Mexico / DATE: 2020 / STATUS: Built / AREA: 9365 sf – 870 m^2 / PROGRAM: Rooftop PROJECT TEAM: Carlos Bedoya, Wonne Ickx, Abel Perles, Víctor Jaime / STRUCTURAL ENGINEER: Kaltia Consultores / LANDSCAPE: PlantaDB / PHOTOS: Onnis Luque

The project is located in the center of Mexico City, on the rooftop of an early 20th century palace where cultural and festive events are held. In order to prevent occasional rains from interrupting the activities organized in the courtyards, the owner of the property requested that the three existing patios be covered. Instead of making three independent interventions, one single proposal was generated: a continuous roof structure, measuring more than 50 meters in length, connecting the patios in a straight line and generating new covered areas in between the patios. The structure consists of 45 lightweight metal trusses, each 1.2 meters apart, dividing the weight evenly over the existing construction, and accentuating rhythm and perspective along the roof. The triangular roof section is designed asymmetrically so that one side could incorporate a covered circulation.

Light and industrialized synthetic materials such as a PVC deck, polycarbonate sheets and railings made of nylon nets, seek to reduce the weight of the construction and generate a strong contrast with the materiality of the historic building. Two different types of polycarbonate were used (translucent and transparent) to filter the sunlight while still allowing visitors to see the sky from the courtyards. Additionally, textile screens (borrowed from the agricultural industry) are integrated in specific places to mitigate the solar incidence.

The geometric rhythm of the structure is complemented by another series of elements such as the planters that overflow the patios and delimit the new terraces, or the light fixtures that highlight the intervention in the city's skyline.

ROOFTOP PRIM

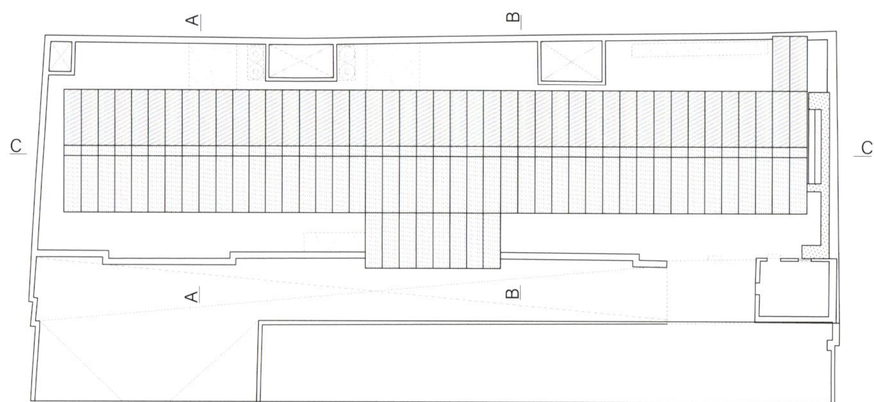

Roof Plan

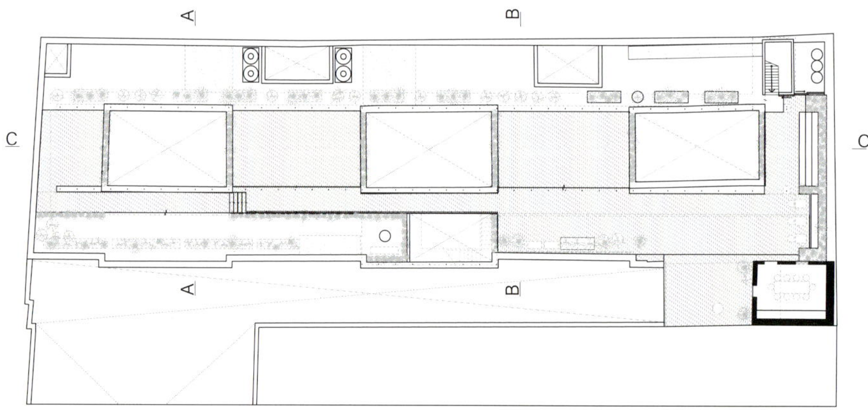

Terrace

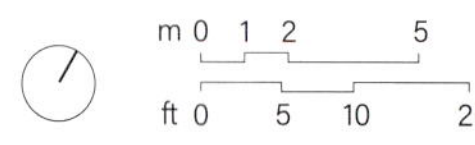

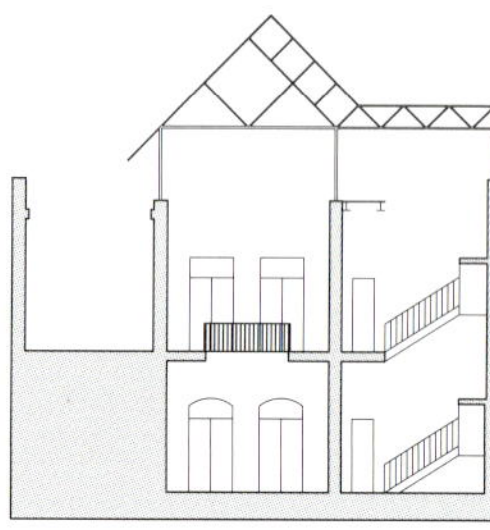

Section A-A

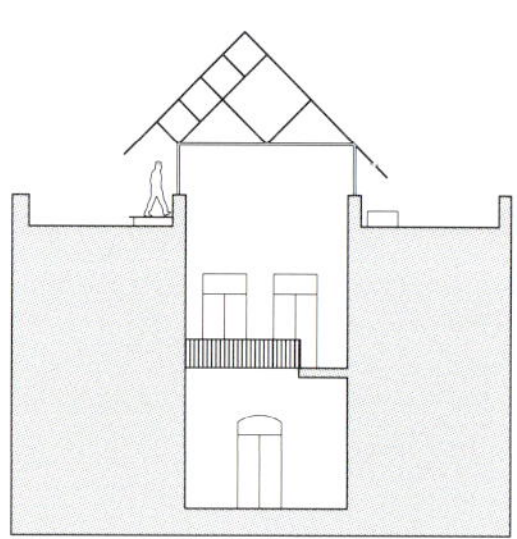

Section B-B

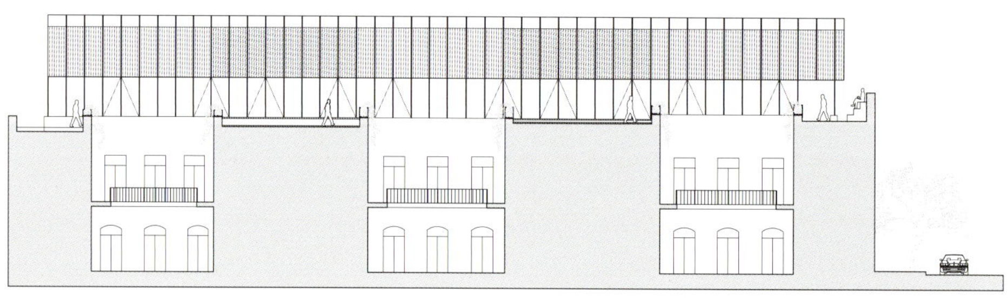

Section C-C

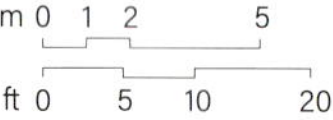

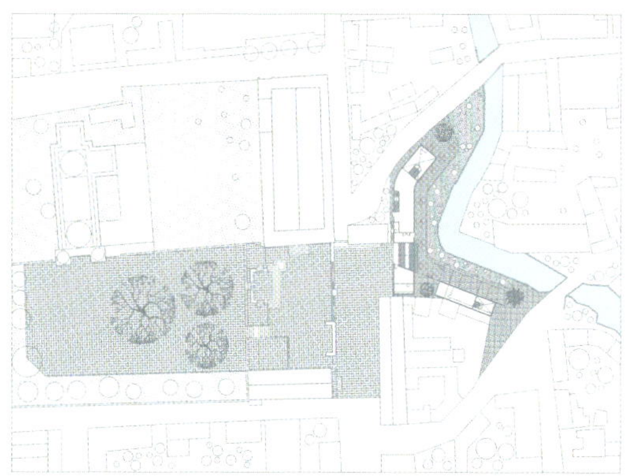

LOCATION: Teotitlán del Valle, Oaxaca, Mexico / DATE: 2016 / STATUS: Built / AREA: 18,300 sf – 1700 m^2 / PROGRAM: Cultural Infrastructure / PROJECT TEAM: Carlos Bedoya, Wonne Ickx, Abel Perles, Víctor Jaime / COLLABORATORS: Rosalía Yuste, Josue Palma, Pamela Martínez, Antonio Espinoza, Andrés Rivadeneyra, Iván Villegas / CONTRACTOR: Bonarq / STRUCTURAL ENGINEER: Kaltia Consultores / TECHNICAL ENGINEER: BioE / LANDSCAPING: Entorno Taller de Paisaje / CLIENT: Municipality of Teotitlán del Valle / PHOTOS: Luis Gallardo

This Community Cultural Center exhibits the archeological and textile wealth of Teotitlán del Valle, a village in the Mexican state of Oaxaca. The main volume, facing the village square, houses the museum which hosts the collections and activities of the Teotitlán Museum of History. In formal terms, the project is governed by the aesthetics of the immediate context, which determine the height, color, and materials used. The secondary volume contains the Municipal Library and a service zone. The area occupied by both buildings represents just 18% of the whole site, leaving a large public space made up of a plaza and gardens. This helps to improve the pedestrian trails across the site by connecting them with the main square. The public spaces of the Cultural Center become then part of the circuit of existing plazas that defines the village's urban structure.

The volumes present austere, neutral façades. The form and material character of the building, including double-slab sloping roofs, 30 cm-thick concrete walls, and controlled openings, create a passive system that responds to the adverse climatic conditions. This basic strategy helps to regulate the temperature inside the building and provides users with a comfortable space to read a book, work or visit the museum. At the same time it eliminates the need to install air conditioning systems. The interiors present a diverse range of lighting conditions and spatial qualities (double and triple-height spaces), generating different atmospheres for exhibitions and activities. The Cultural Center uses a minimal palette of locally made materials (pigmented concrete, timber, clay tiles, and bricks) in order to blend into its context.

TEOTITLÁN CULTURAL CENTER

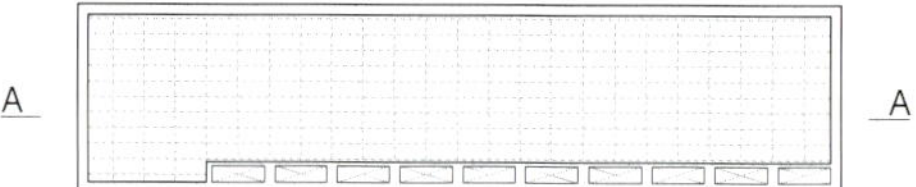

Library - Roof Plan

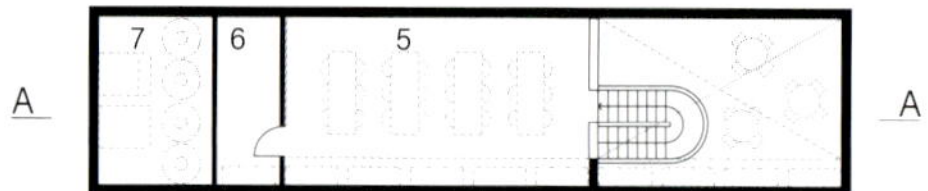

Library – Second Floor

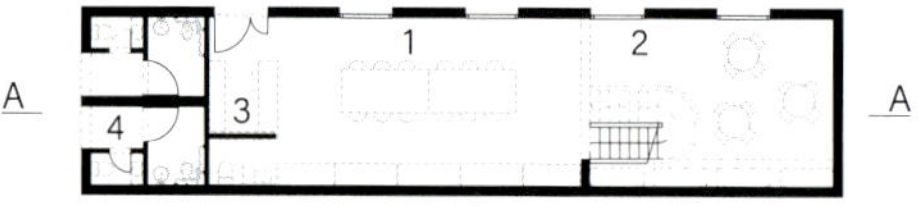

Library – Lower Ground Floor

1. Reading Room
2. Children´s Reading Room
3. Reception
4. Bathrooms
5. Computer Room
6. Storage Room
7. Service Area

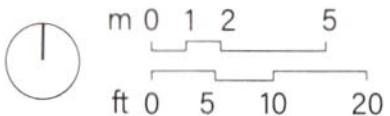

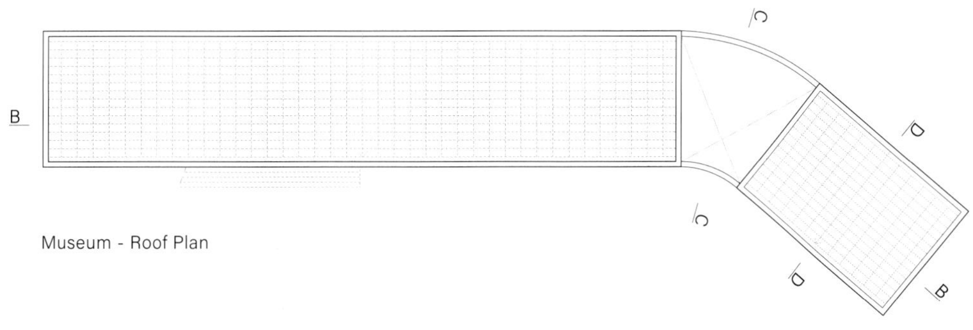

Museum - Roof Plan

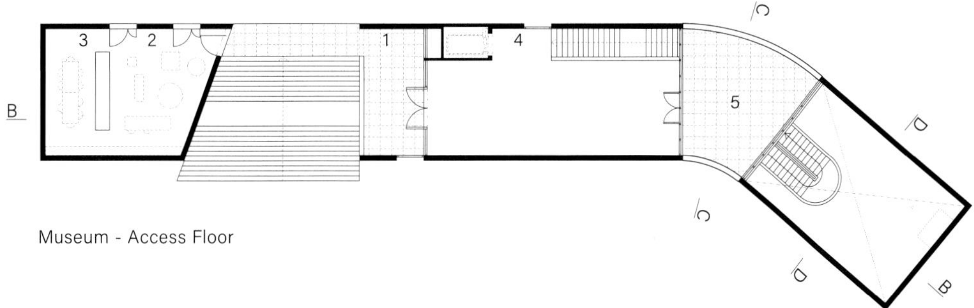

Museum - Access Floor

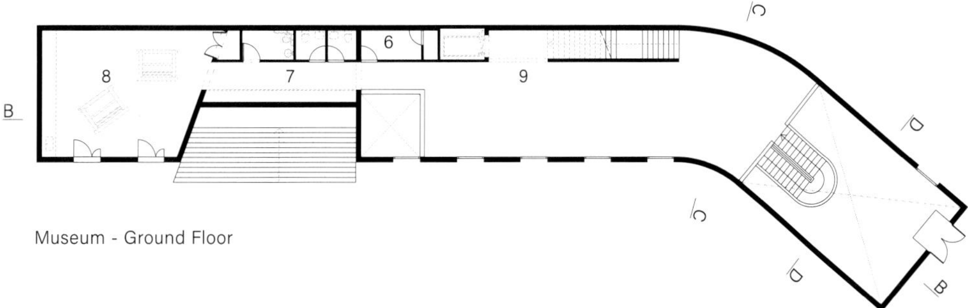

Museum - Ground Floor

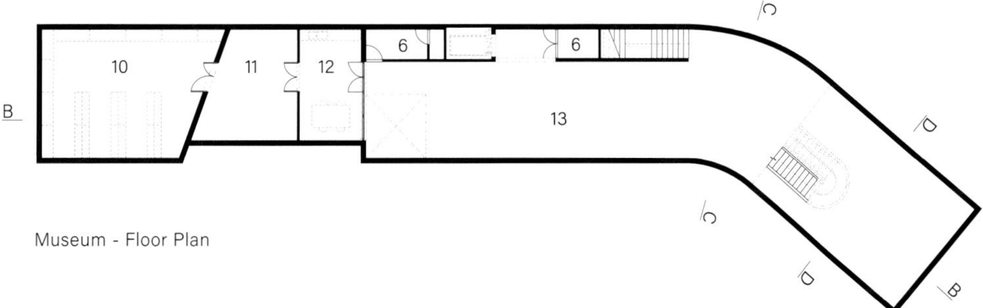

Museum - Floor Plan

1. Access
2. Gift Shop
3. Office
4. Temporary Exhibition Room
5. Patio
6. Storage Room
7. Service area
8. Multi-purpose Room
9. Textile Exhibition Room
10. Archaeology Storage Room
11. General Storage Room
12. Restoration Workshop Room
13. Archaeology Exhibition Room

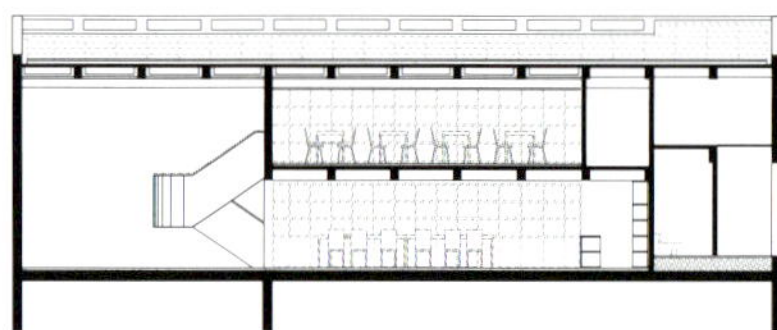

Library – Section A-A

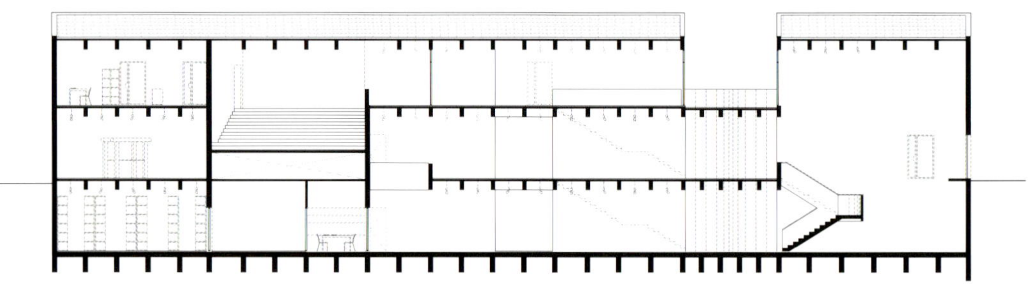

Museum – Section B-B

m 0 1 2 5
ft 0 5 10 20

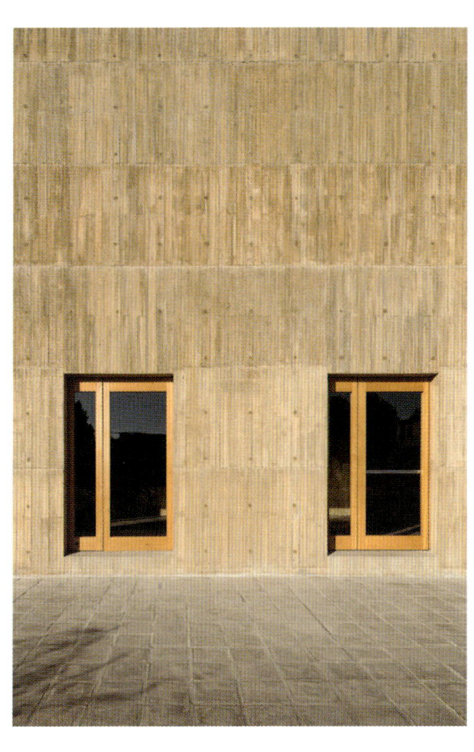

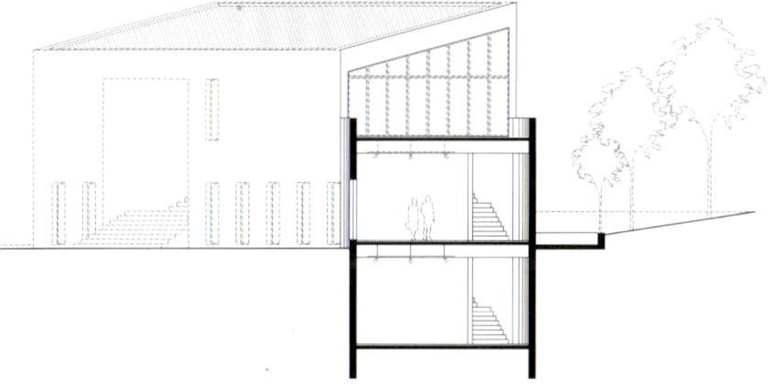

Museum – Section C-C

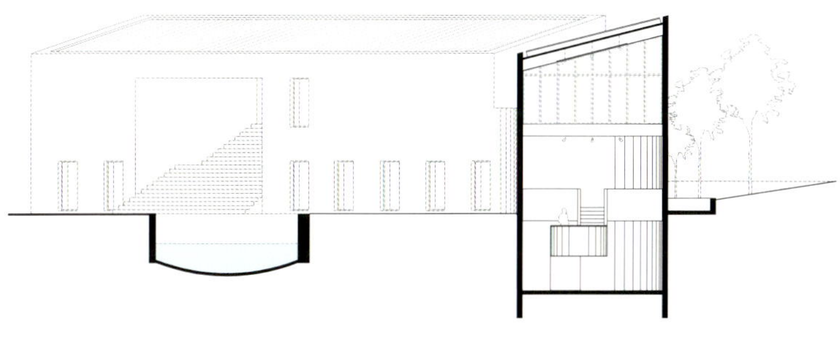

Museum – Section D-D

The Cultural Center uses a minimal palette of locally made materials in order to blend into its context.

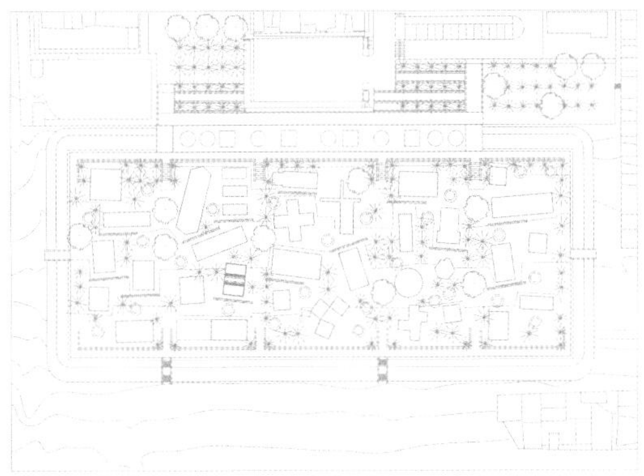

LOCATION: Apan, Hidalgo, Mexico / DATE: 2017 / STATUS: Built / AREA: 700 sf – 65 m2 / PROGRAM: Social Housing / PROJECT TEAM: Carlos Bedoya, Víctor Jaime, Wonne Ickx, Abel Perles / COLLABORATORS: Natalia Echeverri, Oswaldo Delgadillo / CLIENT: INFONAVIT / MASTER PLAN: MOS / PHOTOS: Jaime Navarro

This experimental prototype is part of a housing laboratory promoted by INFONAVIT (Mexico's Housing Authority) to develop innovative, regional housing that could be partly self-built. The complex consists of 32 houses by Mexican and international architects within a master plan designed by MOS Architects.
The proposal, designed by PRODUCTORA, adheres strictly to the budgetary restrictions outlined by the laboratory. The prototype consists of two bays that are interconnected by a central vaulted space, avoiding the need for circulation or hallways. The progressive growth of the house takes place in the central space, allowing the living area to extend by 35%.
The structural layout of the project (square modules of 3.20 meters), reinforced brick walls, and traditional block-and-beam roof slabs, economize the construction. The central vault is built using fired brick. Informed by local conditions, the proposal considers that the building site may vary from rural context to a more urban one. Therefore, the house can also be developed on smaller plots of land or in between party walls.

HOUSE IN SAN FRANCISCO DEL RINCÓN

Elevation

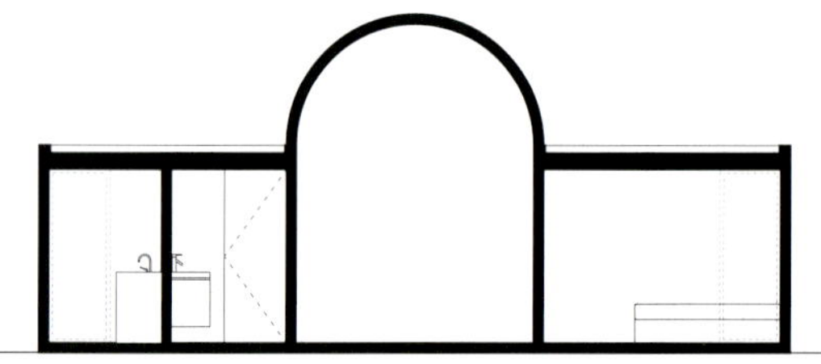

Section A-A

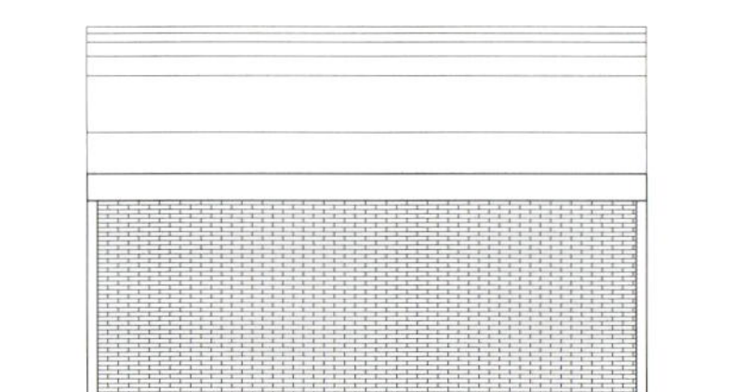

Elevation

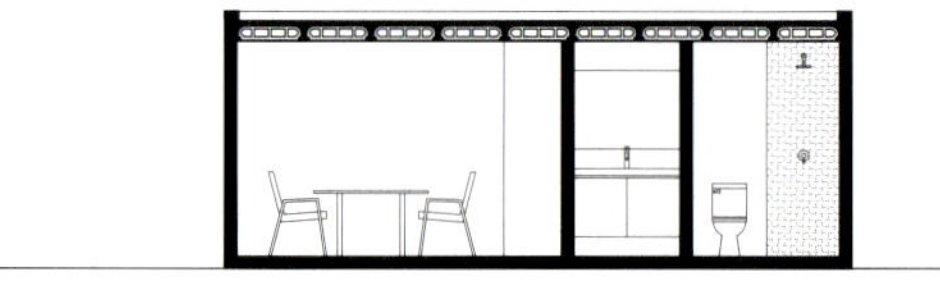

Section B-B

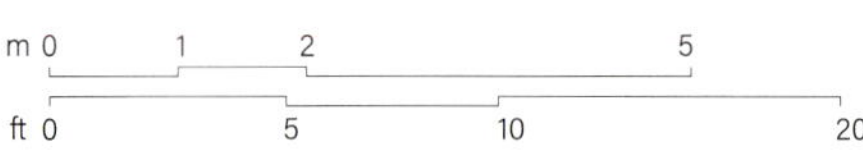

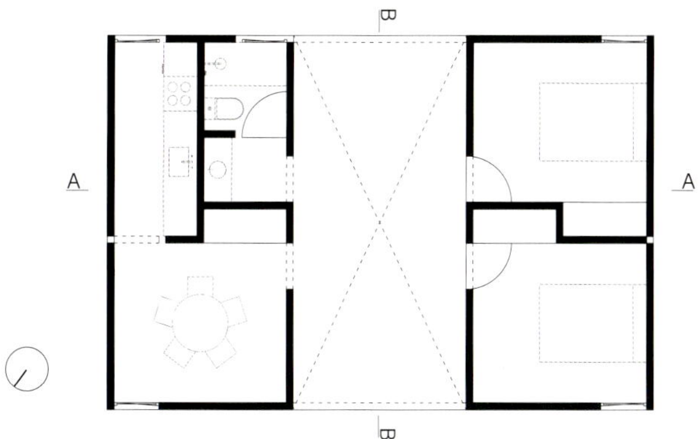

Ground Floor

A flexible central space allows for connections between the different rooms.

•MOS

Ph. Courtesy MOS

Michael Meredith • Hilary Sample

MOS is a New York-based office that fudges typical definitions. Even though the practice's statement is only explicit about their wish to be "horizontal and fuzzy as opposed to tall and shiny"—as the anagram of their name may already suggest—, the work they produce speaks to much more. Meredith and Sample are part of a transforming architectural culture which includes designing in different scales, doing books, exhibitions, works of art, everyday objects, and videos, among other explorations. They experiment, they make, they reflect and write, and all the while, they are also committed to teaching. All of these fragments are part of the same cosmos, in which inquiries about very practical and concrete issues are perceived as extraordinary.

A USUAL MIX OF TOO MANY THINGS

Michael Meredith in conversation with Florencia Rodriguez

As in almost everything this year, the screen was the mediator of this conversation. A shared drive and lots of things around each of us—including dealing with kids' homeschooling, adapting to the challenges of permanent remote work, and the many other things we went through during these unexpected and unprecedented times—forced us out of any comfort zones, and the luxury of abstraction. This short conversation is proof of that. Michael Meredith points out the need of other kinds of engagement, making it clear that theory, some modes of practice, academic research and other forms of intellectual speculations, have not exactly been "reading the room" when facing the contemporary. Even though it is still too early to have answers regarding what will come, many of us probably feel that we expect this moment to be a turning point in some ways, and that we have to be active in choosing or debating what will follow. That questioning spirit, an active bit of discomfort, and the courage to revise and explore further, are relevant ingredients of what we think define Hilary Sample's and Michael Meredith's MOS. Their objects address genealogies without solemnity, they seem common and extraordinary at the same time, they have a quality in between openness and closure that would not fit easily in stereotypes, they explore the diffuse in terms of program but look consolidated. And yet they are not ambiguous, nor dialectically defined; they are something else. And they manage to make that something else feel strangely familiar.

FLORENCIA

Hi. As it is not that easy to break the white page in a written Google-Drive conversation, I would like to propose to begin with some short definitions. Let's play and explore. So, I invite you to briefly relate or spontaneously reflect on the relation between these pairs of words: objects & space, form & boundaries, beauty & intentions, architecture & discipline.

MICHAEL

These word pairs are our everyday language in schools. And also very abstract. They're sometimes useful, but they can also be twisted around, misinterpreted, or misused. If someone wants to say, in some gestalt manner, that objects are the opposite of space, they can. If someone wants to find a way to say there is no difference between objects and space, they can. Both sound right to me. Things can sound plausible in the abstract. I guess the purpose of these is to talk about what architects do, to communicate, but they avoid and abstract what architects really do in the world. Most architects provide a service for a client. Of the dialectic pairings, I think boundaries, objects, form, proportions and beauty (perhaps) are abstract but less abstract. You can experience them. They are physical and material, whereas space, intentions, architecture, and discipline seem more conceptual and vague to me at this moment. I could probably change my mind by the time we finish this conversation.

FLORENCIA

Believe me, I'm not a fan of pairs either, but when reading your text I arrived at two different lines of thought that I would like to explore here. One is directly related to your practice and how do you deal with abstraction vs. a more direct relationship to construction in your own design process. The other one is regarding education and its distance from the profession, but we can discuss that later.

MICHAEL

Well, as you can probably tell, lately I've been thinking abstraction is a problem. Accelerated by modernity and corrupted within capitalism. Labor, goods, and life become economic values. We've all become increasingly comfortable with very abstract thoughts, even with abstracting ourselves. And then we're asked to negotiate abstractions within and through other abstractions: people are abstracted into groups and values, architecture is abstracted into ideas, ideology, or words, and so on. These abstractions produce distance, remove us from the object or act itself. Academia for the past decade has been filled with work focused on things that have nothing to do with most people. Experiments that have little relevance. Sometimes they are done in the name of others without their involvement, sort of unwanted gifts for some abstract community. In a way we are trained to do this in school, working without real clients in the imagined service of a community. It can produce an abstract idea of a client. We can start to think we know what others want. And there are the abstractions of buildings through writing, drawing, and modeling that are presented as ends in themselves, self-satisfied or comfortable within their own representational territory. I'm all for playing and experimenting, but there has to be a way to remind ourselves that this is all a construction and only useful until it isn't. Nowadays, we are trying to focus more on being directly engaged, making things, interacting with others, being engaged in the physical, material economies of production. I'm probably going through a sort of midlife crisis, a self-criticism of previous work that focused on medium and post-medium specificity. Recently, I've become more interested in just really thinking about how the world is constructed and the world of architecture, of development, of governance regarding building or housing. It's truly horrible, we need to fix it by engaging it more directly, not as an abstract set of ideas or proposals. Maybe it's probably better to focus on what we're doing. The stuff we're doing at the moment is affordable housing and cabins, houses, furniture, research, proposals. Actually one of the proposals is on vacancy, vacant storefronts in New York City... We've lived here for about ten years, and it is one of the things we've noticed pre-COVID but it's become even more pronounced nowadays.

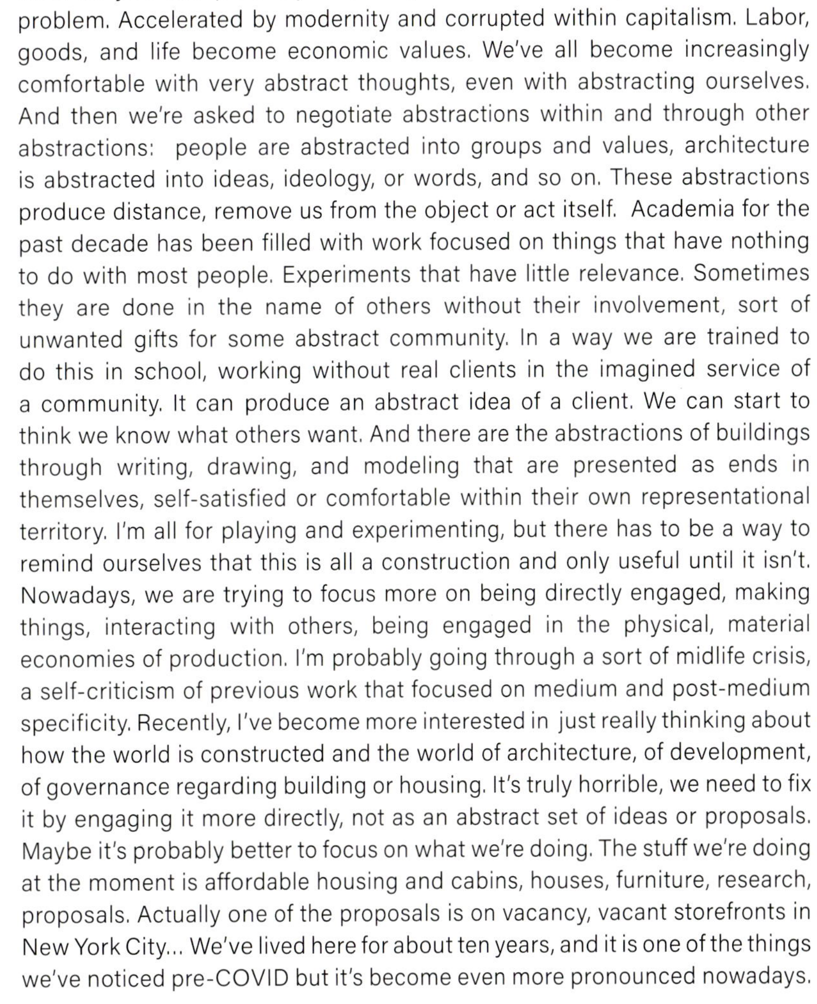

All images courtesy MOS

Anyways, our office is the usual mix of too many things, most of the projects are underpaid or pro-bono. Someone contacts us and says, hey we want to do such and such, and we need it completed in a month and we have no money—can you do it? We usually say yes, although it's getting a little tiresome. We are basically part-time average working architects, our clients generally don't care about our body of work, they don't care that we're involved in academia. They just want someone that can help them make a building, and take on liability for it. There is almost no intellectual discourse, just a purely technical one-how does this work, how much does it cost, how to get approvals, etc... I don't say this to complain, we enjoy what we do, and this is not a problem of the client, but a deeper cultural problem beyond architects, about what we value as a society. I just think there is a reason America looks like it does, we have horrible housing, unsustainable development, profiteering from developers, not because of bad architects, but because of the situation. Architects don't hold much direct influence on general culture, even the so-called star-architects.

FLORENCIA

And why do you think architectural discourse became so separated from general cultural interests? Do you think it is on our side to do something about it?

MICHAEL

I wish I knew. Architecture just requires so much money and time perhaps. Perhaps it's always been associated with an expression of class, aristocracy, and the state/government. It feels out of reach for many. Modernism and Postmodernism tried to reach out to new audiences (supposedly), but it's still pretty limited. The buildings we admire and promote in schools many don't like. They're cold, or ugly, or weird, or unpopular, etc... I remember being at Harvard, and everyone other than those in Architecture (and Art) hated the Carpenter Center. The only building people less liked was Gund Hall (Harvard Graduate School of Design). The recurring joke for most schools is that the architecture school is in the ugliest building on campus. The question is—what can we do about it? How do we build an audience for difference, for experimentation, for willing to pay for qualities over quantity, etc.. Design is one of those things that is very much part of the market, but also distinct from it, a lot of developers don't really have a way to measure good design in their proformas, etc... it is added value, but how much etc... is somewhat indeterminate.

FLORENCIA

This made me remember Tom Wolfe in "From Bauhaus to Our House," which in Spanish was curiously translated as *Who's afraid of the fierce Bauhaus? ("¿Quién teme al Bauhaus feroz?")* He says that Modernism is the moment in which general taste splits off from critics' and architects' taste. And there is something to care about in that statement, and in the idea of fear, if we are thinking that architecture is something that general audiences feel so distant to. At this particular moment I feel we should work on a certain reconciliation, but without falling into pure pragmatism. One of the main programs in your work is the house. What is the basis of your exploration? What motivates you?

MICHAEL

I love the translated title. Maybe things have changed since it was written. Then, there was a more singular cultural narrative. Now, it's more fragmented multiple narratives, as if there is any consensus on critic's or architect's taste. Modernism has a boutique following in mainstream culture. Prefab houses have become luxury items, even though they started as housing for masses. Aesthetic genres, tastes, co-exist without much concern. I'm unsure there is a truly populist architecture. I don't think Classicism is a populist language, although Trump seems to think so. Classicism was supposedly representative of democracy, then facism, then wealth... If anything it's a sort of suburban or comfy hotel design sensibility that the market promotes. We will spend years on projects and then the sales/marketing people will come in and say oh you need to change this, this is what the market wants. Architecture makes less and less sense as an intellectual project. If knowledge is power, and the point of education is to empower students to go out and make a

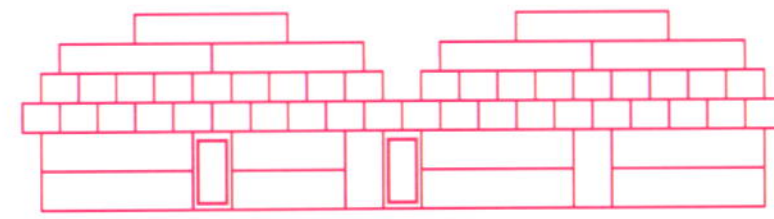

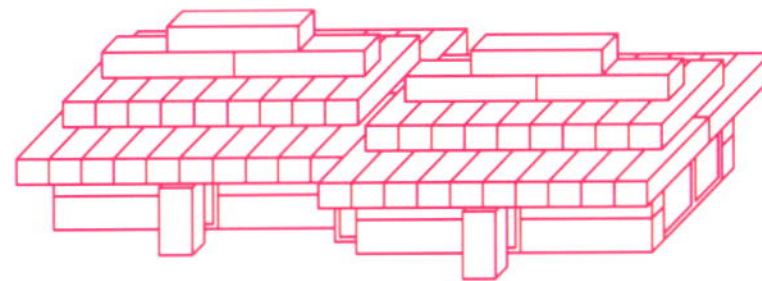

House No. 12, A Foam House with 98 Blocks of Foam and 8 Doors

better world, then we have not done this well. We think ideas can change things, which they can, but there are so many ideas and nobody seems to explicitly argue for one being better than another–learning how to build, run a business, and operate in the world as an architect seems as valuable if not more. This is the moment to reevaluate our values as a discipline. For decades we've been caught up in trying to be ahead of everything, ahead of the market, models of complexity, expressing a technological cutting edge, or an aesthetic project that is out of reach for most construction, and out of reach for most people. Avant-garde. This might be the moment to just be present, neither overly concerned with an architecture from the future or the past, the forefront or the rear waves of culture, and instead try to work with the situation at hand, to remake the present. So yes, a sort of reconciliation, but I just wish architects had more involvement and say in the built environment. Most architects are in a service industry working for clients, while a few star architects operate as artists. It shouldn't be so elite. Part of me wishes architects could become developers, or policy makers, that we could take the lead in rebuilding things, but the reality is currently we have very little agency in making the world. (Despite what we are taught.)

Regarding houses, you can find everything in houses. Shinohara's body of work is a great example of this. It's at a scale where you are very involved in details, construction, furniture, site, in a way that you're not in some other programs. They're compact, like poems. I like the closeness of the outside, their intimacy. The hard part of them is that every client is very invested in their house, and every client has a different idea of function. They can be a lot of work, and tiring. That said, it's not that we can engineer the program we get, its just what we've gotten, and we would prefer schools or housing or community centers as programs, but houses are okay too. A house can be a school, or multi-family housing, or a community center at different times. What's the basis of exploration? It's a great question, what motivates someone to do what they do. I can't answer it. I don't know. There is a sort of pleasure to see things built, to make things. Maybe a desire to have a voice, to be in the conversation. Maybe another way of asking this is what do you value in your work. We really just have very few projects at a time, small things, research, some buildings. Hilary wanted to be an architect at a young age, she was very clear about it. I feel like I could have been anything where I'm making things, art, music, design, writing, ceramics, carpenter, video game designer, and so on. I made music and art, primarily, before architecture.

Model Furniture

Reproductions of Reproductions of Reproductions (or Model Furniture).

An obsession with the stuff that occupies the background of architectural representation, the things we fill spaces with, led us to look at furniture made for architectural models. Think: close-ups of generic, nearly notational chairs; fields of wobbly stools lightly out of alignment; the most mundane shelving systems imaginable; abstracted blocks turned modular benches or cabinets or who-knows-whats; non-descript tables and displays; reproductions of reproductions of reproductions of mid-century modern chairs; indescribable things distorted by humidity; clumsy, ergonomic 2D extrusions; tables with an impossible materiality; seats proportioned a little too high or low; an economy of pieces cut and pasted together; replicas of some other design; etc... These miniature objects, made by armies of interns and careful craftspersons alike, populate models by architecture offices large and small. They're a sort of low-resolution representational default, a reduction to the bare qualities of an object—handmade ready-mades. Works in the "Model Furniture" series are translations of these translations: from a table to a model to a table again, something that oscillates between reality/reference/reality. They are both something and not.

While working on this series, we have collected a myriad of photographs of model furniture into a single catalog, An Unfinished Catalog of Model Furniture Without Architecture. We have used various bad images as a starting point for translations of our own design in a new furniture series, titled "Model Furniture."

1

SHELVING

Model Furniture No. 4

Project Team: Michael Meredith, Hilary Sample, Andrew Frame, Michael Abel

Ph. Michael Vahrenwald

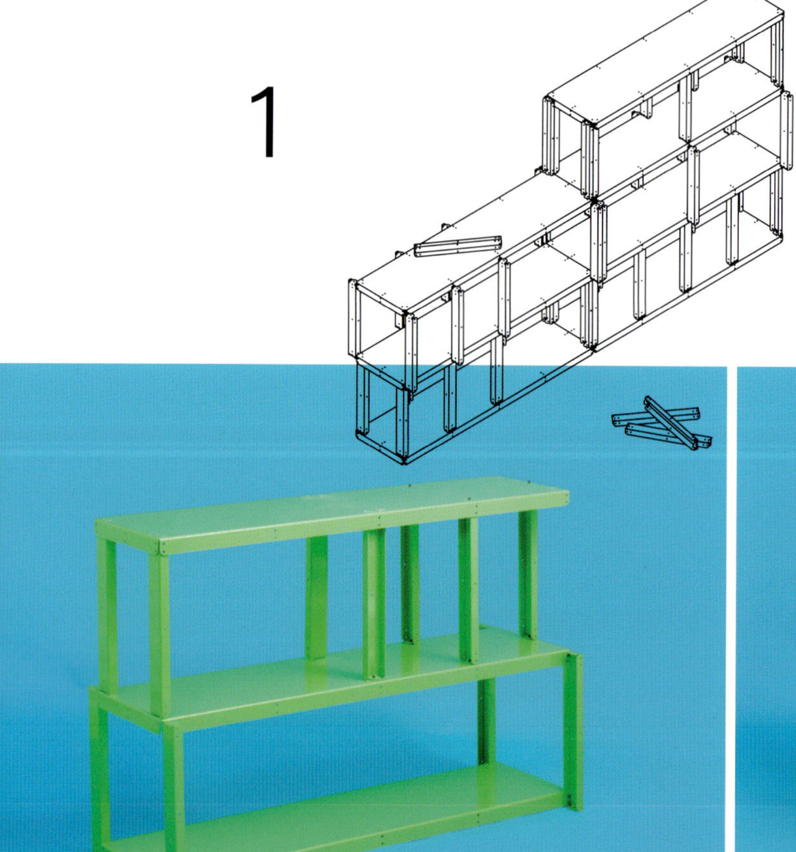

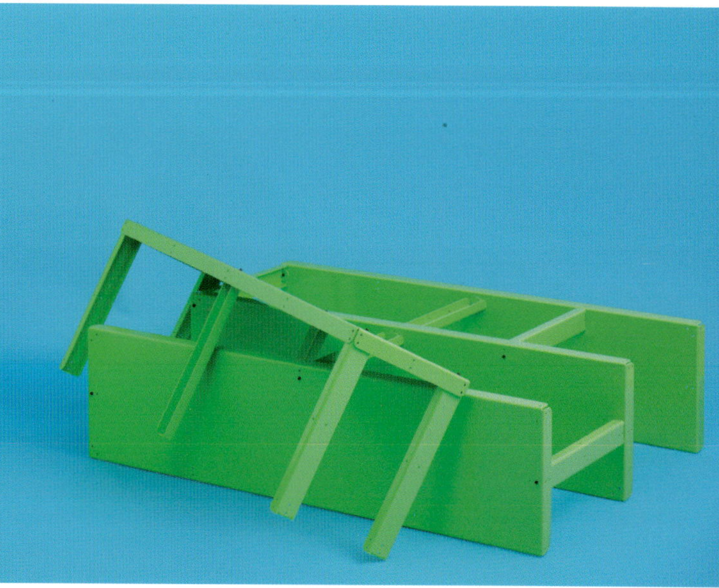

2

CHAIR

Model Furniture No. 2

Project Team: Michael Meredith, Hilary Sample, Andrew Frame, Michael Abel, Fancheng Fei

Ph. Michael Vahrenwald

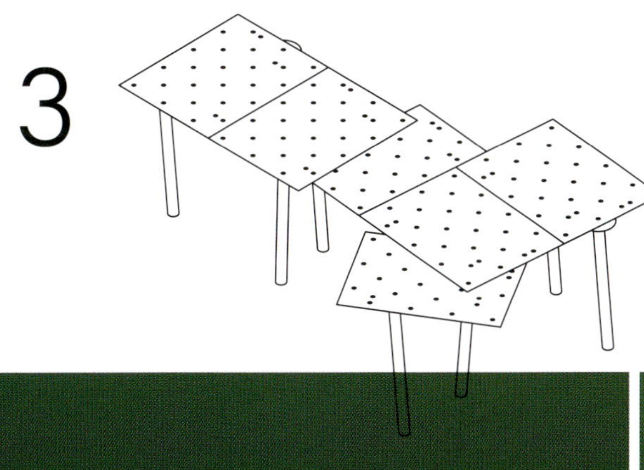

3

CUT AND PASTE TABLE

Model Furniture No. 7

Project Team: Michael Meredith, Hilary Sample, Paul Ruppert, Lafina Eptaminitaki

Ph. Michael Vahrenwald

4

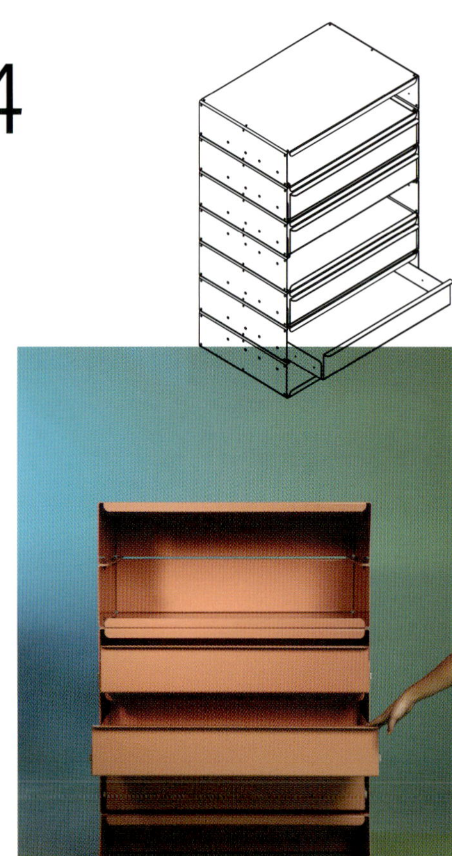

CABINET

Model Furniture No. 1

Project Team: Michael Meredith, Hilary Sample, Andrew Frame, Michael Abel

Ph. Colin Todd

6

LADDER

Model Furniture No. 6

Project Team: Michael Meredith, Hilary Sample, Michael Abel, Nile Greenberg

Ph. Michael Vahrenwald

5

STOOL

Model Furniture No. 3

Project Team: Michael Meredith, Hilary Sample, Andrew Frame, Michael Abel, Fancheng Fei

Ph. Michael Vahrenwald

7

TABLE

Model Furniture No. 5

Project Team: Michael Meredith, Hilary Sample, Paul Ruppert, Mark Acciari, Fancheng Fei

Ph. Michael Vahrenwald

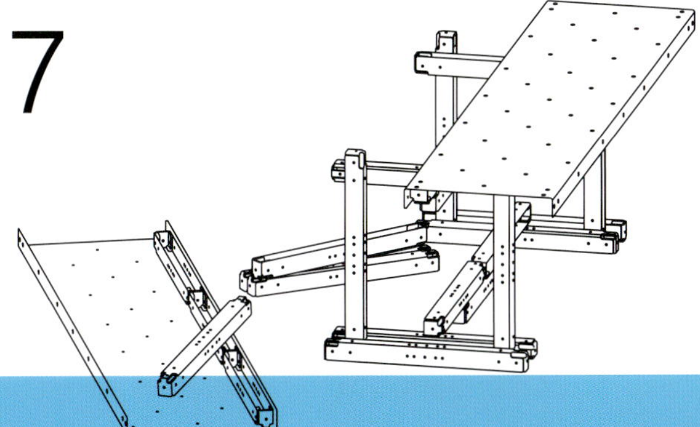

Installation No. 15 And Benches, Platforms, Partitions, Shelving, Activity Books, Uniforms

It all started with two aluminum elements, the 'Horizontal' and the 'Vertical.' The 'Horizontal' is 100 inches long; the 'Vertical' is 16-5/16 inches high. After countersinking 336 holes into the 'Horizontal' and drilling 42 holes into the 'Vertical,' they can attach together: 'Verticals' to 'Horizontals'; 'Horizontals' to 'Verticals'; 'Verticals' to 'Verticals'; and 'Horizontals' to 'Horizontals.' One 'Horizontal' plus three 'Verticals' make a single bench... But 'Verticals' can become horizontal and 'Horizontals' vertical. All of these are attached by 'People,' and we've found that 'People' don't like to follow directions. They bend or break the rules. You can, for example, construct something with 'Horizontals' and no 'Verticals,' or vice versa. This logic of addition repeats until you simply run out of parts or money or both. Everything is aggregated, arranged, and rearranged by 'People.' Everything is mirrored. Everything reflects everything else. 'People' assemble and disassemble 'Horizontals' and 'Verticals' while wearing beautiful shimmering 'Uniforms'—silver mylar, pleated-nylon coats full of pockets for storage—designed in collaboration with 'Slow and Steady Wins the Race'. These 'Uniforms" store and conceal their tools. These 'Uniforms" make the labor seem incredibly fun, which it is not. (It is slightly fun, if you're into that sort of thing.) While working, 'People'carry wonderful 'Activity Books,' designed in collaboration with Studio Lin. These 'Activity Books' inform and distract them from their work. But the 'People' are a nomadic workforce. They don't want to be doing this full-time. They want to be somewhere else. They want to be distracted... Each 'Activity Book' has 100 configurations—and a lot of stickers—that document a small portion of configurations made from 'Horizontals' and 'Verticals:' a bus stop; park bench; bed; catwalk; partition; auditorium; riot barricade; pop-up shop; A.A. (architecture anonymous) meeting space; breakdancing stage; performance review niche; community theater; avant-garde coffee shop; phone booth; bedroom ensemble; bulk storage; secret society hangout; temporary museum; graphic designer support space; a place to forget your wallet; gluten-free cooking arena; artisanal mugs craft fair; yet another makerspace; lecture hall; nondenominational chapel; pretentious market; design night school; global art fair; open-source archive; revolutionary activity organization . . . We cannot anticipate what will happen, or all the possibilities for A/D/O, itself a workspace, design school, retail outlet, gallery, restaurant, and many more things all at once. It is a platform. It is an ever-changing assembly like the installation itself. We don't completely understand what it will become. What we do know is that the 'Verticals' and 'Horizontals' are bolted together with ¼"-20 flat-head screws.

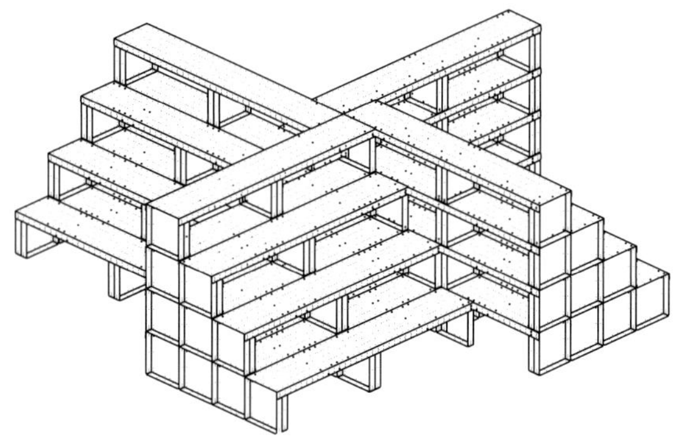

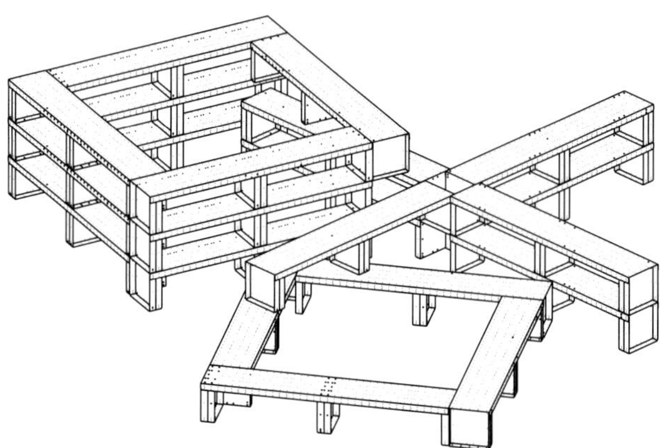

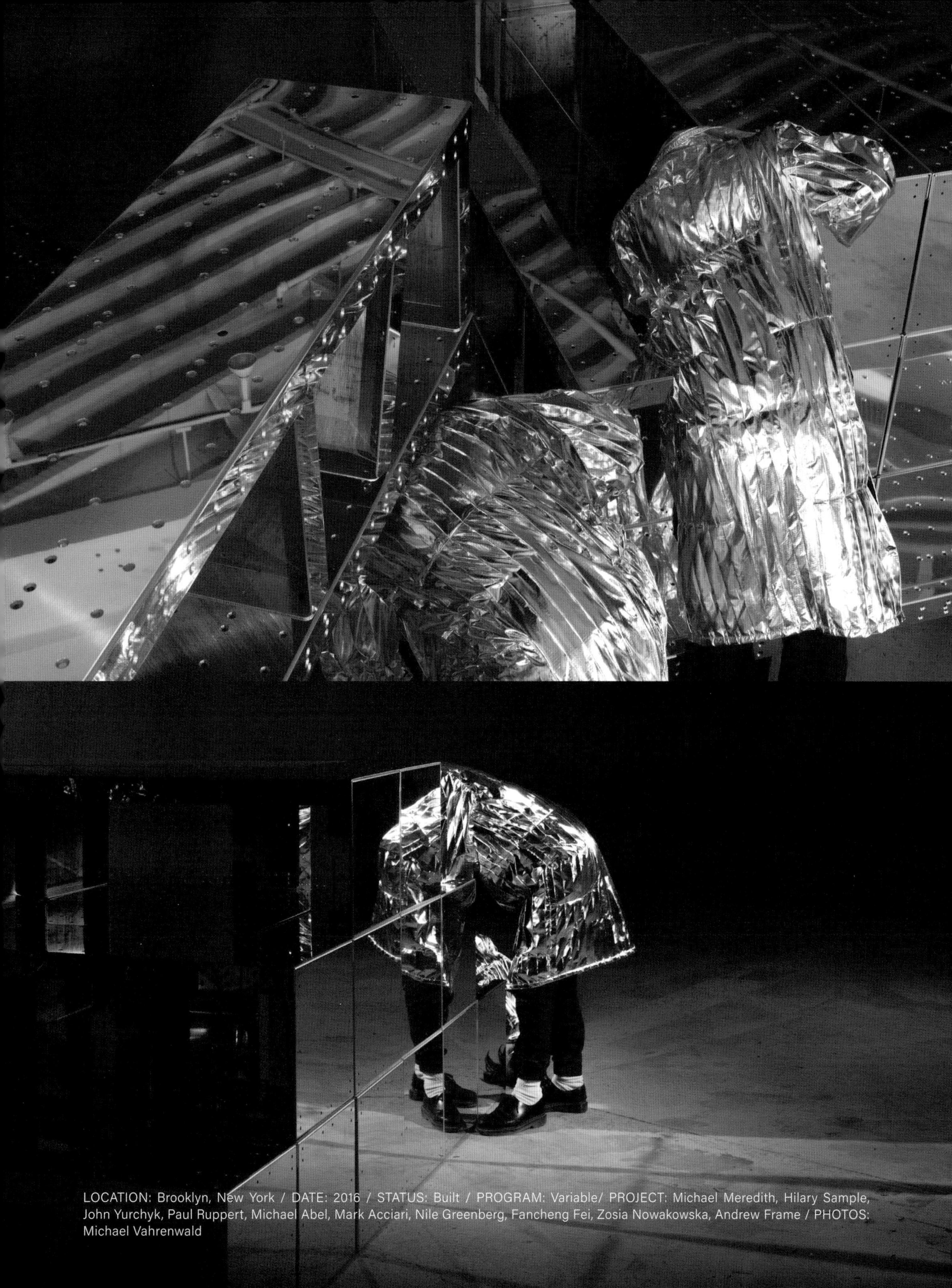

LOCATION: Brooklyn, New York / DATE: 2016 / STATUS: Built / PROGRAM: Variable/ PROJECT: Michael Meredith, Hilary Sample, John Yurchyk, Paul Ruppert, Michael Abel, Mark Acciari, Nile Greenberg, Fancheng Fei, Zosia Nowakowska, Andrew Frame / PHOTOS: Michael Vahrenwald

School No. 3
Petite École

Petite École is a one-room, open-air design school for young children. It is a place for looking and making and for making and looking. It is 688 aluminum pieces modelled, flattened, cut, folded, prefabricated, shipped, and then assembled onsite by a few people in a few days. It is made to be reassembled. It could be constructed anywhere and elsewhere. We imagine different contexts. It looks low-tech. We made large paper models by hand. It looks high-tech. We made parametric fabrication files. We photographed. We sketched. We looked at various angles. We adjusted the elements. We lowered the eaves. We tried other proportions. These look good for the moment. It looks industrial. It looks familiar. It looks abstract. It is made of building elements: a long, low roof with columns and stacked beams holding it up. It is made of folded aluminum. It has a sign made of folded aluminum. It has furniture made of folded aluminum. It is meant to be looked at. It is meant to be inhabited. It is meant for others' enjoyment. It is a stage. It makes other stages. We look. It looks. We make. It makes.

LOCATION: Versailles, France / DATE: 2019 / STATUS: Built / AREA: 1,152 sf / PROGRAM: Workshop, Studio, Lab, Classroom, Atelier
PROJECT TEAM: Michael Meredith, Hilary Sample, Paul Ruppert, Lafina Eptaminitaki, Charles Dorrance-King, Julia Muntean
STRUCTURAL ENGINEER: Bollinger + Grohmann Ingenieure, Paris / PHOTOS: Iwan Baan

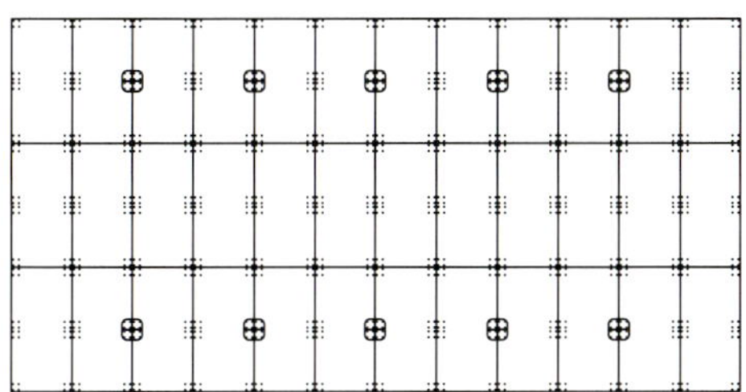

Petite École

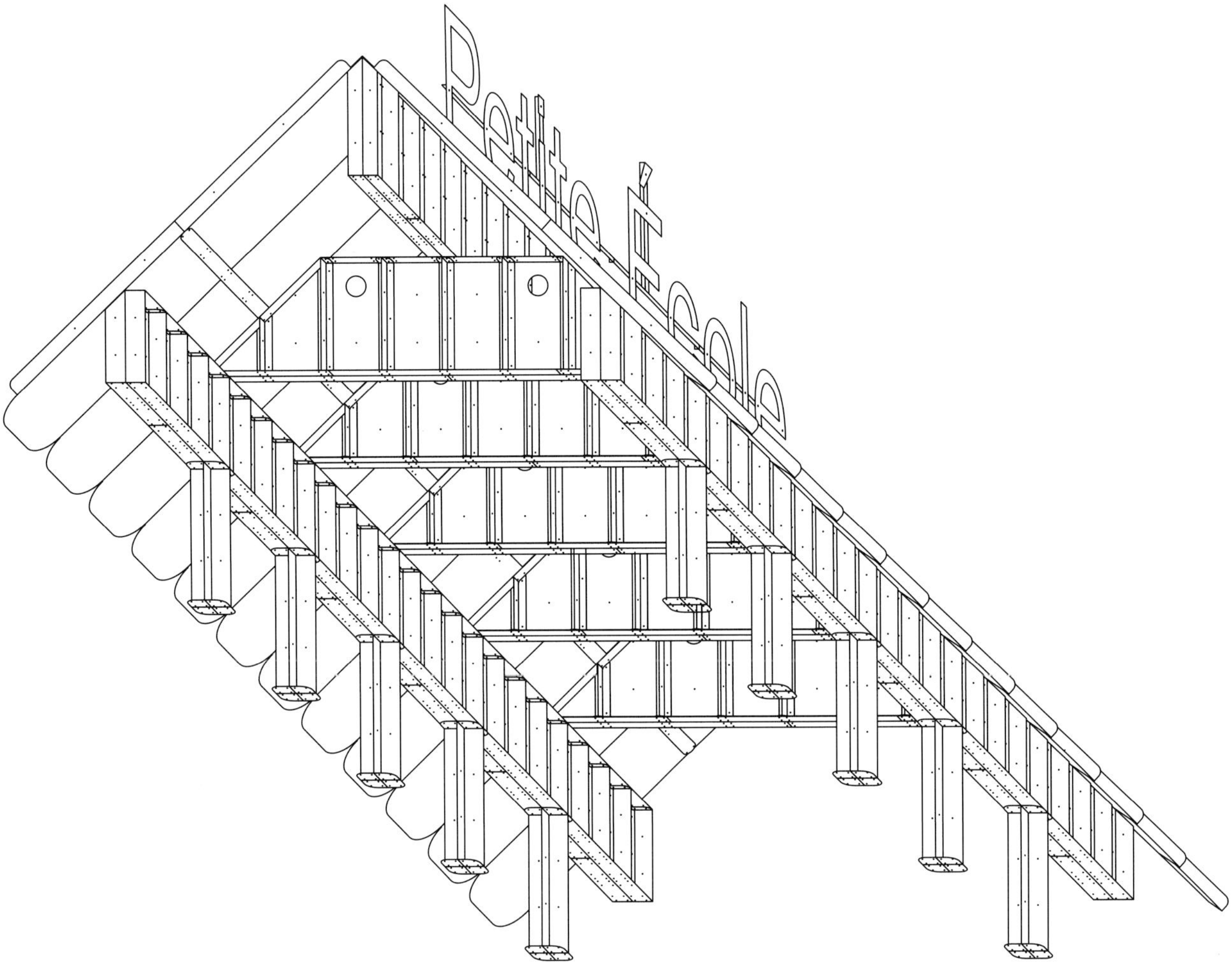

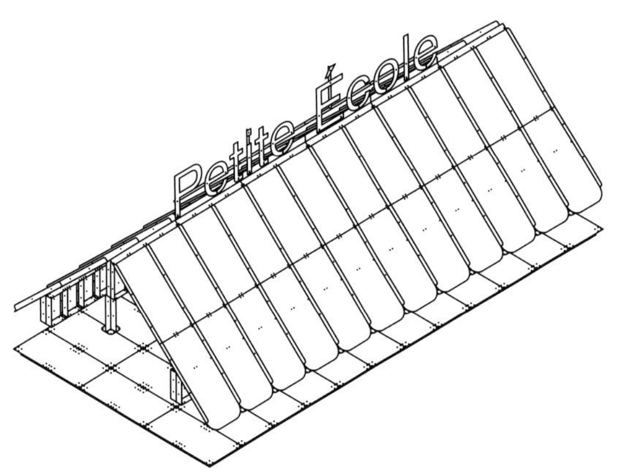

Petite École

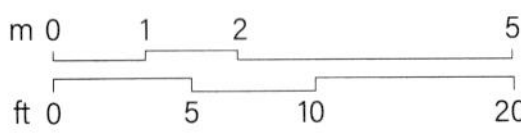

m 0 1 2 5
ft 0 5 10 20

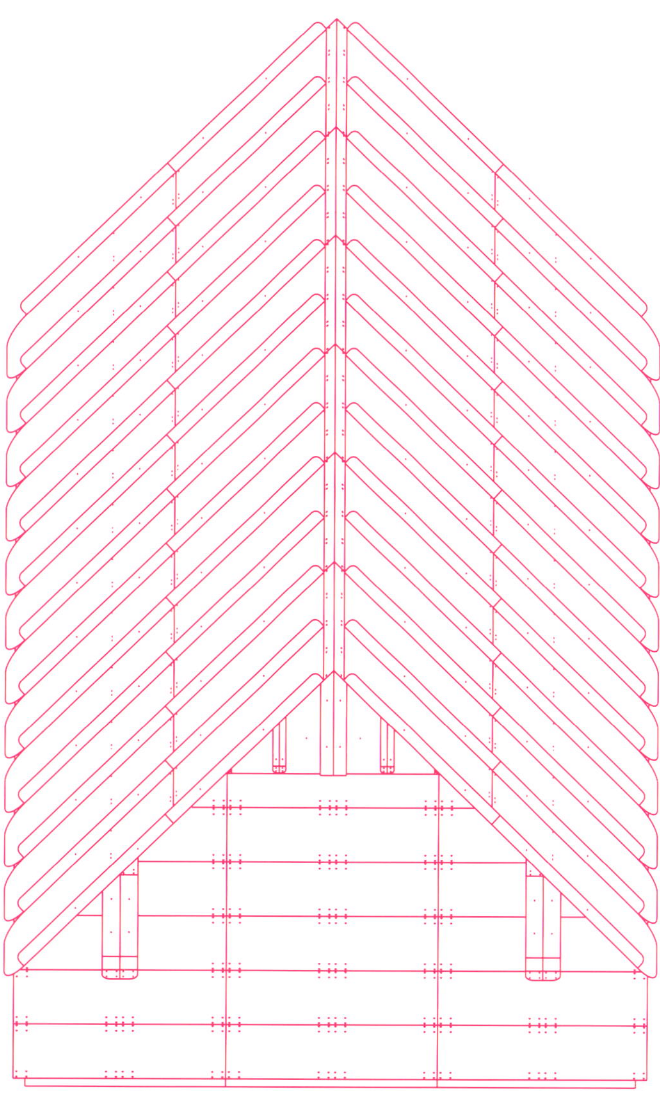

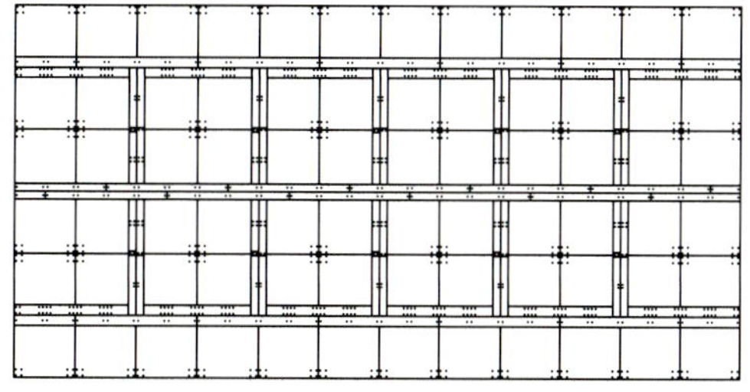

House No. 14
A Room, Chimney, Cistern, and Roof

This is a house, assembled: one roof; three windows; one door; one chimney; two skylights; one fire pit…

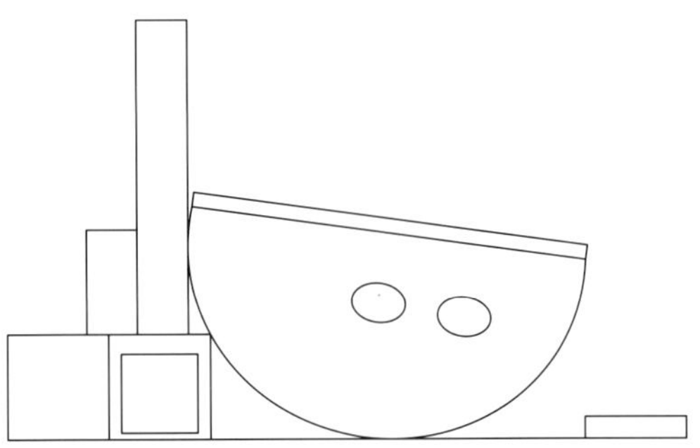

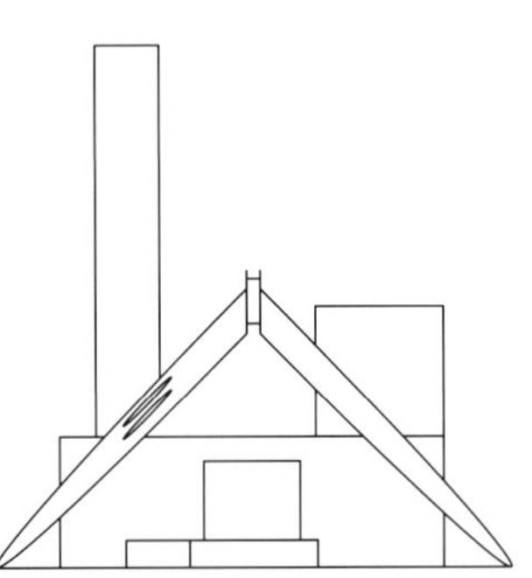

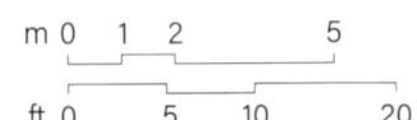

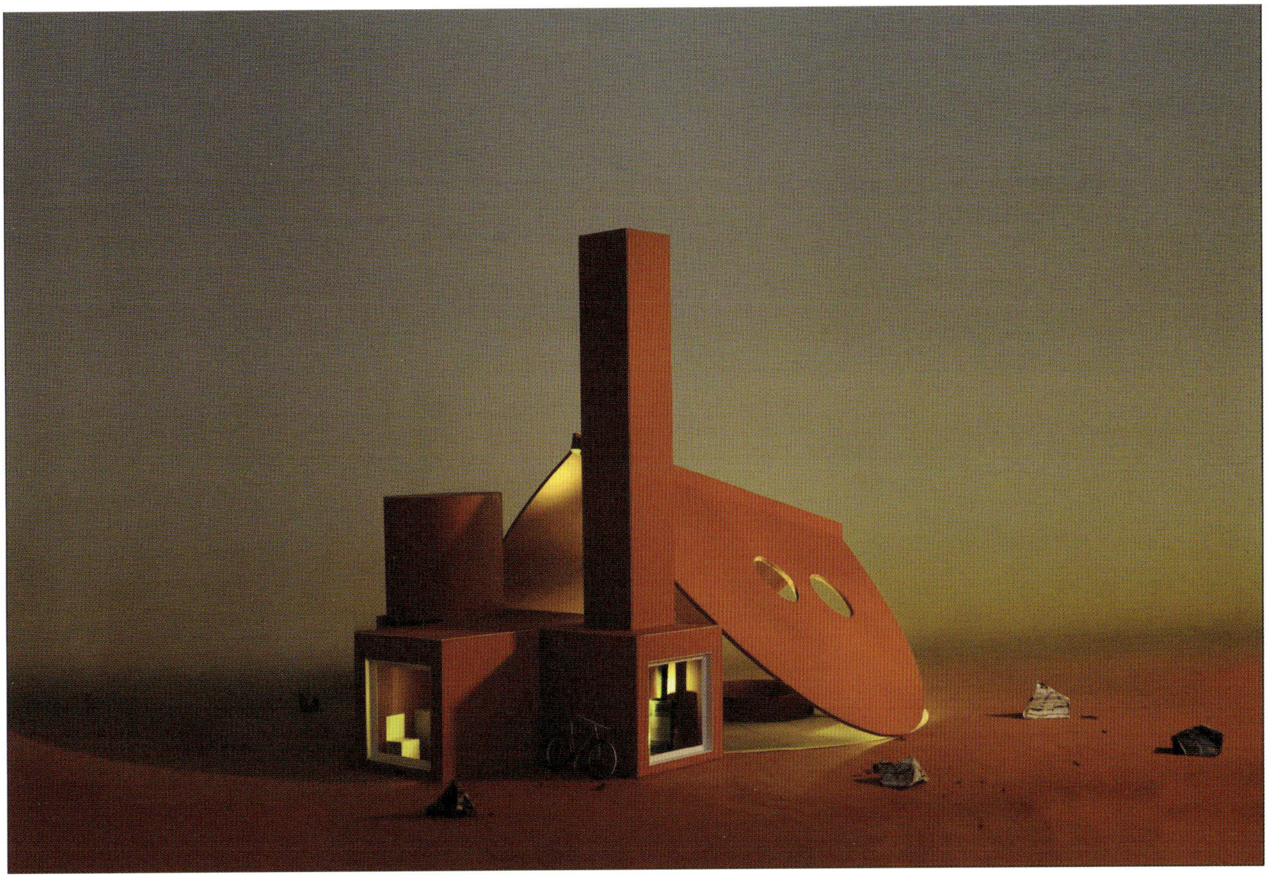

LOCATION: Various / DATE: 2018 / STATUS: Proposal / AREA: 1,065 sf / PROGRAM: Café, Kitchen, Patio, Fire Pit / PROJECT TEAM: Michael Meredith, Hilary Sample, Paul Ruppert, Yam Chumpolphaisol, Lafina Eptaminitaki, Clarie Logoz

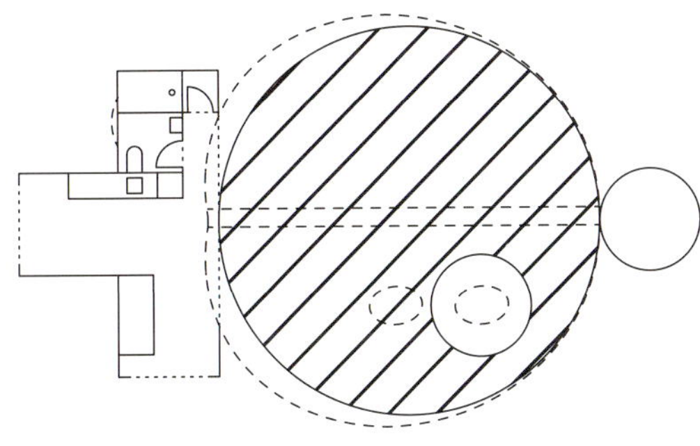

Studio No. 4
Studio with Flat Roof

A studio for making things. Art, architecture, anything. It is an assembly of 120 foam blocks and more than 600 pieces of bent aluminum. While the foam feels scaled for infrastructure, for highways and roads, the metal resembles that of a mail-order shed, a piece of furniture, or an old tin toy. Things look simple. All this sits atop a stepped slab, floating amidst a field of trees. The present configuration arranged three almost identical volumes. But needs might grow, and volumes may be added. Three might become five, or seven. Or everything might come down, to be moved to another site, another field. All services and storage are held to the studio's center, alongside a spiral stairway to the roof. The flat roof can become a surface of things, a stage, a backyard, a basement, a combination, a personal junkyard. For everything in progress, forgotten, imagined, referenced, bought, sold...

LOCATION: Withheld at Owner's Request / DATE: 2020 / STATUS: In Progress / AREA: 1,632 sf / PROGRAM: Art Studio / PROJECT TEAM: Michael Meredith, Hilary Sample, Lafina Eptaminitaki, Paul Ruppert

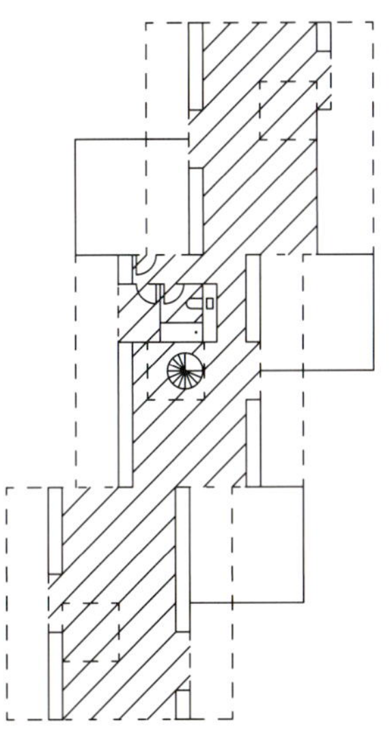

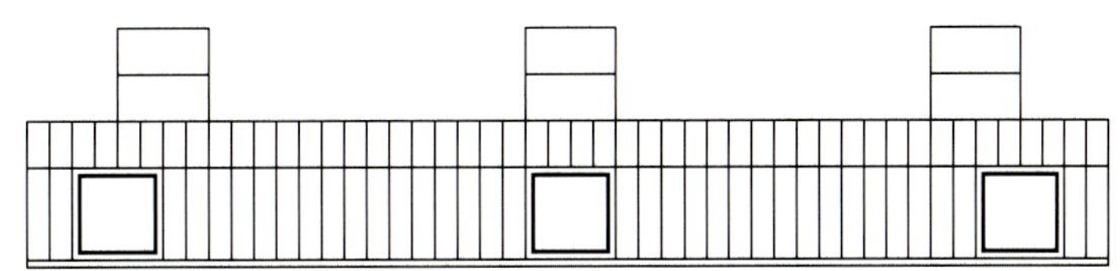

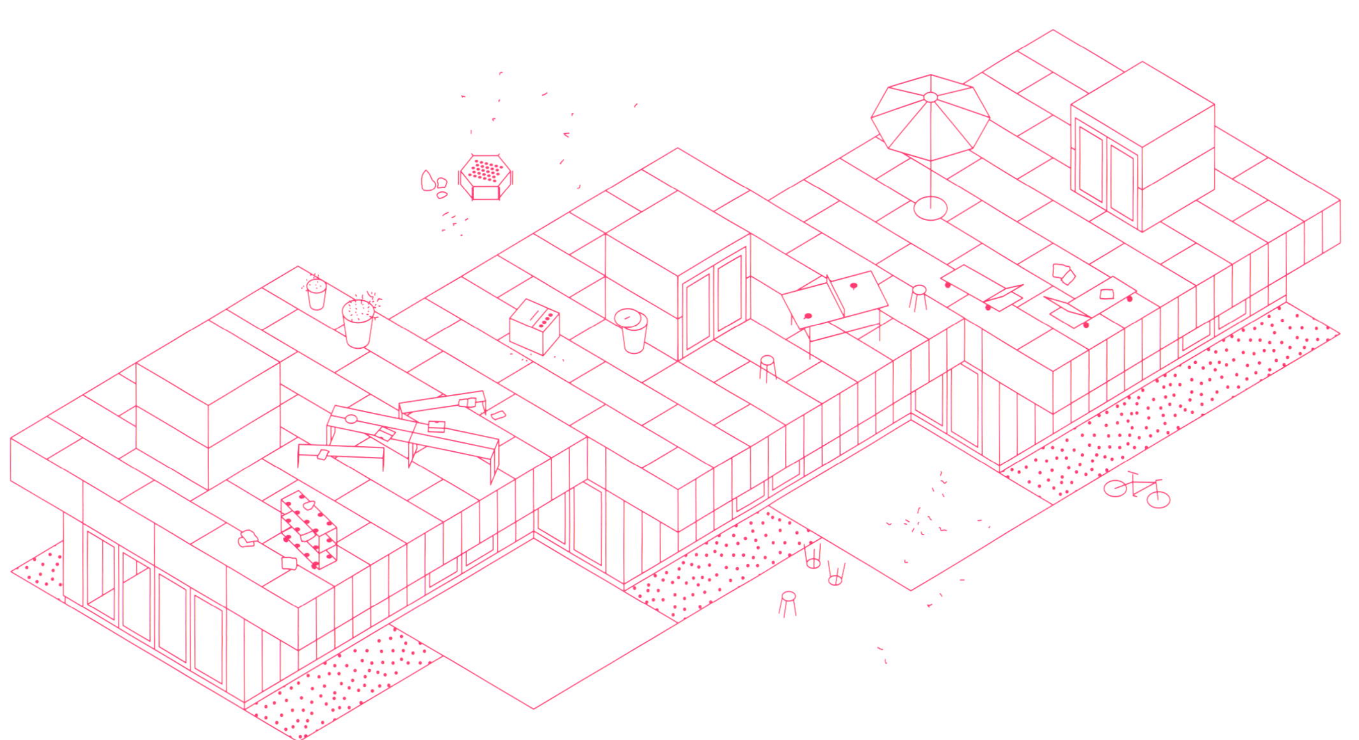

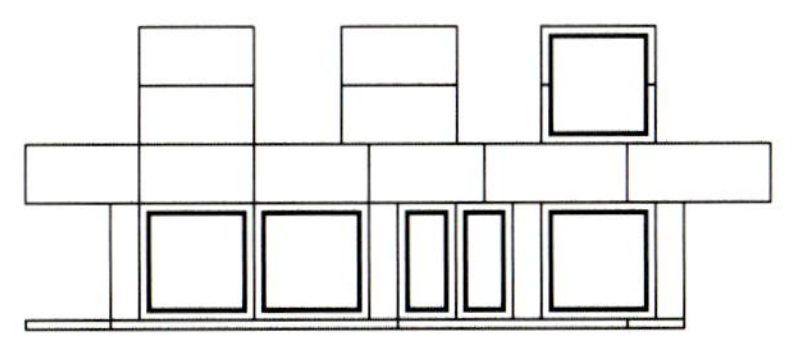

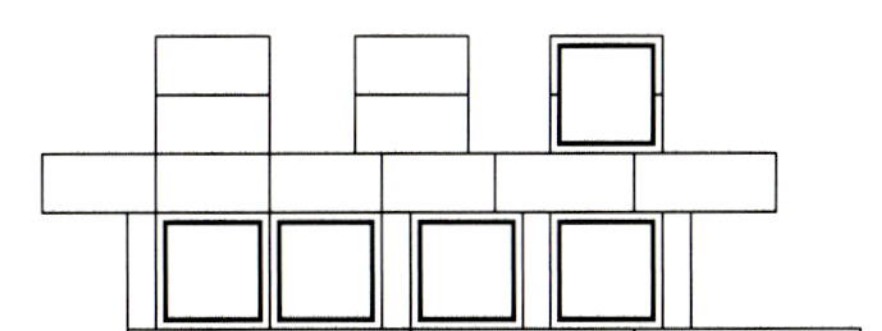

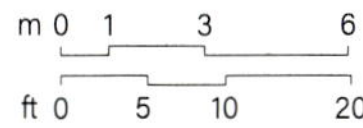
m 0 1 3 6
ft 0 5 10 20

House No. 7
Artist's Residence

This house occupies a single level and provides direct access to the surrounding landscape from every interior space. It is an agglomeration of two hollowed-out, pitched-roof vernacular house volumes with large overhanging eaves. The two structures are joined perpendicularly to form a T-shape and are clad in an industrial, galvanized standing-seam siding. Square openings perforate the siding, providing access, light, and air. The longer extrusion services private programs while the shorter serves as the main living and dining space. The interior spaces are hollow, with low, freestanding object-volumes inserted into them to allow for bathrooms and bedrooms. The interior is both a continuous, free-flowing space and a collection of discrete volumes. The house has an informal relationship with its surroundings, providing both intimate and expansive views of the landscape.

LOCATION: Columbia County, New York / DATE: 2015 / STATUS: Built / AREA: 4,900 sf / PROGRAM: Residence / PROJECT TEAM: Michael Meredith, Hilary Sample, Ceri Edmunds, Ivi Diamantopoulou, Jerico Prater, Joel Stewart, Mathew Staudt, Andy Rauchut, Paul Frederickson, Benas Burdulis, Alexandra Karlsson, Iggy So / STRUCTURAL ENGINEER: Nathaniel Stanton, Craft Engineering Studio PHOTOS: Michael Vahrenwald

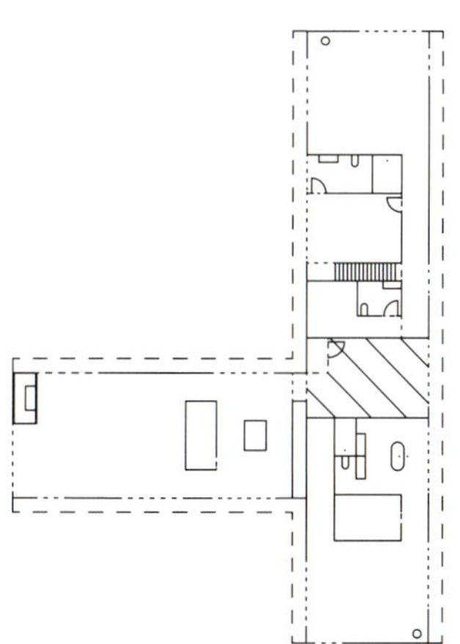

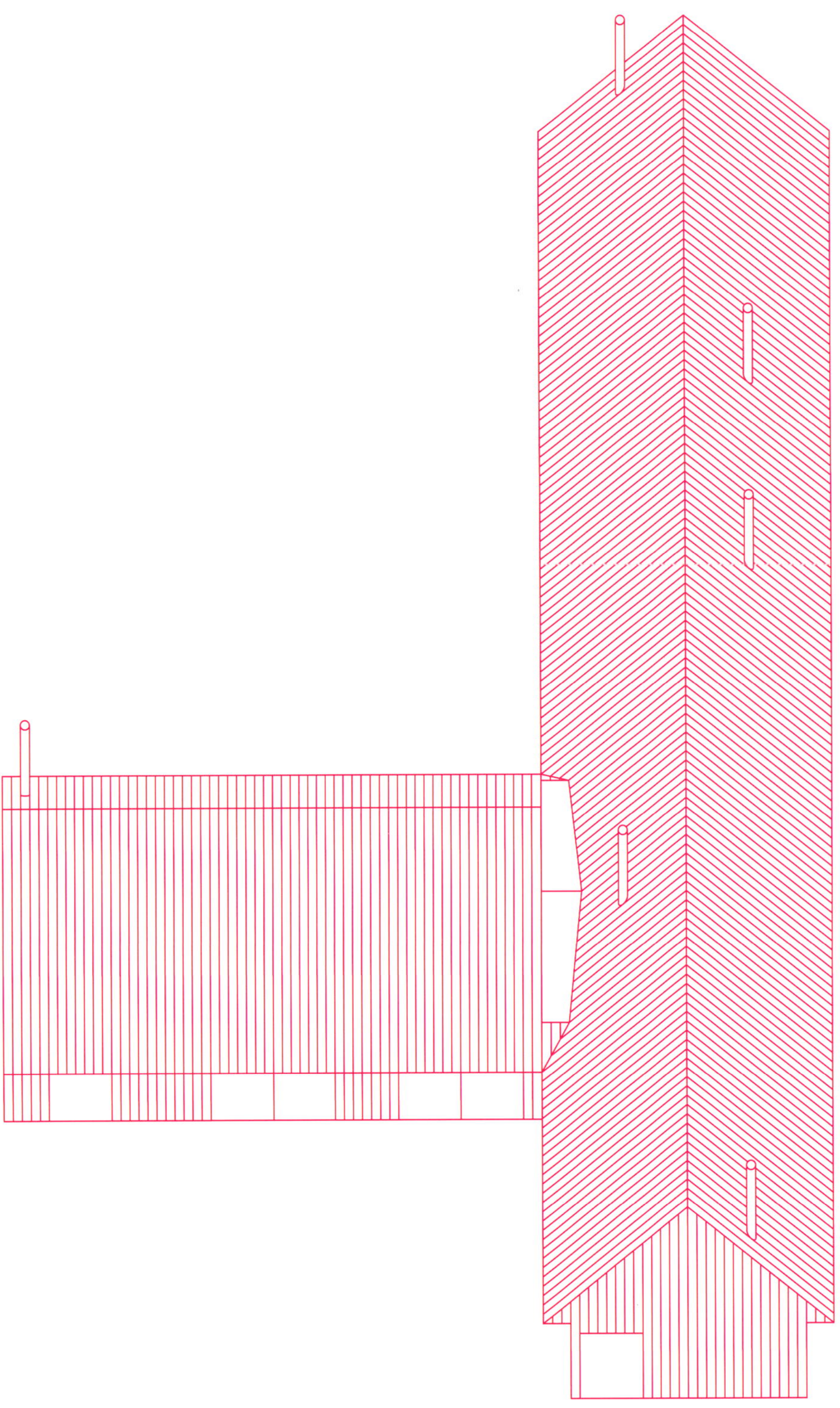

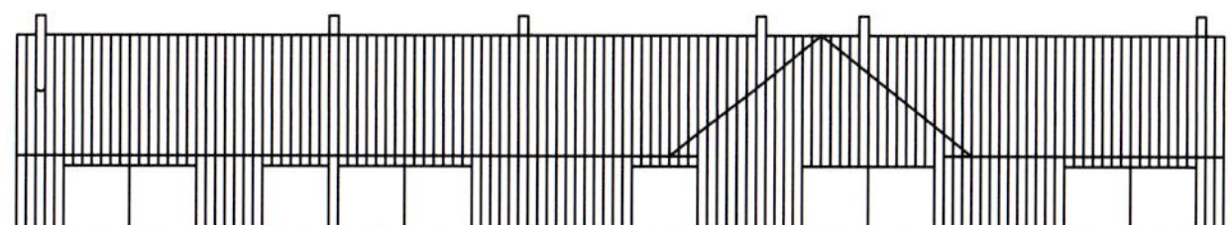

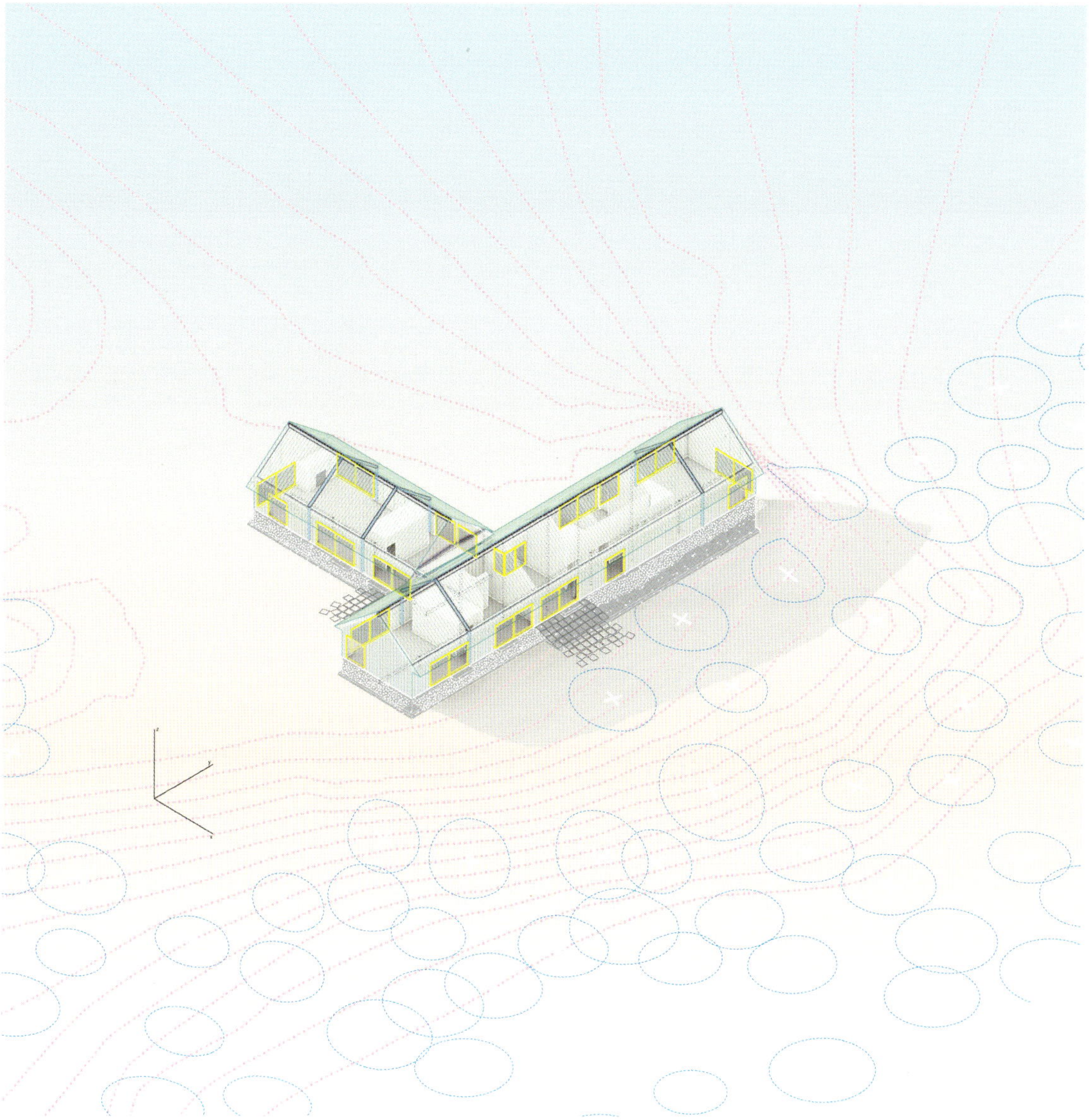

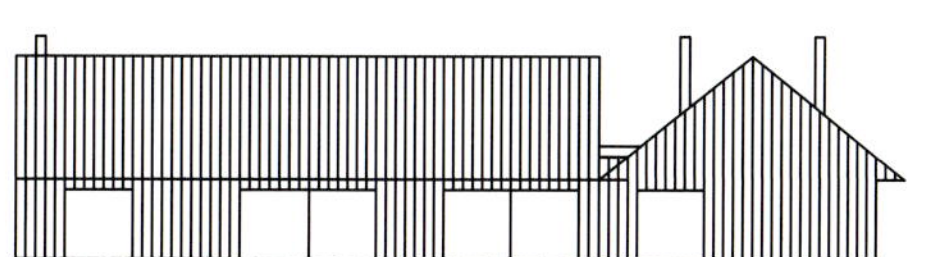

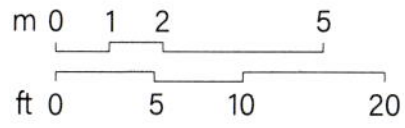
m 0 1 2 5
ft 0 5 10 20

House No. 10
House with Courtyard

There are many ways to describe this house.
Through its parts: five volumes, one courtyard, three beds (could be two, could be one), one shower, five sinks, three tubs, six entryways, 35 windows, 21 doors, 15 plywood trusses, one stove...
Or through metaphor: The house is a hand reaching into the landscape or waving to a Google Earth satellite.
Or through formal organization: The house is an informal aggregation of five house-shaped extrusions with a square courtyard volume subtracted at its center.
Or through personal narrative: The house is shared by a family—a changing family with multiple generations and multiple family members. There are visitors. There are children. There are pets. The family loves to be outside. They love to look at the stars. They love to wake up with the sun. They love to garden. They keep their most precious herbs in the courtyard. At night, Sam watches Mom pick mint for tea through the courtyard's large glass windows. Dad falls asleep in an uncomfortable metal chair in what looks like a hallway but is actually his favorite place to read. Charlie sits alone in his room, out of sight, looking into the endless woods through large sliding doors, wondering what might be lurking in the forest beyond. Someone stops by for a moment. Someone leaves.
Or through verbs: The house or houses are flattened, a splat, a splatter. The house is splitting. The house is adrift. The house is gathering, collecting.

Or through its aesthetic: The house is pretty generic. It is agricultural looking. It is boring.

Or through the iPhone note one of us wrote before screenshotting and sending it, asking for advice: 6:45AM Maybe, what if there is no master bedroom, no his and her sinks, there is no living room, no dining room, no garage? What if everything floats, sinks float, beds float? There are no rooms, no doors inside, it's all one space and many, pulling apart, extending, where there are many fronts, you can walk inside to outside to in and out again. What if it is both looking inward at the garden court and out at its surroundings, and things are incomplete, barely held together, things happen in the spaces between other spaces, hallways and corridors are treated as rooms, rooms are like corridors? The views collapse—in out in out in out. What if the center is not a solid hearth but a garden that changes constantly?

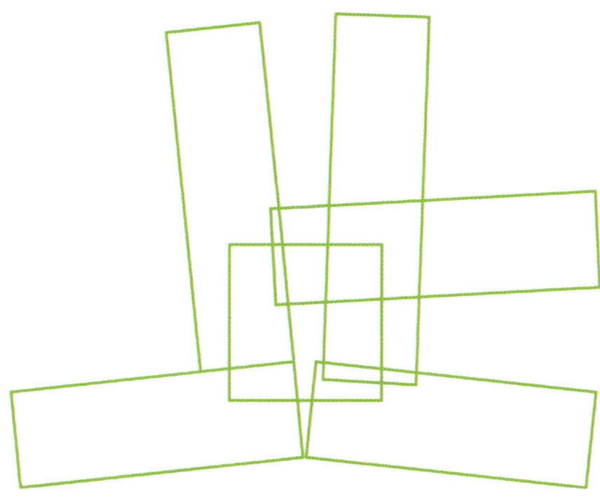

LOCATION: Withheld at Owner's Request / DATE: 2019 / STATUS: Built / AREA: 2,500 sf / PROGRAM: Residence / PROJECT TEAM: Michael Meredith, Hilary Sample, Stefan Klecheski, John Yurchyk, Andrew Frame, Fancheng Fei, Mark Acciari, Michael Abel, Paul Ruppert, Michaela Friedberg / PHOTOS: Michael Vahrenwald

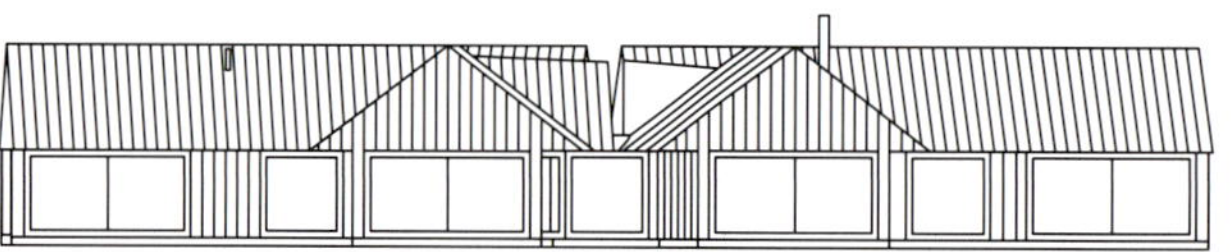

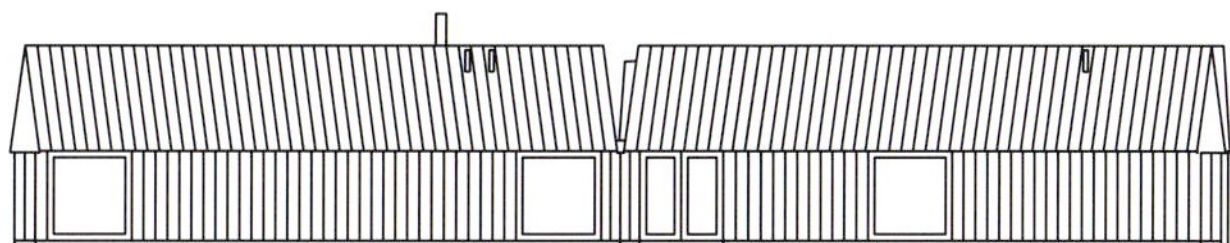

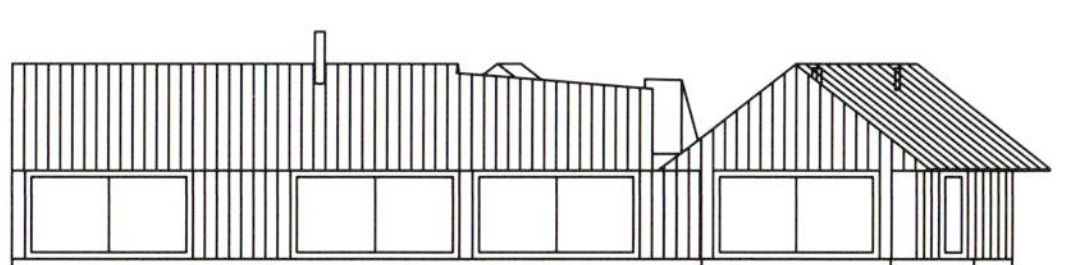

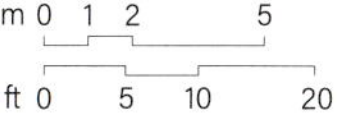
m 0 1 2 5
ft 0 5 10 20

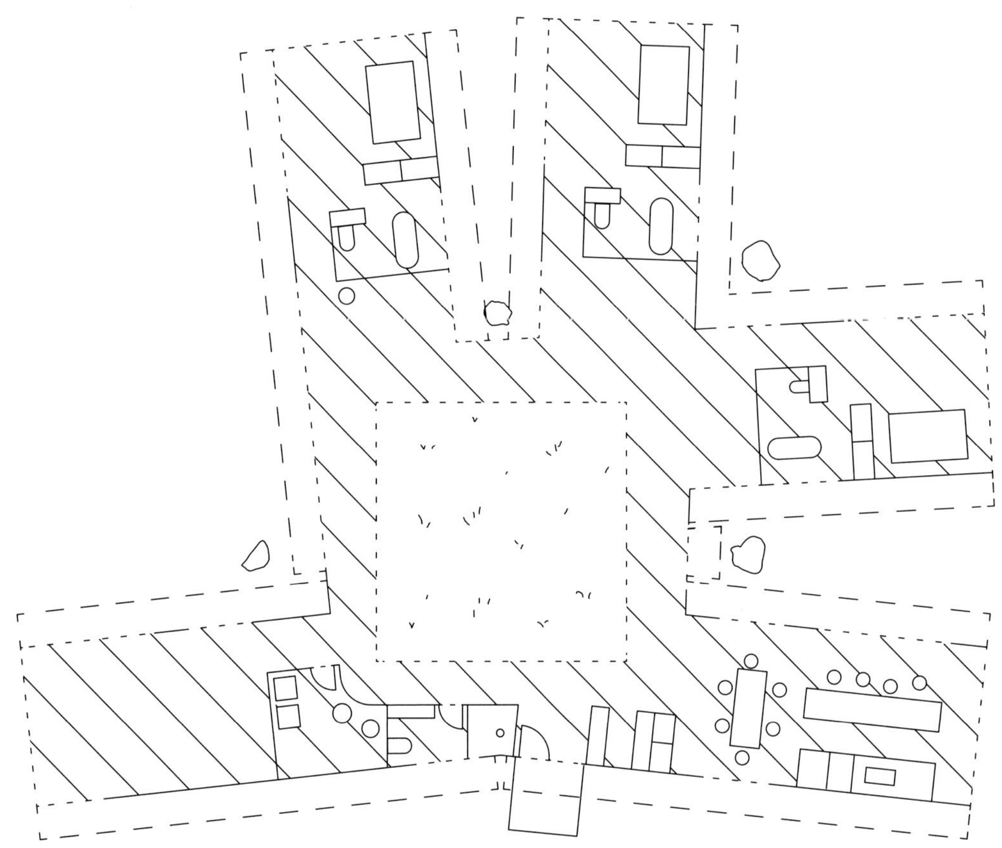

m 0 1 2 5
ft 0 5 10 20

House No. 5
Element House

The Museum of Outdoor Arts Element House is a modular building constructed from structurally insulated panels (SIPs) and designed to operate independently of public utilities by integrating passive systems and on-site energy-generation. The house functions as a guest house and visitor center for Star Axis, a nearby land art project by the artist Charles Ross. Using simple sustainable building practices to increase environmental performance, the building is stripped down to basic components.

The organization of the house is based on an additive geometric system of growth, expanding outward, one module after another. The chimney is transformed from its traditional role as a central solid mass to a decentralized field of vertical skylight openings and solar chimneys designed to cool the building. The chimney's volumes feature remote-control operable windows for passive ventilation. An exterior cladding is composed of raw-aluminum shingles with a small air gap between the shingles and the structure. The continuous interlocking cladding works as a heat sink to distribute solar radiation over the entire surface of the house from the hot side to the cooler, shaded side, thereby reducing heat gain and the need for air conditioning.

LOCATION: Star Axis, New Mexico / DATE: 2014 / STATUS: Built / AREA: 1,500 sf / PROGRAM: Visitor's Center, Residence / PROJECT TEAM: Michael Meredith, Hilary Sample, Ashley Bigham, Jason Bond, Ryan Culligan, Gideon Danilowitz, Michael Faciejew, Steven Gertner, Jason Kim, Kera Lagios, Ryan Ludwig, Gabrielle Marcoux, Meredith McDaniel, Elijah Porter, Michael Smith, Mathew Staudt, Marrikka Trotter STRUCTURAL ENGINEER: Edward Stanley Engineers / CLIMATE ENGINEER: Paul Stoller, Atelier Ten / PHOTOS: Florian Holzherr

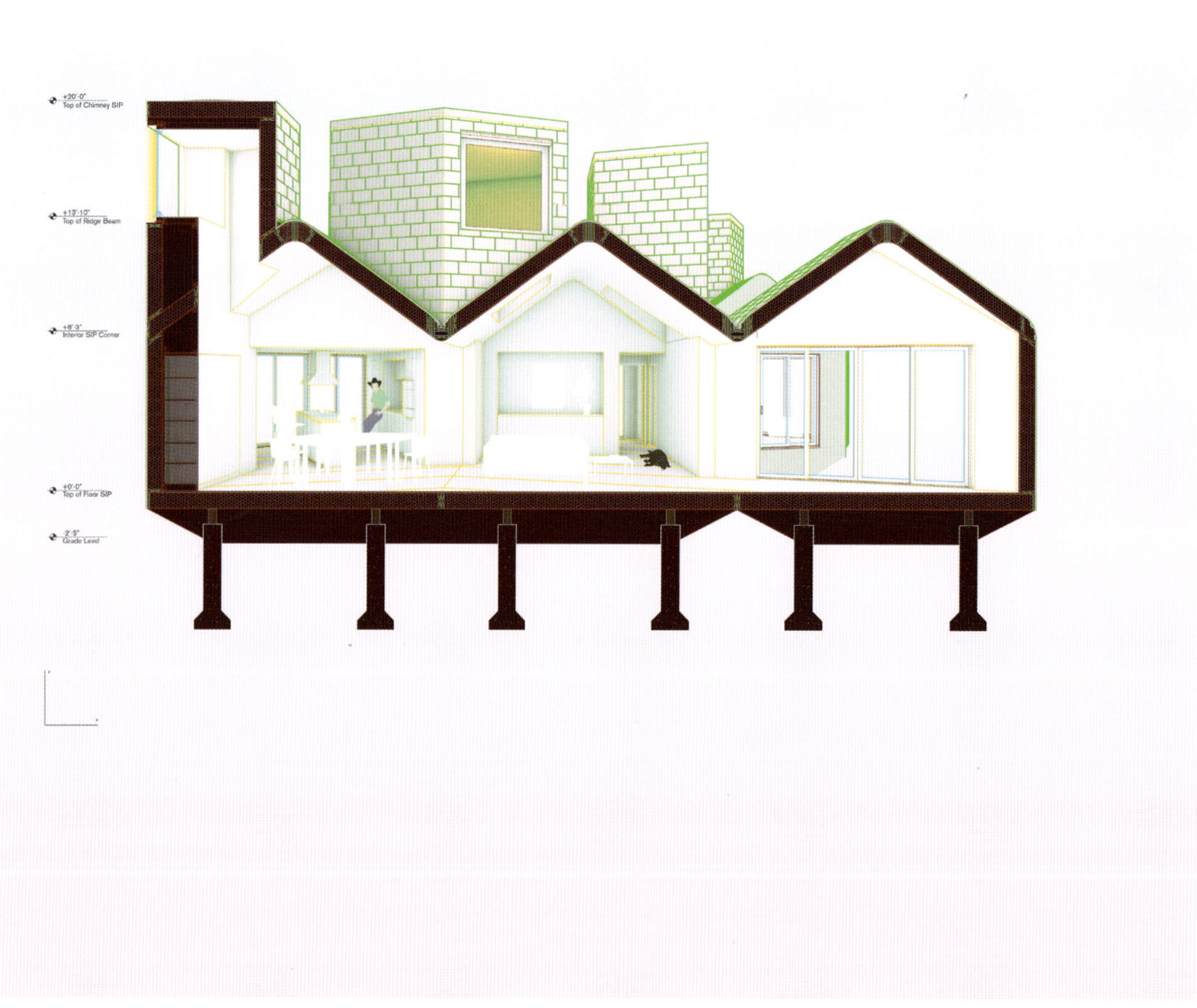
+20'-0"
Top of Chimney SIP
+13'-10"
Top of Ridge Beam
+8'-3"
Interior SIP Corner
+0'-0"
Top of Floor SIP
-2'-5"
Grade Level

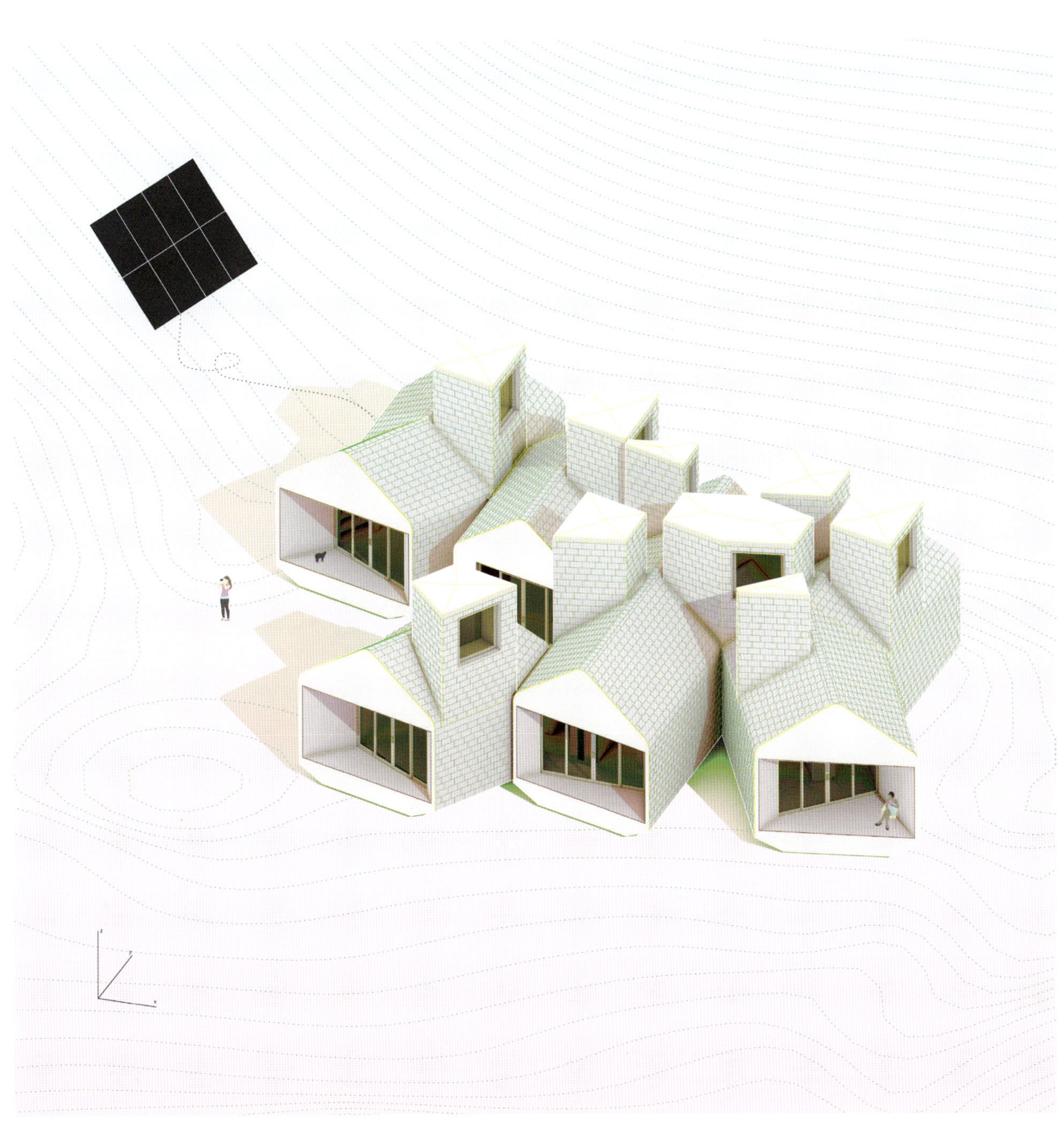

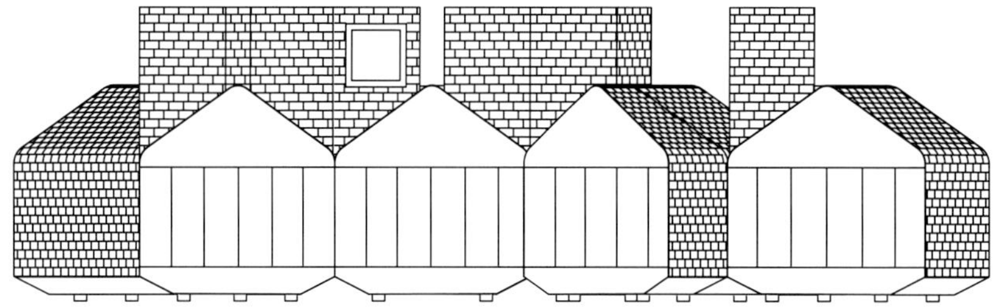

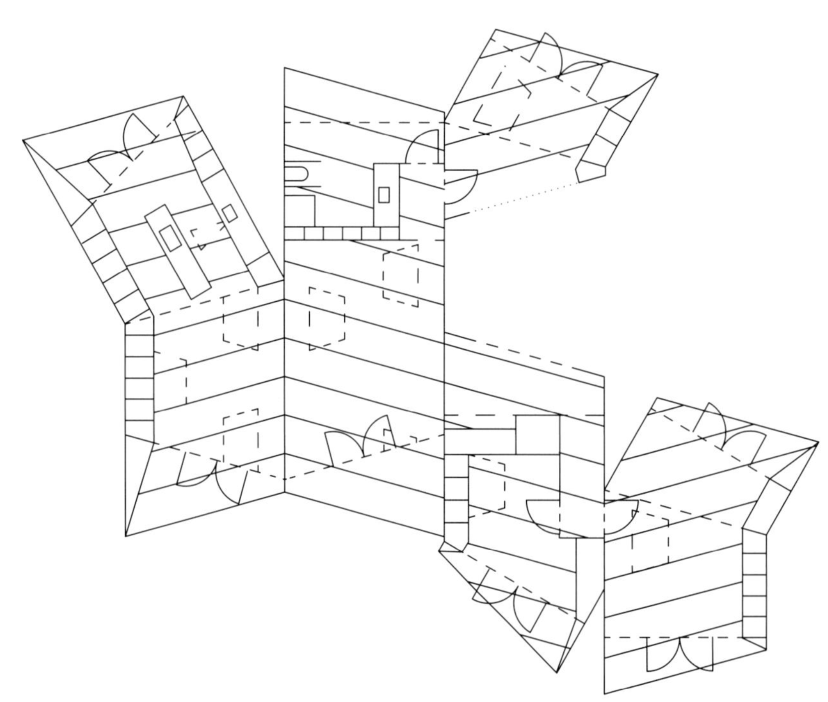

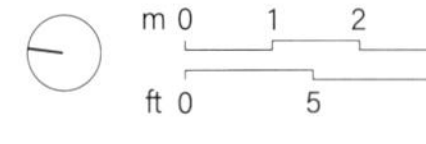
m 0 1 2 5
ft 0 5 15

Housing No. 8 Laboratorio de Vivienda

The 32 projects selected exhibit an architecture of primary (architectural) elements, straightforward geometries and proportions. Each proposal exhibits potential for growth by aggregation, simple repetition, or various strategies of extension, infill, and addition. It was important to consider how these proposals, assembled into a collective, would work together to create not an estate, but a community for Apan. The selection process revealed various categories and themes by which the projects could be classified. Some projects rethink the fundamentals of low-income housing's spatial organization (corridors, courtyards, roofs), some rework labor and construction, and some recast structure or material. The forms of these works are generally economic but, unlike early-modernist projects at the Weissenhof Estate, their tone is not one of a radical break. Today's public will not protest flat (or pitched) roofs and today's architects will not claim to usher in a new style. If anything, these works relate to the vast, varied world of vernacular construction—to the majority of the built world that architecture glosses over. Specifically, here each house responds to one of the nine climatic zones of Mexico. At first glance, many of these works might not appear radically different from existing low-income housing. But upon closer study, the ingenuity of the projects selected function as a totality yet retain their individual identities.

The problem of low-income housing demands the thoughtful attention and expertise of architects like those included here. For, given the limited resources of such works, each decision gains greater significance and has greater impact on the design and on the life of its inhabitants.

Ph. Jaime Navarro

LOCATION: Apan, Hidalgo, Mexico / DATE: 2018 / STATUS: Built / AREA: 9 Acres (Master Plan), 8,600 sf (Welcome/Education Center PROGRAM: Master Plan, Welcome-Education Center / PROJECT TEAM: Michael Meredith, Hilary Sample, Cyrus Dochow, Paul Ruppert, Fancheng Fei, Michael Abel, Mark Acciari, Lafina Eptaminitaki, Mark Kamish / PHOTOS: Jaime Navarro, Isidoro Michan

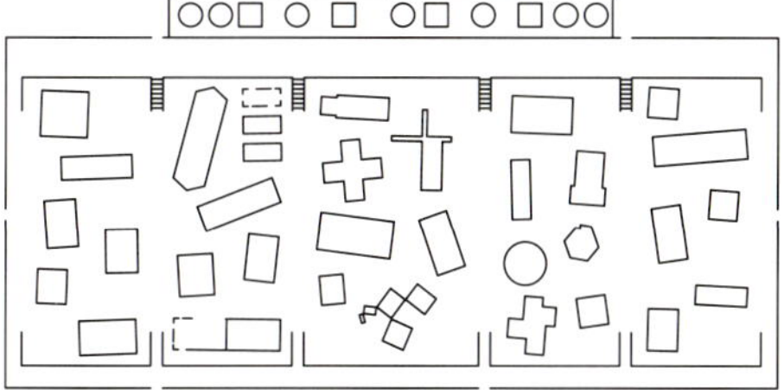

Ph. Isidoro Michan

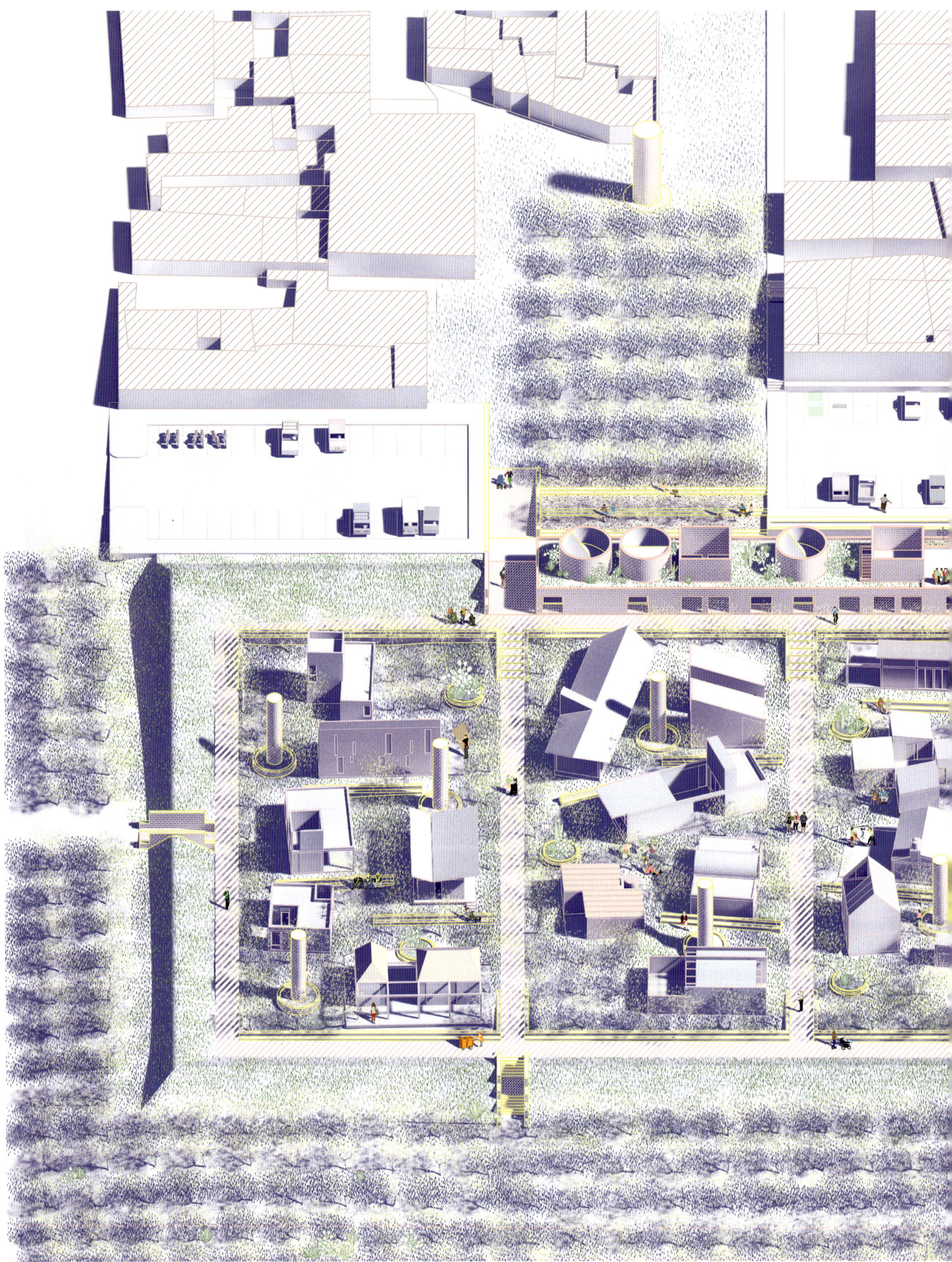

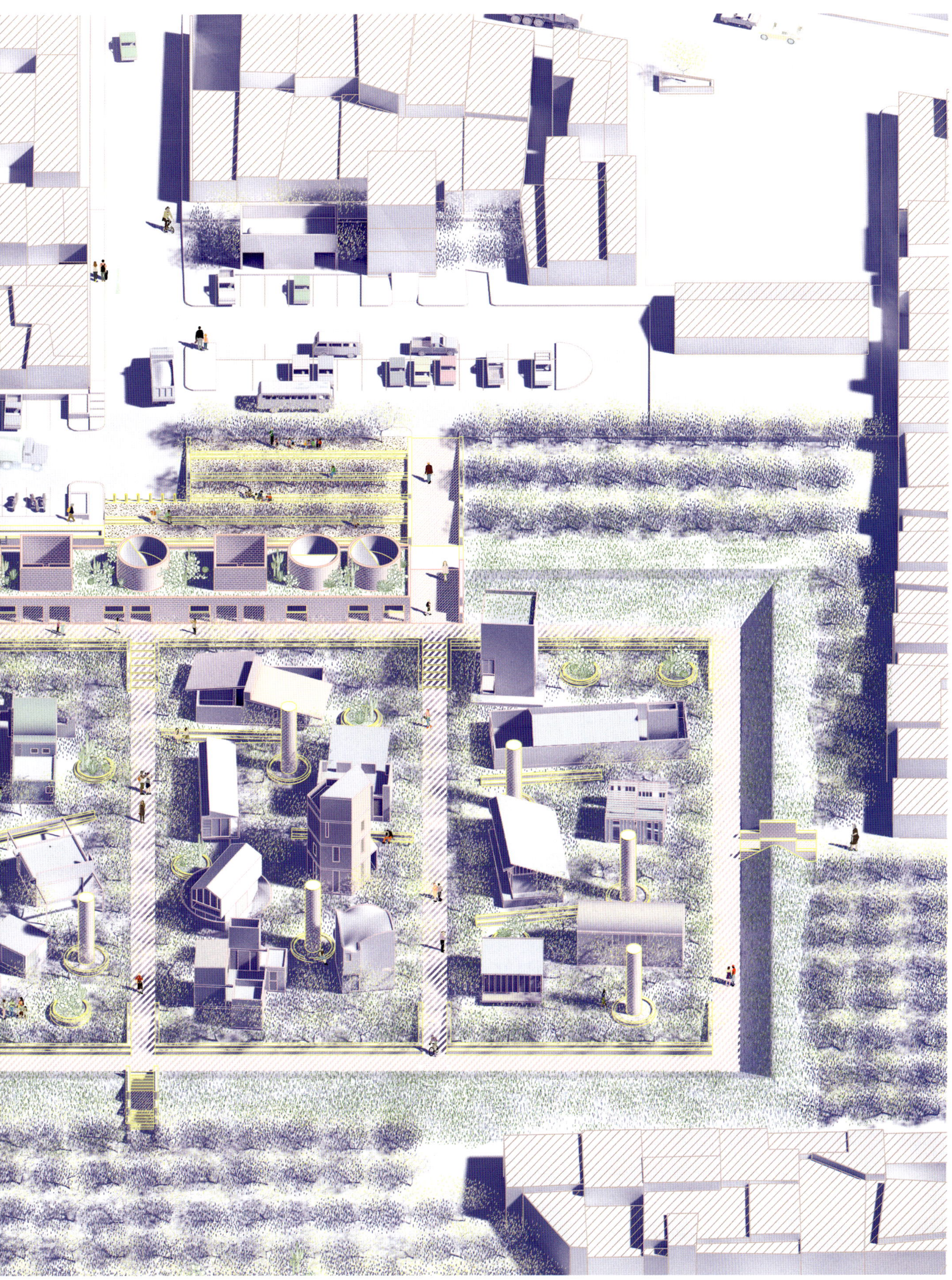

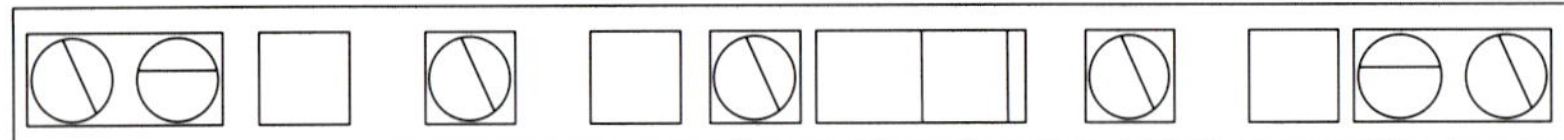

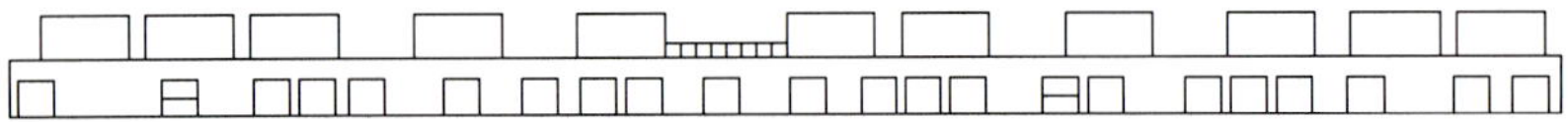

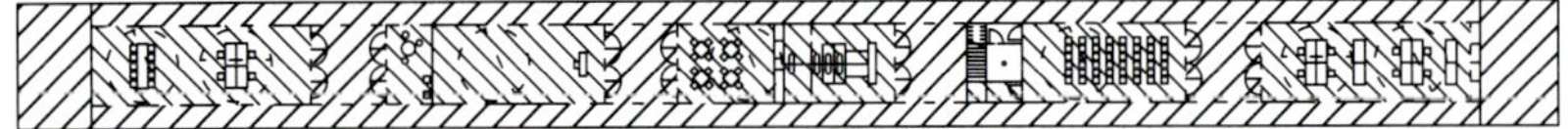

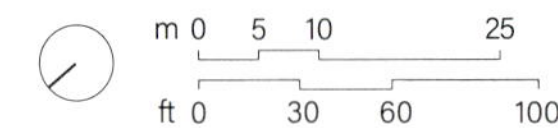

Ph. Isidoro Michan

Ph. Jaime Navarro

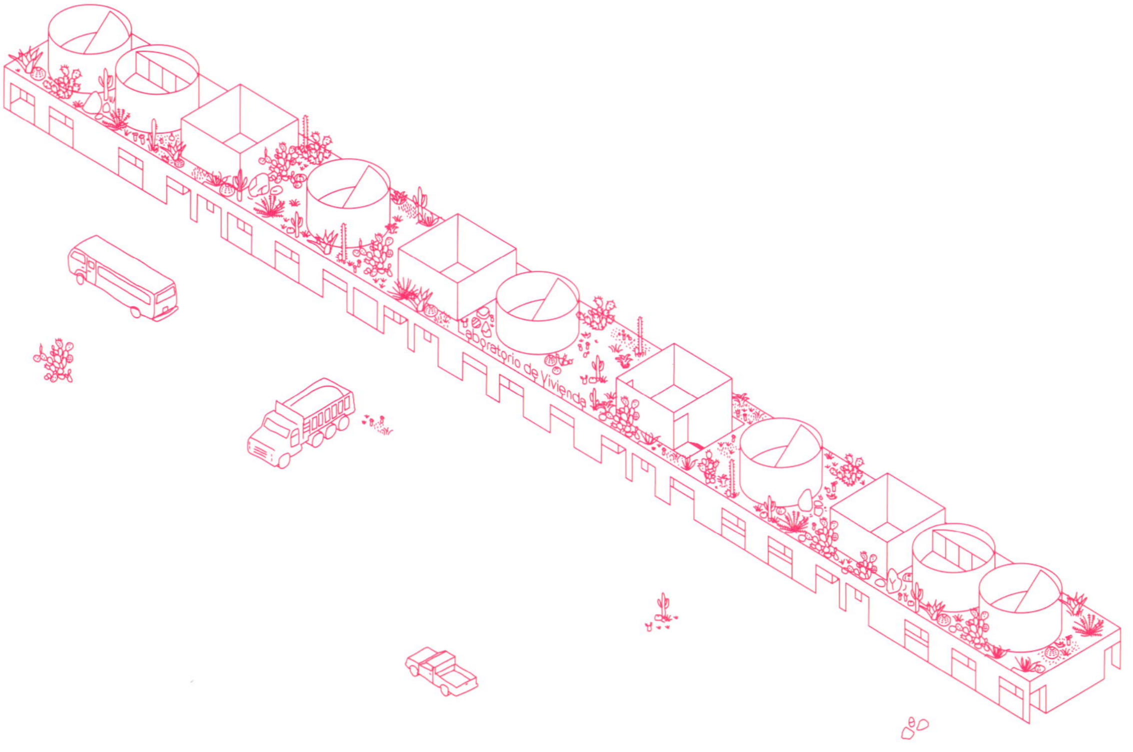